SOCIALISM, SARVODAYA AND DEMOCRACY

SOCIALISM, SARVODAYA AND DEMOCRACY

The Theoretical Contributions of M.N. Roy, J.P. Narayan and J.B. Kripalani

Eddie James Girdner

GYAN

ISBN : 978-81-212-1198-7

₹ 900

First Published 2013

Published by

Gyan Publishing House
23, Main Ansari Road, Darya Ganj
New Delhi-110002
Phones : 23282060, 23261060
Fax : 011-23285914
E-mail: books@gyanbooks.com
Website: www.gyanbooks.com

Laser Typesetting: Rudra Computer Graphics, Delhi
Printed at: G. Print Process, Delhi

Cataloging in Publication Data—DK
Courtesy: D.K. Agencies (P) Ltd. <docinfo@dkagencies.com>

Socialism, Sarvodaya and Democracy : The Theoretical Contributions of M.N. Roy, J.P. Narayan and J.B. Kripalani/ Eddie James Girdner.

p. cm.
Includes bibliographical references (p.) and index.

ISBN 9788121211987

1. Socialism—India. 2. Sarvodaya movement—India. 3. Democracy—India. 4. Roy, M. N. (Manabendra Nath), 1887-1954. 5. Narayan, Jayaprakash, 1902-1979. 6. Kripalani, J. B. (Jiwatram Bhagwandas), 1888-1982. I. Title.

DDC 335.50954 23

Dedicated to

Terrie and Scenery

Contents

Abstract

The purpose of this book is to explicate the theoretical writings of M.N. Roy (1889-1954), J.P. Narayan (1902-1979) and J.B. Kripalani (1888-1982) which contributed to the Indian concept of socialism or *Sarvodaya*. Since the French Revolution, the growth of the nation State, political and economic centralization, concepts of social and historical determinism and a utilitarian ethic have obscured the classical view of a morally autonomous individual in an organic community. The fundamental problem is how to revive the classical notion of a moral community and release the human potential to progress toward a democratic and humanistic society.

From the broad political debate in twentieth century India has emerged the concept of *Sarvodaya*, grounded in classical Indian thought and influenced by classical Greek thought, Renaissance Humanism, Liberalism, Utopian Socialism and anarchist thought. Chapter One outlines the parameters of *Sarvodaya*. Chapter Two delineates M.N. Roy's views on democratic socialism, in terms of his materialist cosmology and concept of historical materialism, his critique of Marxism and Liberalism, and his vision of decentralized socialism and partyless democracy.

Chapter Three explores M.N. Roy's Radical Humanism, particularly his view of human nature and freedom, science, rationality and consciousness, radical self-transformation, and social change.

Chapter Four reconstructs J.P. Narayan's views on democratic socialism including his perspective upon Marxism and nationalism, and his later sharp critique of Marxism and Western Socialism. Chapter Five delineates J.P. Narayan's views on *Sarvodaya*, including his critique of parliamentary democracy and the State, his conception of partyless democracy and communitarianism, and his movement for "Total Revolution."

Chapter Six explicates J.B. Kripalani's perspective on democratic socialism, including his philosophy of socialism and the State, his philosophy of history and his critique of the Marxist concept of class struggle. In Chapter Seven, J.B. Kripalani's interpretation of Gandhian democracy is reconstructed in terms of the non-violent revolution, Gandhian economic principles, decentralization, *Sarvodaya* and Basic, Education.

In conclusion, decentralized non-violent socialism or *Sarvodaya* provides a basis for the fundamental revolution which includes the moral renovation and structural transformation of society, disarmament, human solidarity, human welfare and the emerging global community.

1

Introduction

The search for a moral community is a universal quest which has engaged social and political thinkers from Plato to Marx in the West and from Asoka to Gandhi in the East. In the late twentieth century, the challenge has become more urgent as a result of the sweeping historical transformations since the French Revolution. During this period there emerged individual autonomy, propertied democracy, individualism and social atomism. Moreover, the widespread faith in social and historical determinism has diminished the incentive and capacity of the individual to exercise free will and effective autonomy.[1] The enfeeblement of contemporary society and creative initiative have been greatly reinforced by the centralized institutions of the State and mammoth corporations in conjunction with the pervasive logic of rapid and ruthless technological change. The fundamental question facing societies has been sharply stated as follows:

Can we now revive the notion of a moral community and provide a purely rational basis for it, without leaning toward extreme social determinism, without an appeal to sectarian religious belief, and without losing the gains in tolerance that have occurred from different forms of relativism? Can we rescue morality from the abyss of subjectivism and liberate the notion of community from the jungle of ideology?[2]

The nationalist revolutions of the twentieth century have opened up exciting opportunities for widespread social experimentation in the continuing search for community, in accord with indigenous traditions and diverse philosophical frameworks. The basis for the construction of a viable society requires rigorous thinking about the nature of man and community as well as a broad and vital conception of the political. Contemporary assumptions concerning human nature, the State, the relationship between the individual and society, the nature of power, social and historical change, individual and social morality, the relationship between means and ends, the role of technology, ideological concepts of Liberalism, Socialism and Communism and individual and collective welfare, must be thoroughly examined and questioned. At the root of this enterprise is the removal of ideological blinders from contemporary thinking.

The Indian Debate

In India during the twentieth century there has been a high level of social and political debate as well as a good deal of social experimentation. This broad debate has contributed in significant ways to the shaping of the contemporary Indian polity, although so far the response has been generally disappointing. This wide-ranging debate and social critique has centered around a number of crucial problems which are at the heart of the larger enterprise, the moral renovation of society and politics.

First, the problem of overcentralization of power in both the political and economic spheres and the interrelation between the two has been examined in terms of the impact upon society, whether under liberal capitalism, socialism or Communism. At the heart of this problem is the growth of State power in relation to society. With regard to liberal society, it involves Tocqueville's paradox of equality and freedom. Tocqueville feared that when citizens became more equal they would each demand much assistance from the central government, leading the government to subject ever more of society to central legislation. With the progressive destruction of society, both individualism and central power would grow.[3] Under Western Socialism and Communism, there is a similar growth of the power of the State at the expense of society, although without the protection of individualism.

Secondly, the nature and methodology of social change have been widely debated, especially the question of the necessity and acceptability of the use of force and violence as a means of social change. Out of this extensive debate a broad consensus has emerged that in principle and largely in practice, the use of violence and the establishment of a moral community are, ultimately, incompatible.

A related debate has examined the relationship between means and ends. Following Gandhi, most theorists agree that moral ends can never justify immoral means and conceive of means and ends as inextricably linked. Contemporary Indian theorists have also questioned the dichotomy, largely accepted in the West between immorality in the public sphere and morality in the private sphere. For the most part, Niebuhr's conception of moral man in immoral society has been rejected and many theorists have insisted upon the increased relevance of morality to the public sphere. Another stream in the debate has examined the presuppositions implicit in dialectical materialism. For the most part, the Indian response to this debate has been critical, selective, assimilative and eclectic, with a categorical rejection of the materialist reductionism found in the Structuralist School of Marxism. While the importance of historical and material factors is recognised, the human potential to overcome such factors through the will is strongly asserted. A radical humanist rather than a dogmatic materialist and reductionist perspective has emerged as a dominant theme.

Similarly, most theorists have recognised the inadequacy of the Marxist concept of class as a basis for the analysis of Indian society. Although this concept is deemed useful in at least one dimension of analysis, e.g. the socio-economic, it is generally recognised as only one dimension of the many faceted problem of the analysis of social groups in the sub-continent. The dimensions of caste, language and religion are recognised as often revealing greater cohesion among groups than the factor of class. Many cross-cutting allegiances are recognised which confound the more simplistic Marxist formulation. It is also objected that such a reductionist and often mechanistic view of society does not account for the human potential to transcend group consciousness.

The debate in India has also examined the illusions of liberal democracy, particularly in regard to the institutions of the Party, the State and majority rule. Another important aspect of the debate has centered upon the role of technology and the relationship between moral principles and the application of science and technology.

At the center of these exchanges has been the examination of the relationship between the individual and society. Indian theorists have tended to reject both the Western atomistic view of society and the Marxist view of society in which the individual is merged in the collective. The Indian notion is, instead, a classical one in which the individual is conceived as both morally autonomous and an integral part of the community. A balance, therefore, must be maintained between the two. Whereas capitalistic and individualistic society has lost sight of the organic and communal nature of society, the collectivistic society has sacrificed the individual in the collective, thus losing sight of the true nature of man, as one who requires individual moral autonomy to be truly human.

Finally, twentieth century Indian thought has sought an integration of theory and practice, involving the creative potential of all within the human community and has recognized the universality of the enterprise to transform society. Utilitarian concepts of human welfare and economic formulations based on the concept of the "economic man," have been found insufficient. The basis of the emerging Indian conception of socialism is grounded in the classical Indian conception of *Sarvodaya* or the uplift of all. *Sarvodaya* may be defined as non-violent socialism; social good, the public interest, or universal welfare.

Within the Indian context, the goal of human history differs from that conceived by Western political thinkers. Whereas for Western Socialists and Communists, the goal of human history is the perfection of society, often at the expense of the individual and his moral autonomy, for the Indian thinker, the goal is self-realisation, most typically seen in spiritual terms. Society must provide the material and moral basis for the unfolding of human potential in all.

In Indian political thought, sovereignty resides in the autonomous individual. No individual may relinquish his basic personal sovereignty. This is in contrast to Western Liberal political thought where sovereignty resides in the people, conceived as the majority, and Socialism and Communism in which sovereignty is seen to lie in the collective ego, particularly the proletarian class.

Asian and Indian Socialism

Today several countries in South Asia claim socialism as the official creed, including India, Sri Lanka and Myanmar, and socialism is viewed as "respectable" throughout the rest of South Asia as well.[4] Myrdal viewed indigenous strains of socialism in South Asia as "ideological compromises," whether "Islamic Socialism in Pakistan," "Buddhist Socialism in Burma" or "Sarvodaya Socialism" among Gandhians in India. He hastily dismissed the claims that the "ideals of socialism are immanent in the indigenous philosophy" with the judgement that they amount to nothing more than "intellectual contortions" and verbal jugglery."[5] It appears that Myrdal's contempt for the indigenous conceptions of socialism stems from his narrow definition of socialism as conceived in the West. A proper appreciation of South Asian concepts of socialism, and in particular of *Sarvodaya*, requires a broader approach and a greater willingness to examine the philosophical roots of Indian political thought as well as the impact of Western thought upon the resulting synthesis.

Myrdal's approach led him to conclude that in South Asia "the vague leftist tendency implied has everywhere a common historical origin in the opposition to colonial domination and is clearly connected with nationalism and especially with the egalitarian ideology that is an integral part of Asian Nationalism."[6]

This view, however, fails to account for those elements of Asian socialism which pre-date the period of colonial domination. Myrdal's appraisal and close identification of Mahatma Gandhi with the Western-educated liberal intellectuals in India tends to neglect the profound influence on Gandhi's thought of Indian religious literature.[7] Myrdal sees only those elements of *Sarvodaya* which correspond with Western concepts of socialism as genuinely socialist, and consequently fails to identify the broader elements integral to *Sarvodaya*.

For Myrdal, "Indian socialism is an ideology propagated by an intellectual elite, who are convinced that socialism is desirable on rational grounds as a means for development and for achieving greater equality".[8] He identified the main elements of socialism in India as firstly, "egalitarianism, often in conjunction with political democracy, with the problem often stated in terms of the utilitarian principle of the common good." Secondly, "it is held that the caste structure is incompatible with a socialist society." Thirdly, "it is also held that socialism must be brought about without resort to violence."[9]

Myrdal's analysis of socialism in Asia proceeds in terms of his commitment to nationalization and state ownership and management of a large section of the economy. His treatment, then, not only neglects fundamental elements of *Sarvodaya* philosophy but also includes elements such as statism, centralization, accumulation and large scale industrialization within a Western paradigm of development and growth clearly foreign to those concepts embodied in the goal of *Sarvodaya*.

A more cogent and accurate description of Indian Socialism has been made by V.K.R.V. Rao, who notes seven major themes. Firstly, Indian Socialism does not believe in the use of violence. It is held that "A socialist society established by persuasion and free democratic methods has a greater chance of survival than one established by force." Secondly, the Indian conception of a socialist society not only rejects the use of violence but also employs education and in many cases self-suffering to establish a new pattern of society. A third element concerns the perceived relationship between the individual and society. There is an insistence upon democracy with human dignity and ensuring the opportunity for individual development. Rather than "merge the individual with the society," the "Indian socialist wants the development of each individual but requires this development to be such that it leads to the upliftment of the society as well." Fourthly, Indian Socialism seeks the guarantee of positive welfare, ensuring that all who want can work. It insists upon the elimination of poverty and unemployment. Fifthly, there should be a successive narrowing of inequality. Sixthly, there is the conception of "a political democracy that not only functions at the national and the state levels but also at local levels and gives the people ... political participation." It is expected that power will be decentralised and maintained by the decentralization of economic activity. Industries which by their nature must be of large-scale are to be publicly owned and controlled. The economy should provide a high enough rate of growth for the elimination of poverty. Seventhly, perfect social equality is to be a goal with respect for each individual. Values, institutions and practices must promote the implementation of this concept of human equality.[10]

In summary Rao states:

> [T]he basic values underlying the Indian approach to socialism can be derived from Indian spiritual traditions. Buddhism, Jainism, Vedantic and Bhakti Hinduism, Sikhism, Islam and Christianity have all contributed to this heritage, not to mention the individual contributions of great Indians in more modern times like Vivekananda, Gandhi, Nehru, Vinoba Bhave and now Jaya Prakash Narian. Indian socialism is rooted in respect for human dignity and human equality. While imposing restrictions on the right to private property even to the extent of abolishing it where necessary in the social interest, it permits private enterprise in economic activity and makes for a mixed economy rather than a completely socialised economy. It abhors violence and class war and pins its faith on non-violence, sacrifice, and dedication to the service of the poor. And as a natural consequence, its implementation is envisaged through parliamentary democracy and the rule of law rather than through a violent revolution or a proletarian dictatorship... While Indian socialism has certainly been influenced by the writings of Western socialists, its roots are derived from Indian thinking and adopted to Indian conditions. It is conspicuously Indian in its stress on peaceful change, its belief in the constitutional process, its reliance on parliamentary political democracy, its avoidance of collectivisation of land and its bias for village *panchayats*, and its preference for decentralisation to the

> maximum extent possible, of industrial production. Indian socialism is, thus, much more mixed and pragmatic, if not eclectic, than what one found in the West during the early days of its socialist movements.[11]

The writings of Vinoba Bhave shed further light upon the origins and nature of Indian Socialism. In Bhave's conception, human history has known only two powers for the transformation of society. These are the power of violence (*himsa-shakti*) and the power of law' (*danda-shakti*). Bhave spoke of a "third power," that of love, inherent in early Christianity.[12] This third power was "people's power" or *lok-shakti*. He wrote: "By an independent people's power I mean a power inhering in the people, which is totally opposed to the power of violence, but other than the power of the law, and which it must be our task to call into being."[13] Jayaprakash Narayan observed that in the past the third power or love was applied to individuals only. Today, he thought, this power must be applied to institutions to change the very structure of society.[14] For Bhave, the third power was equivalent to a natural law tenet. He wrote, "The third power is inherent in man as man."[15]

Bhave pointed out the origin of Gandhi's theory of trusteeship, which was derived from the concepts of *aparigraha* (non-possessiveness) and *Samabhava* (sense of equality) found in the Bhagavad Gita.[16] For Bhave, the concept of *Sarvodaya* or the uplift of society was grounded in Bhakti.

> .. The old concept of *Bhakti* should be reinterpreted as *sarvodaya*. Formerly the experience of oneness with all living beings would come to some solitary sage in his ectasy, and he would see all differences as unreal, as things to be overcome. This experience of unity must become in our day the common property of mankind.[17]

Sarvodaya, then, is rooted in the spiritual integral image of interdependent humanity, characteristic of many historical schools of thought in the East, as opposed to the spiritual individualism rampant in the West.

Bhave noted that non-violence and co-operation are complementary aspects of *Sarvodaya*. He wrote:

> *Sarvodaya* work is based in two principles, non-violence and co-operation. The non-violent approach is based on the experience of the unity of the soul. It is a spiritual idea. *Sarvodaya* therefore unites the spiritual and the scientific ..[18]

The idea of interdependence is seen in Bhave's statement that "The aim and purpose of *Sarvodaya Samaj* is to secure the welfare of all.

.. We realise that humanity is one... For us... humanity is the supreme value, and the soul of humanity is one."[19]

Kumarappa used the term "Villagism" to describe Indian Socialism, and to distinguish it from capitalism and Western Socialism. Rejecting the concept of "economic man," he saw man as a complex being. The fundamental principle of villagism was described as all round development of the individual and the ultimate goal was seen as spirituaL "... [V]illagism is nothing but socialism decentralised and freed from violence...", he wrote.[20] Kumarappa saw villagism as grounded in the traditional Indian society, particularly the institutions of the joint family, caste or varna, the traditional system of division of labour, village self-sufficiency and barter. The conception of villagism is a universalistic and utopian image of man and society.

> Work in such a society will be worship in the real sense of the word-a means of identifying oneself, not merely in thought but in deed, with the wider self of the community, and thus with the universal self of all being. Economic life will then be raised to a spiritual level, and instead of work being degraded into servitude done ... merely with the idea of earning ones bread, it will become transformed into a means of reaching the Divine, a labour of love, done for the good of ones neighbours, and leading the individual out of his own little self into the wider self of the community and thus to Universal Self which abides in all alike.[21]

The Indian conceptualization of socialism is similiar to the multilevel-equal-access model constructed by Robert C. North. North conceptualized three models of society, the tooth and claw model, the competition welfare model and the multilevel-equal-access model. The tooth and claw model entails a Hobbesian view of man in which human progress arises only out of struggle, either in the neo-Darwinian or Marxist Leninist mold. For the Darwinians, history is on the side of the strong, whereas for the Marxists it is on the side of the weak. The competition welfare model sees competition as necessary and benign. There is a doctrine of minimal rights and freedoms.[22] The multilevel-equal-access model is described by North in the following way:

> [It] derives from the idea that human beings, like all other creatures on earth, are parts of nature, not masters over it, and are subject to nature's laws. No individual group, or nation properly holds title to the earth and its resources, but merely enjoys use of it for a period of time. From this premise it follows that unequal access to and unequal distribution of resources and other earthly benefits

> are arbitrary arrangements created by human beings and without natural justification. This model also assumes that social stability, as well as justice, is enhanced to the extent that a gain or loss of the society as a whole is shared as equally as possible by all ... In social, political, and economic terms there are three basic points of reference for human affairs: the planet and its resources as a whole, mankind as a whole, and the individual person... The fundamental, natural, and irreducible human unit is the individual person ... [23]

In this model, individuals are responsible for their own actions and their impact upon others and the entire society.

> Everything pertaining to the individual is affected by interactions with the physical environment, with people, and with other living creatures. This means that what I do to you today, will be motivated and shaped, in part at least, not only by what I did to you yesterday, but also by what you did to me yesterday. Thus, each of us is partly responsible for the other's behavior and plight.[24]

It is also recognized that both competition and cooperation are part of human nature. In terms of the institutional framework:

> Both political and economic institutions within this framework operate to keep differences in access to resources and benefits within relatively narrow limits. The pursuit, maintenance, and regulation of all human affairs and enterprises are carried out on a variety of levels and within many different jurisdictions including the family, the neighbourhood, the community, the province, the nation, the region and the world. As many decisions as functionally possible are made at the individual, family and community levels. Only those decisions that cannot be carried out effectively at the local level are delegated to a higher level.[25]

The individual retains political sovereignty in the model as in Indian Socialism. Lawmakers would be chosen by election, lot, rotation or a combination of these. Use of more than one's per capita share of resources is considered a violation, in the same way as theft. Work is shared as equally as possible with inverse feedback mechanisms (rather than positive ones) built into the system to facilitate equality.[26]

If the State is considered as an institutional framework in which a single group exercises legal monopoly of force, as North defines it,[27] then it is possible to argue that in the Indian conception of socialism or *Sarvodaya,* there is no State in the conventional sense. In the Indian model, State authorities do not function through the use of force but rather democratically through the use of non-violence, to the greatest extent possible, to maintain order. They also do not seek to maintain a class hierarchy, but rather to do away with it.

Sarvodaya, then, in terms of power distribution, is pre-statist, or perhaps, more appropriately, post-statist. And it is consciously so, even in the face of existing technology which gives it the ability to monopolize violence. Thus it asserts moral and ethical values over technology so that the moral sphere controls the material.

According to Tandon, the term Sarvodaya has been found in the Jain scriptures. In any event, Mahatma Gandhi paraphrased the thesis in John Ruskin's *Unto This Last* as *Sarvodaya*. For him, it meant the uplift of all and a balanced all-round well being and development of the whole man. Human considerations, particularly the ethical, moral and spiritual, must take precedence over others.[28]

It has also been noted that the Indian conception of democracy is inherent in Buddhist principles and monastic practices, that Islam is egalitarian in principle and that Hinduism has a highly developed tradition of natural law.[29]

Finally, the ultimate goal of spiritual emancipation or *moksha* in egalitarian society in the Indian conception of socialism grew out of the synthesis found in modern Indian political thought between the Hindu tradition and the Western spirit of inquiry. Brown emphasized two major tendencies in modern Hindu political theory: a reaffirming of the ancient principle of *Dharma* and an emphasis on reform and universal ideals.[30] "The most distinguished note of the Indian Renaissance" (late eighteenth and nineteenth centuries) is "the fulfillment and realization of the universalism of the *Upanishads*."[31]

The emphasis upon the spiritual is seen again in Rabindranath Tagore who wrote : "Political freedom does not give us freedom when our mind is not free ... Man's truth is moral truth, and his emancipation is in the spiritual life."[32]

M.N. Roy, Jayaprakash Narayan and J.B. Kripalani

In this work we shall examine the theoretical contributions of M.N. Roy, Jayaprakash Narayan and J.B. Kripalani to modern Indian political thought. Each of these highly independent thinkers contributed in unique and significant ways to the development of Indian Socialism. Assimilative in nature, threads of Renaissance Humanism, Liberalism, Utopian Socialism, Humanist Marxism as well as ideas and ideals from the Indian philosophical tradition are woven into their writings. Their conclusions were often arrived at through a long, arduous and painful process of intensive thought and action during the Nationalist struggle. Each demonstrated remarkable conceptual flexibility, critical insight, intellectual honesty and a willingness to make new starts.

M.N. Roy, whose real name was Manendranath Bhattacharya, entered politics as a revolutionary in Bengal, engaging in acts of political terrorism on behalf of the nationalist movement. His political activities soon took him abroad to the United States and Mexico, where he became an orthodox Marxist, and worked in the Communist International. Shortly after his return to India, he was imprisoned for a period of six years, during which time he studied widely, completed several of his basic works on Western and Indian thought, and began his gradual disillusionment with orthodox Marxism.

Roy's study of philosophy as well as of Stalinist repression in the Soviet Union led him to reject economic determinism. He became a Radical Humanist while remaining a philosophical materialist. As a Radical Humanist, Roy's ideas largely paralleled those of the young Marx.

Influenced by Mahatma Gandhi, Roy came to insist upon morality in politics, but he saw morality as essentially secular-rational. Reason in man, for Roy, was an expression of reason in nature. In contrast to the other two thinkers in this study, Roy rejected traditionalism and religion, being strongly influenced by Feuerbach. He saw Vedic Hinduism as reactionary and argued that historically it arose as an attempt by the Brahmin elite to destroy the materialist enlightenment which came with Buddhism, and reassert their ideological and cultural hegemony. As a result, he considered central elements in Gandhi's thought as reactionary and opposed to the progressive movement in history, the end of which he saw as the supreme goal of human freedom. Although he remained a materialist, human freedom or liberation was conceived in spiritual terms, as *Moksha*, in accord with the mainstream of Indian thought.

Roy's experience and observation of practical politics led him to criticize severely the institutions of bourgeois democracy, including the State, the Party and the parliamentary system of government. He came to advocate partyless democracy and a decentralized institutional structure of society similar to that conceived by Gandhi, Jayaprakash Narayan and J. B. Kripalani. He also saw education as somewhat of a panacea in the creation of a humanist society.

Roy's life, an arduous and often tortuous path of self-discovery was, in many ways, tragic. His early dogmatism and late dynamism made him a fascinating but largely inconsistent thinker. The language of

Marxism, in which his ideas were expressed during his active political career in India, lacked popular appeal, attracting only a small intellectual elite. The Indian Communist Party tended to march out of step with the Nationalist movement and alienated Nationalist leaders, including those in the Congress Socialist Party, through its uncooperative tactics. Roy's Radical Democratic Party, based on materialist ideology, lacking a concrete program for the attainment of political independence, and often in opposition to the programs of the Indian National Congress, failed altogether. Roy's Westernized and intellectual approach could not appeal to the masses and so could not take root rapidly in Indian soil and nationalist politics. Roy ultimately came to see Gandhi's non-violent approach as more suitable to Indian political conditions.

M.N. Roy was a brilliant thinker and critical theorist. His conception of partyless democracy was influentual in shaping the thought of Jayaprakash Narayan.

The writings of Jayaprakash Narayan (J.P.) contribute enormously to shaping twentieth century Indian Political thought. J.P.'s desire to work for national freedom was sparked by two events in 1919, passage of the repressive Rowlett Acts, which authorized imprisonment without trial, and the Julianwala Bagh massacre in Amritsar. After a period of study in the United States, during which he became a Marxist and a socialist, he returned to India in 1929. He was excited by the awakening of the Indian people under Gandhi's leadership but held to his conviction that the establishment of Marxian socialism through class struggle was the only solution to India's bondage.

J.P. became the acting secretary of the Indian National Congress in 1932 and helped to form the Congress Socialist Party in 1934, serving as its general secretary. In the 1940's J.P.'s thinking moved closer to that of Gandhi and he began to advocate a democratic socialist transformation of Indian Society, rather than a violent one waged through class struggle. The Sarvodaya conception of a decentralized and democratic society became his conception of a future free India. In 1952, J.P. announced a final break with Marxism and in 1954 vowed to withdraw from party and power politics. During the 1950's and 1960's, J.P. became active in the *Bhoodan* Movement. Increasingly his thought concerning the ideal institutional structure of society tended to merge with that of Gandhi. The earlier Marxist influence remained evident in his thought, however. Late in life, J.P., remaining an influentual force in Indian politics, called for a partyless democracy and "Total Revolution."

J.B. Kripalani also contributed immensely to the development of Indian Socialist thought. Kripalani's participation in the Nationalist

Movement began in 1917 with Mahatma Gandhi's campaign to improve the social conditions of the peasants in Champaran. In 1923, Kripalani became the principal of the Gujarat Vidyapith, the national college which Gandhi founded at Ahmedabad. In 1934 he became secretary of the Indian National Congress and remained in this office until elected president in 1946. After independence, Kripalani continued to participate actively in Indian national politics.

Kripalani's theoritical writings provide both a systematic interpretation of the ideas of Gandhi as well as a critique of modern industrialized society and Marxism. Kripalani's analysis of Indian society and the Indian Nationalist Movement is also important.

Beginning from diverse standpoints, ideologically, these three thinkers came to see economic and political decentralization as necessary for the establishment of a democratic society which could insure individual moral autonomy. Following Gandhi, they worked for the renovation of society and politics through the application of moral values to the public sphere. Rejecting economic determinism, they believed that the will was capable of triumphing over material factors. Consistent with the Indian cultural tradition, they saw freedom as spiritual self-realization, man's ultimate goal in a free society.

References

1. Raghavan Iyer, *Parapolitics* (New York: Oxford Univ. Press, 1979), pp. 5-6.
2. *Ibid.*
3. Reinhard Bendix, "Social Stratification and the Political Community," in *Philosophy, Politics and Society,* eds. Peter Laslett and W.G. Runciman (Oxford: Basil Blackwell, 1964) p. 217.
4. Gunnar Myrdal, *Asian Drama*, 3 Vols. (New York: Pantheon, 1968), 2: 799.
5. *Ibid.*
6. *Ibid.*, p. 801.
7. *Ibid.*, p. 805.
8. *Ibid.*
9. *Ibid.*, p. 807.
10. V.K.R.V. Rao. *Indian Socialism* (New Delhi: Concept Publishing Co., 1982), pp. 98-101.
11. *Ibid.*, pp. 101-102.
12. Vinoba Bhave, *Third Power* (Rajghat, Varanasi: Sarva Seva Sangh Prakashan, 1972), pp. VII-VIII.
13. *Ibid.*, p. 21.

14. *Ibid.*, p. XI.
15. *Ibid.*, p. 35.
16. *Ibid.*, pp. 11-12.
17. *Ibid.*, pp. 65-66
18. *Ibid.*, p. 69.
19. *Ibid.*, p. 77.
20. Bharatan Kumarappa, *Capitalism, Socialism or Villagism* (Rajghat, Varanasi: Sarva Seva Sangh Prakashan, 1965), pp. 108-115.
21. *Ibid.*, p. 189.
22. Robert C. North, *The World That Could Be* (Stanford, California: Stanford Alumni Association, 1976), pp. 60-69.
23. *Ibid.*, p. 69.
24. *Ibid.*
25. *Ibid.*, p. 72.
26. *Ibid.*, pp. 73-75.
27. *Ibid.*, p. 35.
28. Vishwanath Tandon, *The Social and Political Philosophy of Sarvodaya After-Gandhiji* (Rajghat, Varanasi: Sarva Seva Sangh Prakashan, 1965), p. 1.
29. Iyer, p. 199.
30. Mackenzie Brown, *The White Umbrella* (Berkeley: University of California Press, 1958), p. 84.
31. *Ibid.*, p. 82.
32. *Ibid.*, pp. 120-121.

2

M.N. Roy on Democratic Socialism

The evolution of M.N. Roy's political thought continued from his youth to his embrace of radical humanism late in life. Beginning in an isolated village in Bengal, Roy's political activities took him to the Far East and around the world, bringing him into contact with many nationalist and revolutionary leaders and thinkers. He gained an enormous knowledge of contemporary nationalist and revolutionary movements through his prolonged political activity. Roy's prodigious study during his imprisonment expanded his wide-ranging intellectual interests. His efforts to merge into the mainstream of Indian Nationalist politics and create a leftist vanguard influenced his thinking about the Party and the State. After a brief biographical sketch, this chapter will explore the roots of Roy's materialist perspective and his interpretation of history. Secondly, Roy's critique of Liberalism and Utilitarianism will be expounded. Finally, his ideas regarding democratic socialism, decentralization and partyless democracy will be delineated.

There were four major phases in Roy's political thinking. During the first period from 1900 to 1919, Roy's thinking was shaped by the Bengal Revolutionary nationalist leader, Jatindra Nath Mukerji and the intellectual influence of Vivekananda. Roy's political activities during this period consisted of terrorist activities in Bengal and efforts to secure arms for the revolutionary nationalists in India after 1915. During the second period from 1919 to 1931, Roy became a dedicated Marxist and Communist beginning with his conversion under the tutelage of the Bolshevik Michael Borodin in Mexico. This period ended with Roy's imprisonment in India in 1931. The third period from 1931 to 1948 was a transition period. During the first six years in prison, Roy's views on Marxism began to change and he rejected the theory of economic determinism. Upon his release he modified his views on Nationalism, moving closer to the Indian National Congress. Finally, he organised the Radical Democratic Party in opposition to the Congress. The last period from 1948 until Roy's death in 1954 began with the disbanding of the Radical Democratic Party and its transformation into the Radical Humanist Movement.[1]

Narendranath Bhattacharya (M.N. Roy) was born in the Bengal village of Urbalia, 24 Parganas District, near Calcutta in 1889 in a Brahmin family. His father was a priest and school teacher. Narendranath attended the National University founded by Aurobindo Ghose where he participated occasionally in political activities associated with the Nationalist Movement. He was influenced by Vinayak Damodar Savarkar, leader of revolutionary youths. He joined the Yugantar group, a Bengal revolutionary organisation at age fourteen. Its leader, Jatindra Nath Mukerji became Roy's revolutionary Guru.[2]

In 1907, Roy was first arrested for participating in a raid on the village railway station. He moved to Calcutta and continued his revolutionary activities. In 1910, he was tried in the Howrah Conspiracy case, accused of conspiring to wage war against the King and was sentenced to twenty months in jail. While in jail Narendranath was influenced by the study of religious literature. Upon release from jail he resolved to become a sannyasi, joining the Ramakrishna Mission. But the squalid condition of the people wherever he travelled rekindled in him the desire to work for political emancipation and he returned to the world of underground political activities.[3]

In 1915 Indian revolutionaries began to contact German diplomats in the Far East as part of a plan to smuggle arms into India with their assistance. Roy was chosen for this work and for the next fifteen years moved in the underground world of international revolutionary activity as an ideologist and organiser. He met many of the important revolutionaries of the time, including Sun Yat-Sen, Vladimir Lenin, Leon Trotsky, Joseph Stalin, Ho Chi-Minh and others. As a theorist, he proved to be too creative, honest and humane for the organisational mold of the Communist International. In these respects: he was somewhat like Leon Trotsky. Both were dynamic but ultimately tragic figures in history. In 1914, Roy first left India, travelling to Java to meet with German representatives, but the plot to secure arms failed. He returned with a small amount of money but no arms. In 1915 he again travelled abroad, this time to remain for 16 years. The new plan called for smuggling arms overland from China as well as securing German cooperation in arming Andaman Island prisoners and landing them on the Orissa coast. Again Roy secured money but the Germans declined to cooperate further.[4]

Roy travelled next to Japan, meeting the Indian revolutionary Rash Behary Bose and also Sun Yat-Sen. As a fiery nationalist, Roy secured little encouragement from them. Bose focussed upon the larger "mission of Japan to free Asia from White domination." Sun Yat-Sen believed that the nationalists should let the Japanese drive the colonial powers from Asia, then seek terms with the Japanese. This thinking was based on the "doctrine of racial solidarity."[5]

Nevertheless, a bizarre scheme was discussed with Sun Yat-Sen for securing arms. The Chinese nationalist leader suggested that Roy should seek funds from the German ambassador in China. This money would be used to purchase arms from the rebels fighting the "Third Chinese Revolution," the revolt in Yunan and Szechuan provinces bordering on Burma and India. Roy proceeded to China but the mission again failed when the Germans refused to fund the purchases.

Roy decided to contact German diplomats in the United States and Berlin. He was smuggled back into Japan where, with a German supplied passport and disguised as a Theology student, Father Martin, he secured a visa for the United States. In 1956, he arrived in San Francisco and spent two weeks with friends at Stanford University in Palo Alto. It was here that he took the name Manabendra Nath Roy (M.N. Roy). Travelling to New York, he met Lala Lajpat Rai and heard him speak. At this time he differed sharply in his thinking from the Socialists, Anarchists and Syndicalists whom he met in New York. He wrote, "As nationalists, we disagreed with their doctrine of social revolution; as Indians, we vehemently opposed Marxist Materialism with our spiritual genius."[6]

In his free time Roy visited the New York Public Library to read the works of Marx and soon became a believer in Socialism. Roy found that Indian nationalists in the United States, were suspected of being German agents. He was arrested on the campus of Columbia University but a few days later escaped prison by slipping into Mexico, where he hoped to take active part in a revolution.

In Mexico, Roy wrote a number of pamphlets and articles on imperialism and revolution and founded the Communist Party of Mexico, the first Communist party outside the Soviet Union.[7] He met Michael Borodin, the Communist International representative in Mexico, who had a profound influence on him. In his memoirs, Roy recalled, "He initiated me in the intricacies of Hegelian dialectics as the key to Marxism. My lingering faith in the special genius of India faded as I learned from him the history of European culture."[8]

Nevertheless, Roy had some reservations and detected elements in Borodin's creed that repelled him.

> ...Borodin's remark that Bolsheviks did not argue but obeyed discipline, had rubbed me on the wrong side ... The Bolshevik had to defend his faith in the unchallengeable authority of the party and the revolutionary duty of its members to submit themselves unquestioningly to discipline. It appeared to me that the revolutionary faith of Bolshevism had a religious fervour, which did not harmonise with its materialist philosophy."[9]

But Roy became a dedicated Marxist and prepared to go to Moscow as the Representative of the Communist Party of Mexico to the Communist International.

In November 1919, Roy secretly left Mexico for Europe, and made his way to Berlin and Moscow. In the USSR, Roy met Lenin with whom he discussed the colonial question and drafted an alternative thesis to that of Lenin.

There were fundamental differences between Roy and Lenin on this issue. Lenin believed that nationalism was a revolutionary force and his thesis on the national and colonial question reiterated the principle of self-determination. Roy disagreed with Lenin's view that the nationalist bourgeoisie played a historically revolutionary role.[10]

Roy asked Lenin how the Communist International could develop the national liberation movement in the colonial territories. He did not agree with Lenin's answer.

> He argued that Imperialism had held the colonial countries back in feudal social conditions, which hindered the development of capitalism and thwarted the ambition of the native bourgeoisie. Historically, the national liberation movement had the significance of the bourgeois democratic revolution. Every stage of social evolution being historically determined, the colonial countries must have their bourgeois democratic revolution before they could enter the stage of the proletarian revolution. The Communists, therefore, must help the colonial liberation movement under the leadership of the nationalist bourgeoisie, regarding the latter as an objectively revolutionary force.[11]

But Roy believed that the nationalist movement could not liberate India from Imperialism.

> I pointed out that the bourgeoisie even in the most advanced colonial countries, like India, as a class, was not economically and culturally differentiated from the feudal social order: therefore, the nationalist movement was ideologically reactionary in the sense that the triumph would not necessarily mean a bourgeois democratic revolution. The role of Gandhi was the crucial point of difference. Lenin believed that, as the inspirer and leader of a mass movement, he was a revolutionary. I maintained that, a religious and cultural revivalist, he was bound to be a reactionary socially, however revolutionary he might appear politically.[12]

Roy conceptualized the tactics he would later attempt to put into practice in India.

> I concretised his [Lenin's] general idea of supporting the colonial national liberation movement with the proposal that the Communist Parties should be organised with the purpose of revolutionising the social character of the movement under the pressure of organised workers and peasants ... I maintained that, afraid of revolution, the nationalist bourgeosie would compromise with Imperialism in return for some economic and political concessions to their class. 'The working classes should be prepared to take over at that crisis the leadership of the struggle for national liberation and transform it into a revolutionary mass movement.[13]

Roy felt certain that unless the proletariat could capture the leadership of the nationalist movement, a compromise with Imperialism was certain. He concluded that a base of operations should be established as close to the Indian border as possible.

Roy proceeded to Tashkent in Central Asia to establish his base of operations and raise an army of liberation. The force would be equipped and trained in Afghanistan and with the help of mercenary tribesmen occupy Indian territory and set up a civil government.[14] An Indian military school was founded at Tashkent to train Indian revolutionaries.[15]

Roy also participated in the international congresses of the Communist International, becoming a full member of the Executive Committee in 1924.[16]

In 1926 Roy was sent on a mission to China to assist the nationalists. At this time Michael Barodin was the Communist International representative in China. Roy's mission to China failed, however, with the defeat of the revolution, which insured that he would be subsequently ousted from the Communist International.[17] He returned to Moscow and Berlin in 1927 to write Revolution and Counterrevolution in China.

In September 1928 at the ultra-Leftist Sixth World Congress of the Communist International in Moscow, Roy was accused of putting forward the "Theory of Decolonization." This theory held that "British Imperialism would gradually lead the Indian people to freedom." The charge was unfounded, but was used against Roy as the Comintern had decided to change policy and it was necessary to expel Roy.[18]

In 1929, Roy was expelled from the Communist International, but continued his work in the Indian Nationalist Movement, although many Indian Communists now repudiated him.[19] When the Indian National Congress held its session at Lahore in December 1929, Roy placed before it a programme for national revolution.

On November 14, 1930, Roy left Europe for India, spending the last week with Ellen Gottschalk whom he married in 1937. In 1931, he was present at the Karachi session of the Indian National Congress where he met Subhas Chandra Bose and Jawaharlal Nehru. Nehru recalled this meeting in his *Autobiography*:

> I had come across M.N. Roy in Allahabad some days before coming to Karachi ... I recognised him immediately, having seen him in Moscow in 1927. He saw me at Karachi also. During the past few years Roy had written a great deal in condemnation of me politically, and he had often succeeded in hurting me a little. There was a great deal of difference between us and yet I felt attracted towards him, and when later he had been arrested and was in trouble, I wanted to do what little I could to help him. I was attracted to him by his remarkable intellectual capacity; I was also attracted to him because he seemed such a lonely figure, deserted by everybody. The British Government was naturally after him; nationalist India was not interested in him; and those who called themselves Communists in India condemned him as a traitor to the cause.[20]

Travelling under the name of "Dr. Mahmud," Roy worked to build up the trade union movement until his arrest on July 21, 1931. Roy's arrest may have been accelerated by his denunciation by Indian Communists.

Roy spent the next six years in prison, much of the time in near solitary confinement, during which time he devoted himself to intensive study and writing. He produced an enormous amount of writings, under severly difficult circumstances. In 1935, Roy attempted to get his followers reinstated in the *Comintern* so that they could work in the Communist Party of India, but this effort failed.[21]

Upon his release from prison on November 20, 1936, Roy was welcomed by the Nationalists, except for the Communists.[22] At this point, Roy moderated his views somewhat and argued that national independence should be the immediate goal of the Nationalists. Shortly after his release he travelled to Allahabad where he was met by Acharya J.B. Kripalani, a member of the All India Congress Committee. With Kripalani, he went to Nehru's house where he spent a week.[23] Roy joined the Congress and was made a member of the AICC, but Congress leaders were suspicious of his intentions. Soon after this, Roy attended a series of meetings in Bombay, which included Kripalani and other Congress leaders.[24]

Jayaprakash Narayan was converted to Marxism while studying the writings of Roy while he was a student in the United States in the 1920's. As General Secretary of the Congress Socialist Party in 1936, J.P. was anxious for Roy and his followers to join them in their work. He visited Roy and after the meeting believed that he was assured of Roy's cooperation and support.[25]

But Roy believed the CSP was likely to degenerate into reformism due to the heterogeneous nature of its membership, which included Marxists as well as non-Marxists. Therefore, Roy ordered his followers to join the CSP in order to split the party and absorb the "proletarian elements." In 1937, Roy urged his followers to resign from the party in groups in order to give the impression that the CSP was collapsing. J.P. later felt bitter toward Roy over this incident.[26]

During World War II, Roy's support for the War and his opposition to the Quit India movement led to Roy's expulsion from the Indian National Congress. In December 1940, he organised the Radical Democratic Party. Roy worked feverishly to develop pro-war sentiment in India, also becoming General Secretary of the Indian Federation of Labour, a group which broke off from the All India Trade Union Congress, over the war issue.[27]

During the closing years of the war, Roy arrived at his philosophy of New Humanism, coming to see more clearly the inadequacies of Marxism and Communism. He felt that at this stage of history, society must go beyond both capitalism and Communism. Roy held summer camps at Dehra Dun and Mussoorie to put forward his ideas, developing the "Humanist Manifesto" or "Twenty two Theses."[28]

Roy and several other members of the Party decided that in New Humanism there was no place for a political party and that the party would have to be disbanded to remain consistent with their principles. It was argued that the party organisation prevented people from exercising their sovereignty and was thus an obstacle in the way of democracy. Consequently, the party was disbanded in 1948, after years of organisational work.[29]

J.P. visited Roy twice to discuss the ideas of "partyless democracy" with him, but on both occasions Roy was too ill to speak with J.P.[30] Roy died on January 25, 1954. His wife Ellen continued to work in the New Humanist Movement until she was murdered on December 13, 1960.[31]

Philosophical and Historical Materialism

M.N. Roy adopted a materialist view of the world after becoming a Marxist early in life. Materialism may be defined as "the name given to a family of doctrines concerning the nature of the world which give to matter a primary position and accord to mind (or spirit) a secondary, dependent reality or even none at all. Extreme materialism asserts that the real world consists of material things, varying in their states and relations, and nothing else."[32]

Marxism was the basis for Roy's materialist views, his ideas being reinforced by his study of materialism while in prison. Roy remained a philosophical materialist even after he rejected the Marxist view that history as well as human thought and action are economically determined. Roy studied the history of materialism in order to discover evidence by which to reinforce the Marxist view of the world. He also wanted to dispel the belief, which he considered a myth, that the special "genius" of the Indian mind and Indian society was its concentration upon the spiritual. Roy believed that a study of ancient Indian philosophy would disprove this "myth" and show that ancient Indian thinkers were actually progressive pioneers in developing a liberating materialist view. He believed that he could prove that Vedantic spiritual revivalists who were able to overcome the materialists were motivated by the desire to reassert their economic, political and cultural hegemony over society rather than with the search for Truth. Roy also desired to make materialism both comprehensible and appealing to modern Indians, breaking them out of their obsession with things spiritual. Roy saw such an enlightenment as the basis for the Indian Renaissance.

Roy's study of the history of philosophy convinced him that mankind had made real progress toward freedom and human liberation only in those periods when a scientific and materialist view of the world was emerging. He wrote:

> Every great thinker who contributed anything permanent to human progress advanced the cause of materialism, even if he

> were an avowed enemy of materialism. This proves that materialism is the driving force of all human progress.[33]

Roy believed that the entire history of philosophy and human progress had contributed to the development of materialist thought, although some periods were marked by rapid progress, while in others, idealist and religious views impeded progress. Roy noted at least three periods in history when rapid strides were made by independent and forward-looking thinkers. Firstly, during the classical periods of ancient Greece and India, several thinkers elaborated materialist views of the universe. Secondly, during the Renaissance in Europe, the liberating spirit of scientific materialism re-emerged and man again greatly increased his knowledge of himself and the world. Thirdly, with Feuerbach, man again set out on a new path. "Feuerbach's materialist criticism pulled down the religio-theo-metaphysical super-structure of civilisation, not only Western, but as a whole." [34] Marx and Engels took up the thread with a dynamic conception of man as a social being, who through action in history determines his own consciousness. For Roy, "materialism is the philosophy of revolution. Revolutions are inherent in the process of human development. Therefore, materialist philosophy is a necessity in all ages."[35]

When Roy was imprisoned in India, he planned to write a history of materialism. In his first letter from Cawnpore jail (April 11, 1931), he wrote, "I should like to make a special study of the history of Materialism and of the cultural importance of the Middle Ages."[36] Roy believed that such a work was badly needed in India.

> ...[P]eople have such erroneous ideas about the subject. It must be made understandable to the Indian mind. The arguments and facts, which are commonplace to the European of average education, are still not accepted as such in this country. They are regarded and suspected as products of the materialist western civilisation which is antagonistic to the "spiritual genius"[37] of this holy land.

In *Materialism,* Roy argued that "in the earlier stages of its development, philosophy, by its very nature, was materialistic."[38] He pointed out that Pythagoras defined philosophy as "contemplation, study and knowledge of nature." Before man reached this speculative phase, he had imagined supernatural forces behind natural phenomena. But intellectual growth impels man to begin philosophy, that is to "seek in nature itself the core of all natural phenomena, to find in nature a unity behind the diversity."[39] He wrote:

> ... [M]etaphysics leaves the ground of philosophy in quest of noumenon above and beyond nature, something which is distinct from the phenomena ... Strictly speaking, philosophy is materialism, and materialism is the only possible philosophy. For it represents the knowledge of nature as it really exists-knowledge acquired through the contemplation, observation and investigation of the phenomena of nature itself.[40]

The following account of the history of materialism, written in 1934 during Roy's imprisonment, is based upon these assumptions. At this point in the development of his thought, Roy attributed his philosophical enlightenment to the West, and after sixteen years abroad was repulsed by the Indian frame of mind, which he saw as mystical and fatalistic. At this point he appreciated only those materialistic elements which he found in Indian philosophical thought.

Although Roy was to move closer to the mainstream of Indian tradition in the future as he re-evaluated existing Marxism and its underlying philosophy and developed a critique of the parliamentary form of government, he remained highly critical of religion and "mysticism" as the enemy of human freedom. As a radical humanist, he turned to the social thought of Vivekananda, Aurobindo and Gandhi as an alternative to both capitalism and Communism, while rejecting the tradition of Idealism in Indian thought. In 1951 he wrote:

> The bewildered bulk of the civilised mankind can see only two ways out of intellectual confusion and the resulting moral chaos: one is the line of protection offered by the totalitarian state .. ; the other is religious revivalism. The former is rejected by all who believe that social justice is compatible with individual liberty. But only a few realise that religious revivalism means lowering of the standard of the revolt of man against spiritual slavery...[41]

Roy's statement that "...philosophy is materialism and materialism is the only possible philosophy," amounts, in effect, to a redefinition of philosophy and a narrowing of the meaning of the term. As such, it is a reductionistic approach. Although this is true with regard to both the Western and Eastern philosophical traditions, it is particularly restrictive in dealing with Indian thought where no sharp distinction is delineated between philosophy and religion. Idealism was viewed by Roy as reactionary and often equated with ignorance and slavery. Human freedom, for Roy, was incompatible with idealism. By using this approach, Roy presupposed his conclusion that materialism is the basis of all progress in society.

Roy's account of the development of philosophical materialism proceeds as follows. He traced the origin of materialism to Thales, who began the search for the origin of phenomena in nature itself. This marked the beginning of an "era of free inquiry," in which man set out to "conquer nature" and gain freedom. Man became conscious of his "mission to conquer nature" and an era of science and philosophy began.[42]

Other Ionian physicists, according to Roy, contributed to the "development of materialism. Anaximander found the natural origin of things in air. Diogenes, his disciple, traced the reason that regulated the world to the original substance of air, and saw the universe spontaneously evolving itself.[43]

Roy argued that Anaxagoras raised monist materialism to a higher level by suggesting how motion might appear in a presumably inert mass of infinitesimal fragments of matter.[44] He said that "nous" (mind) which governs and arranges the process of aggregation and segregation of the infinitesimal fragments is not a spiritual force and therefore not dualistic. Heraclitus considered fire to be the original substance and the world to be "an ever living fire-self kindled and self extinguished."[45] Roy declared that the major contribution of Heraclitus to materialism was the science of dialectics which destroyed the "absurd conception of absoluteness." All truth was knowable to the senses and the foundation was laid for the Marxist-Hegelian notion of the negation of the negation.[46] Unity behind the diversity of phenomena was to be found not in the substratum but in the empirical fact of change—what exists is the process of becoming. Protagoras, according to Roy, added to this tradition with the proposition that "man is the measure of all things." For Protagoras, that which can be perceived by man really exists, and that which cannot does not exist. Roy argued that Empedocles, who deviated from strict materialism toward Platonic metaphysics thought that all things were the product of a combination of primary elements, fire, water, earth and air. So he was a materialist in the sense that he held the view that ideas were the result of the impressions of objects received through the senses.[47]

Ancient materialism was developed into a comprehensive system by Democritus, according to Roy, and then further developed by Epicuras several hundred years later. The atomist theory from Democritus and Epicuras became the foundation of modern science. These early scientists conceived of a soul made up of fine atoms. These materialist philosophies were seen by Roy as the "weapon in the struggle for the spiritual liberation of man."[48]

But Roy saw man's project of liberation—his quest for freedom—as repeatedly plagued throughout history by the nemesis of metaphysics. The failure of the ancient materialist thinkers to defeat metaphysical ideas resulted in the domination of human thought by religion, theology and metaphysics for nearly 2,000 years. Roy traced the root of metaphysics to the failure of earlier materialism to explain the phenomena of sensation. The "materialist conception of the origin and evolution of the universe is the mother of science." But philosophy degenerated into metaphysics because man was not yet sufficiently advanced in his conquest of nature.[49]

The Epicureans carried on the struggle for human freedom and happiness, according to Roy, but were severely censored by Christianity. The Roman ruling class suppressed the Epicureans because of the revolutionary potential of their teachings that happiness can be obtained through knowledge. There was a basic "antithesis" between the Epicureans and the Stoics and Christians. The Stoics believed that the highest realisation of individual existence is to submerge the self into the general. But the Epicureans wanted "freedom from superstitions."[50] The Stoics and Christians taught that virtue is its own reward. For the Epicureans, virtue was the means to an end which is happiness.[51]

Epicurus is important in the development of materialist thought because of his modifications of the atomic theory which contributed to later work by Rene Descartes, Isaac Newton, Robert Boyle and others. Basically, to account for the origin of material bodies from atoms, Epicurus conceived of the atoms as deviating from the straight lines of their fall. This improved the previous theory, because Aristotle had refuted the theory of Democritus by showing its main weakness. Aristotle showed that in a void space, all bodies, irrespective of size, would fall with a uniform speed, hence there could be no impingement necessary for the atomic motion to become more and more complex. Epicurus' theory of deviation not only accounted for the origin of substances but also for free will. This modification of theory, according to Roy is in accord with the later Newtonian conception that heavenly bodies gravitated toward each other. Epicurus has a theory of the soul, but this does not make him a dualist, for Roy. The soul is composed of a fine substance distributed throughout the whole body and dies with the body.[52]

Revolutionary as Epicurus' theories were, they were obscured by the "metaphysical deviation of Greek philosophy" which led to the establishment of the Catholic church. Epicurean humanity, according to Roy, was then held in "ignorance and superstition for several hundred years." But the basic cosmology of Democritus and Epicurus survived and again flowered during the Renaissance, when scholars built upon the ideas of classical materialist thinkers. The "rational-materialist foundation of the Aristotelean system," according to Roy, eventually "shook off its metaphysical superstructure to become a powerful lever of modern civilisation."[53]

At the close of the Middle Ages, Aristotelean logic triumphed over the Platonic idealist system, again opening the way for free scientific inquiry and progress toward the ultimate liberation of mankind.

The struggle between freedom loving materialists and metaphysical idealists who, in Roy's view, wished to keep man enslaved, went on in India just as in classical Greece. Not surprisingly, Roy perceived the first true attempts toward science and philosophy in ancient India as attempts to understand nature and self in a materialist way.[54]

In Roy's view, the earliest Indian materialist philosophy was systematized by Brihaspati who authored the *Lokayata Darsana*, and who is known as the founder of the materialist Charvak system in ancient India. According to the *Lokayata Darsana*, (1) only perceptual evidence is authority, (2) the elements are earth, water, fire and air, (3) wealth and enjoyment are objects of human existence, (4) matter can think, (5) there is no other world and (6) death is the end of all.[55] According to the *Charvakas*, "mind is matter thinking," and "morality is natural, that is, a social convention, not a divine command."[56]

The oldest system of Hindu philosophy, the *Vaisheshik*, was founded by Kanada who lived in the sixth century B.C., approximately the same time that Greek thinkers expounded an atomist theory. Kanada, according to Roy, makes no room for the soul in the metaphysical or spiritualist sense of the term. "Intelligence is conceived as a mere adventitious quality of the atoms" and "consciousness is regarded as the product of a complicated combination of atoms."[57] Consciousness develops when, at a certain stage, an atomic aggregate acquires the property of receiving impressions of external objects and relating to them. The *Vaisheshik* system regarded nature not as being but as a process of becoming.[58]

The *Sankhya* system of Kapila deviated from strict materialism and developed a rational-naturalist system of metaphysics. Kapila's theory of cognition, according to Roy, is materialistic. He says that "the origin of the physical world is traced to an endless process of causality, and that process is inherent in nature." Roy saw Sankhya as "free of the dualist fallacy" and "a self contained materialist system." Kapila held that sense perception was the only reliable source of knowledge."[59]

Buddhist thought was rooted in these early theories of materialism and built upon them. Its "point of departure," according to Roy, was the atomism of the *Nyaya-Vaisheshik* system and the rationalistic-mechanistic conception of nature contained in the *Sankhya* system. Generally, Buddhists visualized everything as in a flux and rejected the "absolute truth" revealed in the *Vedas*. They did not think of the ego as a reality but rather conceptualized the individual consciousness as *sanskaras*, that is, activities and impressions man receives throughout life. These constitute a causal series so that the soul is a sum total of impressions.[60]

Roy stated that "no school of Buddhist philosophy admits the existence of any extra-natural or metaphysical intelligence such as God of soul." The ideal of *nirvana* represented the nihilism of Buddhist philosophy. But this was a contradiction in a thoroughly materialistic system and consequently "overwhelmed" the system.[61]

The Jains also, according to Roy, disputed an absolute standard of truth and developed a dialectical logic. They expounded a particular logic (*anekant*) which maintained that contradictory attributes, such as being and nonbeing could belong to one and the same thing. The Jains conceived the soul as composed of soul-atoms.

But the great progress made by these systems toward a systematic science of man and nature, toward human knowledge and progress ceased when they were overcome by metaphysical Brahmanical philosophy. In fact, India differed from Europe in that "a renaissance of the ancient liberating thought was delayed until it was too late."[62] For Roy, the reasons for this were fundamentally economic and he expounded an account relying heavily upon economic factors, in accord with his Marxist world view. First, he says that the priestly ruling class preached the doctrine of renunciation and mortification in order to maintain a dominating position. Here the relationship between the Brahmins and the Buddhist. pioneers of materialist thought is largley analogous to that between the Roman Christians and the Epicureans, for Roy.

The Scholasticism of Shankaracharya "checked all spiritual progress" because of the economic conditions of India. The southern Dravidians (with a more advanced culture and superior markets and trade routes) were overcome by the more primitive and pastoral Aryans. Buddhism, according to Roy, represented a revolt not only of the *Kshatriyas* against the *Brahman* priestly order, but also of the Vaishya or mercantile class as well. In fact, he notes, five hundred merchants had set up the Buddhist University at Nalanda. But while the larger volume of trade, which developed in the south, might explain the persistence of

Hinayana Buddhism, generally, the self sufficient village economy prevented the growth of trade on a national scale. The trading class never attained a position in society equivalent to the class of merchant princes in ancient Greece, whose social position was antagonistic to the power and privilege of the priesthood.[63] Vedic priests represssed the "masses" refusing to allow them to participate in happiness. Most of the land was also held by the Brahmins and Kshatriyas so that a strong mercantile class could not develop. Manu even prohibited sea voyages because of his fear that heretical views would spread.[64] In this way, according to Roy, the ruling elites were able to prevent progress in science and materialist philosophy so rigorously that an Indian renaissance was prevented.

Roy's interpretation of Indian philosophy is highly selective, however. First, there is a great diversity of views in Indian philosophy with six basic systems and several systems of Hinduism, the four schools of Buddhism and the two schools of Jainism in addition to the materialist Charvak school.[65] Radhakrishnan pointed out that "The chief mark of Indian philosophy in general is its concentration upon the spiritual ... Neither man nor the universe is looked upon as physical in essence, and material welfare is never recognized as the goal of human life except by the Charvak."[66] Idealism, rather than materialism has played the major role in shaping Indian thought:

> Materialism undoubtedly had its day in India, and, according to sporadic records and constant and determined efforts on the part of other systems to denounce it, the doctrine apparantly enjoyed widespread acceptance at one time. Nevertheless, materialism could not hold its own; its adherents have been few in number, and its positive influence has been negligible. Indian philosophy has not been oblivious to materialism; rather, it has known it, overcome it, and has accepted idealism as the only tenable view, whatever specific form that idealism might take.[67]

In *Materialism*, Roy continued to trace the evolution of philosophical materialism up to modern times. The Renaissance brought a flowering—a rebirth of classical knowledge. The German classical school eventually culminated in the encyclopedic system of Hegel, embodying a more developed notion of the dialectic, than that developed in classical times by materialist thinkers. Finally, Marx and Engels were able to build on the incisive critique of religion by Feuerbach and develop a science of dialectics to greatly advance man's knowledge of himself and human society.

Roy concluded that the triumph of metaphysics over materialist thought was related to the fear of revolution among the elites. Materialism, by its very nature, and in accord with the nature of man, threatens to greatly increase the knowledge and understanding of the common man, and also to increase his material well being and enjoyment. Therefore, the ruling classes in history sought to suppress materialist ideas and teachings for their own class interests. This was also a way of controlling the surplus produced in society and appropriating it for their own use. Thus the Christians and Romans were concerned to persecute the Epicureans, and the Brahmins in India could not tolerate the liberating and egalitarian ideas propagated by the materialistic Buddhist teachings. Consequently, for Roy, materialism was seen as a progressive, liberating and universalistic force in history, whereas metaphysics was seen to be reactionary and a tool of repression utilized by ruling classes for their own interests. It was viewed as an attempt by those in power to make what is relative, absolute in order to prevent the movement of history and human progress and to prevent man from gaining knowledge and becoming free.

Roy showed how the struggle has continued between those who would preserve a metaphysical view and materialists. Positivism, for example is not a materialistic system because it fails to recognise the objective reality of matter. Since one can never know, as a phenomenologist, whether the world has objective reality, independent of the mind, one is forced back upon the notion of God as the ultimate source of knowledge.

Roy also criticized those who seized upon recent discoveries in physics to argue that there is no objective reality in matter. For example, one such discovery was that electrons demonstrate both a particle and a wave nature. For Roy, this meant that the classical atomist theories must be modified, but that such discoveries in no way distracted from a materialist view of the universe. Also the fact that matter and energy were interchangeable did not contradict the materialist view. He also argued that Einstein's theories of gravitation had solved the ancient problem of "action at a distance," which Newton had tried to solve in his gravitational equations, but had failed. Newton's equations "described action of bodies in relation to one another, but did not solve the riddle of gravitational force." Einstein, on the other hand, had solved the problem with an alternative conceptualization of the problem.[68]

Roy remained a materialist throughout his life. In *Beyond Communism,* he wrote:

> I am of the opinion that materialism is the only philosophy possible; any other philosophy, in the last analysis, takes us outside the physical universe, into the wilderness of a mystical metaphysics over which presides God ... The result in each case is the end of man's freedom on this earth ... All systems of philosophy other than materialism are dishonest religion; they smuggle religiosity in through the back door... [69]

Although Roy continue to view religion as Marx did, that is, as the opiate of the people, yet his materialism did not lead him to downgrade reason or the will. He wrote in *Politics, Power and Parties*:

> Historical determinism .. does not exclude freedom of the will. As a matter of fact, human will is the most powerful determining factor. Otherwise, there would be no room for revolutions in a rationally determined process of history. The rational and scientific concept of determinism is not to be confused with the teleological or religious doctrine of predestination ... Reason is a biological property, it is not the antithesis of will.[70]

While remaining a historical materialist, Roy severely criticized economic determinism and ultimately rejected it. First of all, he argued that the theory of economic determinism is dualistic, whereas a strict materialism is monistic. Secondly, it leads to a contradiction seen in the conclusion that the classless society will lack class struggle and thus be devoid of progress. The "dialictics of history will cease to operate; progress will come to a stand still; humanity will die."[71] This would be a "death sentence for mankind." Third, Marx's ideas about the future of the State proved to be empirically false. "The State does not wither away." Finally, Roy noted that economic determinism does not recognise the autonomy of the mental world.[72] He concluded:

> ... [T]he economic interpretation of history is deduced from a wrong interpretation of materialism. It implies dualism, whereas materialism is a monistic philosophy. History is a determined process; but there are more than one causative factors. Human will is one of them, and it cannot always be referred directly to any economic incentive.[73]

Again in *Beyond Communism* he wrote:

> [The economic interpretation of history is] misapplied determinism... two things happen together, and it is maintained that one is caused by the other. Great confusion is created consequently.. The concept of causality must be freed from the fallacy of dualism, if determinism is to withstand the positivist onslaught. Causality can be conceived as a function of the

> physical and social processes and proved to be so. If it implies two things, one acting upon the other, there is absolutely no escape from ... extravagant empiricism ...[74]

Roy argued that causality was not an empirical but rather a logical concept, and thus causality could not be established empirically.

So the idea of an ideological superstructure, that is, ethical values, cultural patterns and movements of ideas, rising in a deterministic way from an economic base, was rejected by Roy. He wrote:

> It has been asserted that causal relations between ideas and historical events can be established. Yes, but in the reverse direction, not in the Marxist sense. If you mean that sort of causal connection where ideas have the causative force, then you throw away the economic interpretation of history.[75]

Roy moved closer to Hegel in his view of the role of ideas in the evolution of history, while remaining a materialist. Ideas, while playing a vital part in the development of history, rise out of the material world and are a part of it. It could be argued that in this conception, Roy was moving closer to the young Marx, and away from the more economistic elements in the late Marx. In the *Economic and Philosophical Manuscripts*, Marx wrote that the world—all of nature—was an extension of man and consequently his own creation. Man creates the world in accord with his life activity as a species being, according to Marx. For Roy, the world is an extension of man, as a material being, and his ideas as a part of that world have objective reality. "As a comprehensive logically consistent philosophy," Roy wrote, "materialism does not deny the objective reality of ideas, because their origin can be traced in the background of the physical universe."[76]

A dialectical materialist conception of history, for Roy, necessarily entails the view that ideas have a history of their own. They have developed throughout history, but in a progressive rather than in a dialectical manner. "From any point in history, ideas can be traced back to their biological origin, which is embedded in the background of the physical universe."[77]

The evolution of Roy's thought moved him away from a vulgar economic determinism and toward a more sophisticated view of historical materialism. In his view, "fanatical defenders" who were incapable of "appreciating the supreme importance of human spirit" and who "implicitly deny the creativeness of man's mind" had brought materialism to "disrepute." He wrote:

> Materialism must be raised above the level of vulgarity of dogmatic orthodoxy, and developed so as to conform with the

advancing knowledge, from physics to psychology, if it is to carry conviction to all thinking minds and be generally accepted as the gospel of freedom... [78]

The implications of Roy's historical materialism were that one could reconstruct history from a study of the history of human thought. In this way, "gaps in social and political history" could be "filled in by deductions from the history of thought." He noted that philosophical movements always preceded earth shaking social and political, events. Roy used this method to try to understand the evolution of materialist thought in ancient India, even when historical records were lacking. Therefore, "the history of ideas could stand by itself without any reference to social and political history as its incentive."[79]

Roy cited empirical evidence in history which contradicts a strict economic determinist theory of history. For example, he took issue with those who argued that the Renaissance and the Reformation were bourgeois movements and produced the rise of the commercial classes. He argued that this was simply not true. "The prosperous city of Genoa," he said, "did not produce a single man of the Renaissance, nor did Venice." On the other hand, "Florence the birthplace of the Renaissance was not a trading republic." The Medicis, he argued, "were not bourgeois but classical representatives of mediaevalism." And "the source of inspiration was in the ancient pagan culture of Greece and Rome."[80]

Roy did not believe that the future could be predicted, as those who took literally the economic interpretation of history, and defended it dogmatically. It is only possible to have an approximate idea of the future, he said, and anything more than that is of the nature of utopia.[81]

Criticism of Marxism and Liberalism

Roy came to the conclusion that all contemporary political theories are defective in practice. This observation led him to subject Marxism and Liberalism to thorough critiques and to an attempt to go beyond these contemporary doctrines of society to his own conception of Radical Humanism.

Roy believed that Marxism had failed mankind because it had become teleological, deterministic, and consequently a new theology. Man was reduced to a zero in the face of historical necessity and economic determinism. According to Marxism, man must first recognise necessity before he is free. Therefore, "the Marxist conception of freedom means slavery for the individual, and a society composed of voluntary slaves can never be free."[82] The individual is replaced by the collective ego of society.

On the other hand, Liberalism has also failed mankind. It leads to a dictatorship in parliament. "The fundamental defect of parliamentary democracy," he argued, "results from the contradiction between the philosophy and the political practice of liberalism." This was because:

> While true to its humanist tradition, liberalism proclaimed freedom of the individual, its economic doctrine of *laissez faire*, with its political corollary, place the individual in a helpless position in the wilderness of cut-throat competition. In such circumstances, the political and social practice of liberalism having negativated the moral excellence of its philosophy, parliamentary democracy was bound to be discredited.[83]

Consequently, "while parliamentary democracy formally recognised the sovereignty of the individual, in practice, it deprived all but a privileged few of that sovereignty.[84] The doctrine of *laissez faire* gave a few the liberty to exploit the majority under the name of free enterprise. All this had led to a contemporary crisis which man must try to go beyond in order to restore the sovereignty of the individual. Man must be moved back to the center stage of history and again become the measure of all things as for Protagoras.

Roy exposed a number of serious contradictions in the body of Marxist thought. In part, these can be traced to Marx himself. Others, he thought arose through the vulgarisation of Marxism due to dogmatic interpretations. In its essence, Roy believed that Marxism was not "a closed system of thought." He noted that Marxism "is capable of enriching itself continuously with the lessons of new experience." Consequently, Marxism could become the philosophy of the future if .. it was not "debased into dogmatism," as a religious faith. Because of its philosophical heritage, Marxism had two sides, one materialist and the other teleological. The major contradictions arose with those who emphasized its teleology because "they regard determinism as a teleological concept which makes marionettes of men." Believing the enture process of human development to be predetermined, the "social forces," the "means of production," etc. become, in reality, like "modern gods."[85]

But this type of "providential will" was, according to Roy, smuggled into Marxism by Marxist scholastics. Roy wanted creative Marxists to grasp the materialist side of Marxism and develop its humanism, which gained inspiration from the Renaissance and which represented "the revolt of man against God and his agents on earth." To free Marxism from its theology, Marxists must again focus upon man as the creator of his world and as the maker of history. In fact, this was what Marx had done, Roy thought, before "the teleological aspect of Marxism sacrificed man at the alter of the imaginary collective ego of society."[86] As Marx became more concerned with the economic forces, rather than with man, and traced history and social activity to the means of production, human activity and history were seen to be controlled by a superhuman being, just as in the past. But this made man a slave of material forces, and Roy pointed out that man's brain is the "most powerful means of production ever created." So, a crucial fallacy of Marxism was that it "lost sight of man as the root of historical change."[87] Preoccupation with economic forces set the stage for theology to creep back into Marxism.

Roy further explored the roots of these contradictions in *Reason, Romanticism and Revolution*. First of all, Roy pointed out that "Marxism itself contradicted the doctrine that ideologies are created by the economic necessities of particular classes with the object of promoting and defending their respective interests". This is because the most important part of Marxism, namely its economic analysis, contained the fundamental principles derived by the British political economists whom Marx characterized as the "ideologists of capitalism." Marx himself was brought up as a "bourgeois intellectual." Yet, the ideas developed by these theorists "went to feed what was called the ideology of the proletariat."[88]

This insight into a serious contradiction in Marxist thought led Roy to question Marx's notions about the dialectical development of ideas in history. Challenging Marx, Roy argued that ideas "have been in a continuous process of evolution" throughout history. "Ideas have their autonomy and a logic which is not dialectical, but dynamic," he wrote. Consequently, to associate particular ideas with particular classes is "a false practice." Since ideas are created by men, they belong to all humanity. The theories of classical capitalist economics, and principles of Hegelian philosophy contributed to Marxism, the so-called ideology of the proletariat. Roy concluded that "Marxism was not a negation, nor a negation of a negation of the older ideas that it took over. Without those ideas, there could be no Marxism."[89]

Roy pointed out that Marx drew upon the ideas of a great number of thinkers and he criticised him for being ungrateful for their contributions to his system of thought. Marx, he pointed out, was critical of the utopian socialists for example, but ultimately he himself lapsed into utopianism. While Marx did not go nearly so far as the utopian socialists in attempting to chart the future, Roy suggested that Marx's ideas are finally apocalyptic and consequently eschatological and utopian. Roy's criticism of Marxism as apocalyptic was largely derived from the critique by Martin Buber in *Paths to Utopia.*[90]

In criticizing the utopian aspects of Marxism, however, Roy greatly oversimplified Marx's actual position. This debate has been considerably clarified by Shlomo Avineri.[91] He pointed out that Marx did give Saint-Simon, Charles Fourier and Robert Owen credit for critical insights into the class struggle and considered them "revolutionary in many respects." Marx's main objection was that they lacked an "understanding of existing reality as a key to the future." According to Marx, "true knowledge of the shape of things to come is a function of having an adequate understanding of existing social relations." Since this placed severe epistemological limitations on predicting the future, Marx declined to predict the structure of socialist society in any detail.[92]

Roy traced the historical origin of a number of the ideas which became elements in Marxist thought. First, the doctrine that social, political and cultural history is economically determined evolved through the contributions to the study of history of a number of scholars. The "new science" of history was founded by Giambattista Vico. In the eighteenth century, Edward Gibbon and others "revolutionized" historiography. Georg Wilhelm Friedrich Hegel contributed his ideas to the understanding of history, along with French historians. Francois Guizot argued that "to understand political institutions, it is necessary to know the nature and relationships of property." Guizot, according to Roy, then introduced the idea of class struggle in his study of the English Revolution. He noted that Augustin Thierry, Louis de Rouvroy Saint-Simon's secretary grounded political revolutions in the evolution of society. The other French liberal historians who traced social evolution to economic relations were Francois Mignet and Jules Michelet.[93]

Roy also noted that many socialists and moralists of the seventeenth and eighteenth centuries contributed to socialist ideas, condemned the institutions of private property and economic exploitation of labour, and based liberty, equality and justice on common ownership. Philippe Michel Buonarotti believed that society could be reformed only through a violent revolution. Louis Blanc visualized the classless society and Jerome Blanqui advocated the establishment of the revolutionary dictatorship. Roy interpreted this to mean that "the movement of thought from democracy to socialism was not dialectical but continuous."[94]

Roy argued that the emergence of teleology in Marxist thought introduced another contradiction in the system. Thus Marxist historiography contradicts itself in "trying to combine rationalism, the view that history is a determined process, with the romantic view of life, which declares the freedom of the will ... "[95] The argument expounded by Roy was that if Marx intended to combine these two elements into his system of thought, then the system must steer clear of embodying a teleological view of the evolution of history. Otherwise, "the rationalist concept of determinism cannot be distinguished from the teleological doctrine of predestination." Marxism, Roy argued, had with its imposed teleology, absolved itself of the "idea of freedom" and the possibility of choice" for man. That is where Marxism had gone wrong. Free of the teleological view, Marxism might have "fit Romanticism, reconciled with reason and will, into the scheme of a determined evolutionary process." It could have recognised man as a "sovereign force, a thinking being who creates the means of production."[96]

Roy saw Marxism as "idealistic," but he did not see this as a fault, since idealism does not contradict materialism as long as one traces the roots of ideas in the rational scheme of nature. But in Roy's view, Marx failed to do this. He said that Marx created a dualistic system, since he saw ideas and consciousness as a reflection of the external world, the economic forces, rather than arising from the rational scheme of nature. Marx held a romantic view of life and was a revolutionary, Roy argued, but historical necessity in Marx is incompatible with the romantic notion of man as a free human being who makes revolutions and all of history. So at each turn, the eschatological view which crept into Marxism imposed shakles on Man's freedom and introduced contradictions into the theory. In this way, Roy saw Marxism as shot through and through with damaging contradictions.[97]

Roy concluded that the "philosophical implications" of Marxism were not clearly thought out by its founders. And, "they failed to see that thinking man acts upon the process of social evolution not as a *dues ex mechina*; he is an integral part of the process. The human brain is also a means of production of ideas, which motivates action to create history."[98] These pitfalls of Marxism would be avoided by Roy's philosophy of New Humanism, which would embody a thoroughgoing materialism and the idea of man as a free creative being.

Roy came close to contradicting himself when he argued that Marx put so much emphasis upon revolutionary action that "Marxism tipped the scale on the side of irrationalism, to degenerate eventually into a faith." It could be argued that Roy elevated his belief in the rationalism of nature to a faith, and in so doing, limited man's freedom. Roy took pains to show that Marx's economic determinism enslaves man, limits his freedom, and thus runs counter to the romantic idea of revolution. But, on the other hand, Roy argued that man's ability to change the world is limited by the "law of nature" and the "law of man." Man has a "moral right" to change the world, according to Roy, because he is part of a "ceaselessly changing nature." Yet, man's ability to change the world "is limited by the axiom that the whole is greater than its parts." If man "disregards this self- evident truth," as he believed Marx did, then "revolutionary activism becomes irrational and runs up against the law of nature and the law of man."[99]

Roy's Godwinian faith in the rationality embodied in the forces of nature, led him to downplay the potential of human action and will to change the world. In this way, he unwittingly came to limit man's freedom, in much the same way as man would be limited by economic determinism and historical necessity. The proper philosophy for a revolutionary, according to Roy, would be a "judicious synthesis of rationalism and romanticism." Without this caution, he said, "revolution, then only mars the salutory and uninterrupted progress instead of being truly beneficial for mankind as Godwin wanted."[100] Roy seemed to be saying that man should not block the path of the inevitable rational progress in nature by excessive revolutionary activism. Yet, if man is indeed the maker of history, if he is free and has a natural moral right to change the world, how would his revolutionary activity interfere with the rational progress in history?

Roy's reservations about revolutionary activity perhaps stemmed from his concern about the use of violence. The appeal to violence, he claimed, is part of this "romantic extravagance" of revolution, and is basically .."anti-thetical to rationalism." He said that one is the thesis while the other is the antithesis, and the synthesis is that "by changing the world, man changes himself."[101]

Another charge which Roy levelled against Marxism was that its theory of revolution is "cynical." It teaches the "dogma that human beings are never activated by moral impulses." Consequently, Marxism rejects the "belief that human nature by itself is sufficient cause for the endless progress of mankind," and declares that revolutionary action is "the decisive force in history." Roy held that such a view leads to the view of the dictatorship of the proletariat and ultimately to a political dictatorship.[102]

But Marxism had, on the other hand, made positive contributions to progress. One positive value for Roy was its liberal tradition. While

Liberalism proclaimed the principle of individual freedom, it nullified it in practice. "Socialism promised the practice of the principle."[103]

Roy again acknowledged that Marxism made a significant contribution to philosophy, offering a solution to the problem of dualism, which arose due to metaphysical speculation. This problem, Roy believed is seen most acutely in the Cartesian system, with its "split world" of mind and matter. "Philosophy came to the conclusion that there was no bridge over the gulf between the two," he said. This led to doubt about the objective validity of knowledge acquired through the senses and denial of the physical reality of the world. But Marx was able to bridge the gap by "formulating the principles of material monism."[104]

> And since consciousness is determined by being for Marx, mind and matter are aspects of the same world... Matter as a conceptual metaphysical category is the ultimate reality, capable of producing life. Consciousness, cognition, mind, ideas follow in the course of biological evolution. The world of experience as a whole is real; transcendental reality is a figment of imagination. Mind as well as matter, the physical world as well as the world of thought and ideas, are, equally real. But philosophy must have a realistic scientific understanding of their relation. Marx's contribution to this understanding won for him an outstanding place in the history of philosophy.[105]

Roy criticised Marx for not being true to the tradition upon which he built. First, he rejected the humanist tradition of the utopians and secondly, he rejected eighteenth century materialism as being mechanical. Consequently, Marxism came to embrace a "vulgar materialism." Roy continued,

> His subsequent thought-particularly sociological, ... did not move in the direction indicated by the significant point of departure. Marxism, on the whole is not true to its philosophical tradition. In sociology, it vulgarizes materialism to the extent of denying that basic moral values transcend space and time. With the impersonal concept of the forces of production, it introduces teleology in history, crassly contradicting its own belief that man is the maker of his destiny. The economic determinism of its historiology blasts the foundation of human freedom, because it precludes the possibility of man ever becoming free as an individual. Yet contemporary sociological thinking has been considerably influenced by the fallacious and erroneous doctrine of Marxism which does not logically follow from its philosophy.[106]

Roy traced the root of economic determinism and vulgarisation of materialism to Marx's effort to rectify Feuerbach's conception of Man. Feuerbach had conceived of man as an abstraction. Marx, on the other hand, wished to explain the evolution of man as the "maker of his own destiny" in a more scientific way. Seeking the "rational foundation," Marx came to see primitive man's "efforts to earn a livlihood" as the biological struggle for existence. This, Roy believed, led Marx to ground the origin of society in economic motivation. But this basis of Marxist historiography, he claimed, was a mistake. Instead, at the time of the origin of the species, the urge of man was not "economic" but rather the biological urge for self preservation. Man was forced to build tools, and out of this struggle emerged mental development and the search for freedom. So, according to Roy, Marx came to see man as an economic automaton. Man lost his freedom in a deterministic scheme, which could not logically be deduced from materialist presuppositions.

But this treatment is not altogether true to Marx, as can be seen in his discussion of human nature in his early writings, particularly the *Economic and Philosophical Manuscripts*. In "Alienated Labour," it is clear that for Marx, the species nature of man is not to be an economic automaton. Marx believed that,

> man makes his life activity itself an object of his will and consciousness. He has a conscious life activity... only for this reason is he a species being... Only for this reason is his activity free activity. Man produces when he is free from physical need and only truly produces in freedom from such need."[107]

Marx believed that in the realm of necessity, where man was forced to labour for survival, he produces, as an animal, out of need. But such activity is not man's species-activity. Marx thought such labour alienates man from his species-life. It is alienated labour.

Roy's position suggests that Marx was a humanist and a romanticist, convinced of the creativeness of man, basing his works on a moral foundation, but allowing himself to fall into the trap of seeing man as caught up in economic determinism. *Capital*, he said, was a "treatise on social ethics." Marxism, then, with its "libertarian moralist spirit," is for Roy a part of the accumulated store of human heritage and can be a basis for a more comprehensive philosophy, e.g. Radical Humanism, when it has been freed from its contradictions.[108]

Finally, Roy faulted Marxism in practice. The thrust of his argument involved two major aspects. Firstly, history has not unfolded as Marx predicted, and secondly, Marxism in practice had failed miserably. The proletarian revolution, which was expected, never came. According to Marx, the revolution should have first ocurred in England. Its appearance in Russia, Roy argued, was an "accident-the result of a fortuitous combination of circumstances," and "as such, it was itself a negation of the mechanical view of historical determinism."[109]

Further, the revolution itself did not usher in the true history of man, as Marx hoped, but rather became a "terrifying spectre" and ultimately a period of counter-revolution resulting in the rise of fascism. Marx left behind no blueprint for the construction of socialist society, being primarily a critic of capitalism. Socialist reconstruction would be determined by the development of the forces of production. In the realm of political practice, Marx viewed the "proletarian dictatorship as the instrument for breaking down the resistance of the dethroned bourgeoisie." In terms of distribution, he fell back on the "anarchist ideal, from each according to his ability, to each according to his need." Roy said that Lenin dismissed this formula as a "useless slogan," after which Stalin adopted the "tautological statement, from each according to his ability, to each according to his work."[110] Consequently,

> its success in one country pragmatically proved that the new order was not to be a creation of man rising as Prometheus unbound; that human creativeness, in the intellectual, moral and cultural fields, was not to be unfettered; that the new order was to enshrine the collective ego of the proletariat; to claim subordination and sacrifice of individuals composing the class.[111]

Critique of Liberalism and Utilitarianism

For M.N. Roy, the most damaging aspect of Liberalism was the tremendous gap between the principles embodied in the doctrine, and its application in practice. It was because the hope which Liberalism held out to man had withered, that mankind had been driven to take protective shelter under theories which moved the collective to the center stage of history. Liberalism, he noted, was rooted in the ideas of the Enlightenment and "man's struggle against spiritual subservience." It put faith in the individual as a moral entity, building in Stoic and Christian ideas about the nature of man. But Roy argued that the two main concepts of nineteenth century Liberalism were defective, i.e. parliamentary rule in the political field and *laissez faire* in economics. Because of these defective concepts, the realisation of individualism for the common man became a legal fiction. With the rise of the Party, the individual disappeared, and with the rise of utilitarian doctrines, which were morally defective, man lost faith in himself and sought salvation in the collective security of the mass.[112]

Roy traced the origins of Liberalism to the movement to secularize politics and society, although he claimed its roots could be traced all the way back to Greek rationalism. "The development of European thought towards rationalism, naturalism and secularism," he wrote, "was an unbroken process from the Renaissance of the twelfth century to Hobbes... Hobbes' philosophy of scientific naturalism and Locke's psychology of sensation, logically related with it, gave man a new faith—the faith in himself. That was the core of Liberalism."[113]

As a chapter in man's quest for human freedom and emancipation, Liberalism began with the struggle for emancipation from religion and spiritual serfdom. The Enlightenment brought the message of man's creativeness— in the tradition of the Renaissance and ancient wisdom and culture. Simultaneously, preceding the Reformation, the movement for the secularization of politics also contributed to the development of Liberalism, as it produced ideas challenging the established order of both Church and King. Science and humanism also contributed to the philosophical revolution.[114]

But Roy saw Hobbes as the thinker that systematically laid the foundation for Liberalism. For him, "political thought was secular without any reservation." Roy greatly admired Hobbes' approach to political thought as he proceeded in a scientific and materialistic fashion, which Roy believed was necessary. He noted that Hobbes uses a "mechanistic cosmology," is vigorously rationalistic and thus frees political philosophy from theology. For Hobbes, there is no dichotomy between man and nature. "Man is part of nature, and nature is a rational process ... the humanism of the Renaissance becomes scientific naturalism ... Man's spiritual liberation is complete."[115]

Hobbes, then, "laid the most solid theoretical foundation of democracy." Beginning with the presuppositions that human nature is selfish, self-preservation is the basic biological urge, and contending that this selfishness gives birth to reason, "Hobbes constructed a political philosophy which maintains that to promote the individuality of its members is the function of social oganisation."[116]

But Roy held that the fault inherent in Liberalism was that its secularism did not go far enough. Inclined toward "natural religion," it became "metaphysical and came to view reason as something transcendental." Newton had held to "mechanistic naturalism" in which God was *ex machina*, outside of nature, but in the nineteenth century, liberal rationalism revived the belief in a "pantheistic moral order." God was brought back ..and seen to be "immanent in nature." Reason in man came to be seen as conscience which guides and rules over man. This, said Roy, was a return all the way back to the Stoics.[117]

> In the context of the transcendental and teleological system of thought, the liberal doctrine of individual liberty was bound to stultify itself, and be vulgarized in practice. The post-revolutionary revolt against reason had placed a high premium on the idea of free will; the concept of individual freedom had been carried to the extent of irresponsibility; the ideal of freedom had thus appeared to deny morality. A reaction to that romantic extravagance, nineteenth century Liberalism held that human freedom and a rational order of nature were reconciled by the rules of impersonal laws discovered by reason.[118]

With the revivalism of pantheism in Liberalism, the system of thought became deterministic and the principle of individual freedom became a legal fiction.

Roy saw the liberal political regime as shot through with contradictions, and thus faulty in several ways. First, the eighteenth century idea that a good society could be insured by good laws was mistaken, since "good laws can be effective only when they codify already accepted modes of behavior." In the political sphere, the fundamental ideal of liberal thought—the guarantee of liberty and individualism for the citizen, had been lost sight of.

With the rise of the Party and the populous centralised Nation State, the vote of the individual meant little. His sovereignty was effectively swept aside and government became a dictatorship of the ruling party. Elections were conducted in an atmosphere of mass hysteria. With the loss of genuine participation and personal knowledge of the candidate, the ideal of government of, by and for the people was reduced to government for the people. With the social atomization of society, the individual was rendered powerless. Finally, the establishment of utilitarian justifications of government for the people underpinned the dictatorship of the majority party and established the fundamental rationale for the collectivisation of society. But lacking any moral foundation, and removing man from the center stage of history, utilitarianism led to the political bankruptcy of the liberal system.[119]

Roy was disconcerted that a common element in all modern political philosophies was the desire to capture power. This meant that in some respects, there was little difference between systems on the Left and on the Right. This "scramble for power," Roy believed, was bound to lead to a "progressive demoralisation of public life."

> In theory, the vote, under liberal democracy would delegate sovereign power to a group of individuals or party, which became the repositories of the sovereignty for the period between the two elections. Now, the practice of democracy shows that between two elections the people have no possibility of controlling those who are ruling .... consequently, delegation of power, for all practical purposes, has become surrender of power."[120]

Much of the problem can be traced to the rise of the Party, which serves as an effective dictatorship. Individuals cannot vote for a particular candidate according to their own "intelligent judgement," but must vote for a particular party. This indirect or parliamentary democracy, Roy believed, is a "negation of the fundamental principle of democracy." This notion was well expressed in the twelfth thesis of his Principles of Radical democracy:

> The defects of formal parliamentary democracy have also been exposed in experience. They result from the delegation of power. To make democracy effective, power must always remain vested in the people, and there must be ways and means for the people to wield the sovereign power effectively, not periodically, but from day to day. Atomised individual citizens are powerless for all practical purposes, and most of the time. They have no means to exercise their sovereignty and to wield a standing control of the state machinery.[121]

Another limitation of parliamentary democracy is that "the executive cannot be controlled," Roy claimed. He noted that Hitler rose to power democratically, and that many dictatorial regimes claim democratic sanction.[122]

In the shelter of the collective, man cannot be an individual. Candidates appeal to "sentiment" and the "emotion" of the masses. "The electorate is in a state where no discriminating judgement is at all possible, whipped up into a state of frenzy and driven like cattle to the polling stations to cast their votes," he wrote. It is, then, a great irony that a system which envisioned the moral development of the individual, reduced man to a confused, powerless and helpless creature.[123]

Finally, Roy traced the decline of Liberalism to its moral ambiguity. He pointed out that in the twentieth century, Liberalism has been threatened by the rise of Socialism and Communism on the Left and the rise of Fascism on the Right. Roy believed Liberalism fell victim to two equally damaging philosophical trends. The first of these, previously mentioned, was the de-secularization of Liberalism and the restoration of metaphysical and transcendental notions. This was ironic, because Liberalism was born out of man's struggle against spiritual subservience.[124]

The second philosophical trend was that line of thought which originated in Humean skepticism and Comtean positivism", laying the foundation for a crass utilitarianism. Positivism was defective in that it could provide no moral underpinnings for society. Thus "man was destined to be tossed on the sea of skepticism and moral relativism on the one hand, or succumb to spiritual slavery on the other." In either event, man lost faith in himself and sought safety in the collective security of the mass society.

The second defective tenet of Liberalism, the doctrine of *laissez faire*, according to Roy, "served the purpose of rising capitalism ... Liberalism appeared to provide a moral justification of the economic exploitation of man by man ... In economics, the doctrine of *laissez faire* gave a few the liberty to exploit the majority under the name of free enterprise." This ultimately resulted in Liberalism being discredited.[125]

But Roy rejected the idea that Liberalism was created by the needs of the new economic society. It developed, he argued, "according to the logic of the evolution of thought ... It cannot be said that Liberalism was the ideology of the bourgeoisie or the philosophy of capitalism." Liberalism and capitalism, that is, developed "simultaneously." "Religious beliefs, philosophical principles, social changes, economic developments of the same historical epoch are mutually influenced, but we cannot attach primary importance to any one of them."[126]

Roy's attitude toward the doctrine of *laissez faire* was explicated in the thirteenth thesis of his Principles of Radical Democracy:

> Liberalism is falsified or parodied under formal parliamentary democracy. The doctrine of *laissez faire* only provides the legal sanction to the exploitation of man by man. The concept of economic man negativates the liberating doctrine of individualism. The economic man is bound to be a slave or a slave-holder. This vulgar concept must be replaced by the reality of an instinctively rational being who is moral because he is rational. Morality is an appeal to conscience, and conscience is the instinctive awareness of, and reaction to, environments. It is a mechanistic biological function on the level of consciousness. Therefore it is rational.[127]

Socialism, Decentralization and Partyless Democracy

M.N. Roy's sharp critique of liberal and parliamentary democracy led him to reformulate the concept of democracy in accord with his humanist principles. The fundamental flaw or problem which must be confronted, he felt, was that of concentration of power in the modern State. Concentration of power, in turn, could be traced to the political Party, which by its nature was elitist and resulted in society being controlled by a minority. The Party reduced the individual to a legal fiction and rendered the concept of freedom in the modern State an illusion. To rid modern society of the phenomenon of concentration of power and the domination of society by the Party, politics must return to a humanist basis in which man again becomes a rational and intelligent being.

Roy's vision for the transformation of society and decentralization was grounded in his concept of the origin of society, the rise of the modern State and Party, and the ultimate concentration of power. In his account of the origin of the State, Roy differed sharply from Marx. For Marx, the State arose with the availability of a social surplus which made possible an exploitative class. On the other hand, Roy argued that "the State arose to coordinate and harmonize the diverse departments of social activities, so as to promote the welfare of the community as a whole." The State, in this view, was one of several "equally autonomous social institutions, along with the economic, educational and cultural." Where Marx saw the State as exploitative and dominating, Roy saw it as conducive to human development.[128]

Roy's Weberian view of the State as "the political organisation of society," and his view of politics as "the theory and practice of public administration," can be traced to his views concerning the nature of society. Whereas Marx viewed social and human change as resulting from diverse interests, resulting in class conflicts in society, Roy believed that there were both "diverse interests" and "cohesive forces" in society. That is,

> the centrifugal tendency is counteracted by a centripetal tendency. In the history of social revolution, an equilibrium between the two created stability, whereas discord and disharmony led either to the establishment of dictatorships or other autocratic forms of government or to social disintegration.[129]

The fact that an "equilibrium" could be obtained, accounted for the history of civilisation, for Roy.

Consequently, Roy did not reject the State as ultimately alienating and repressive as had Marx. He saw that if one defined the State in Marxist terms as "an organ of coercion, an instrument created by a certain class or section of society with the purpose of exercising its domination over the rest," then one would be forced to conclude that in the ideal society, the State must wither away. But on the contrary, since power is highly concentrated in actually existing communist states, this leads to a serious contradiction. "The ideal of a Stateless society," he wrote, "is an obvious absurdity." One could envision a classless society, but even such a community could not do without a "central organisation" which would "harmonise" the functions of other institutions. In this way the State would again serve its original function as an instrument of public administration. If power could be dispersed, the State would no longer be a "Leviathan" but would become "coterminous with society" and the people would enjoy genuine democracy.[130]

The State, then, in the Marxist sense, as an instrument of coercion, can only "wither away" when power is decentralized or dispersed among the people. Roy defined power as the ability to do a thing. But the problem in the modern State was not power as such. Power would always have a place in history. Rather, the problem, for Roy, was "concentration of power." Eighteenth century liberal doctrine held that the best government is that which governs least. But as power is highly concentrated in the modern State, the fundamental problem of democracy is how to disperse power.[131]

Since the Party is the means by which power is concentrated in the hands of minorities, the possibility of practicing politics without parties must be explored.

> Because it is through the instrumentality of political parties that power is concentrated in the hands of minorities to be abused and misused on false pretenses, the desired decentralisation of power is conditional upon the disappearance of the instrument of centralisation. It must be replaced by another instrument which can guarantee that the sovererreignty of the people will always remain with the people.[132]

The trouble with political parties, for Roy, is that they are not formed for the purpose of ensuring democracy, but rather for the purpose of capturing power and for the ultimate perpetuation of rule by a minority. "They are guided by the dictum that the end justifies the means, and the means often amounts to the corruption and destruction of democracy ..." Party politics, he suggested, "carries within it the germs for the destruction of democracy."[133]

Roy envisioned people's committees as the mechanism for the dispersal of power in society and through which party politics would come to an and. He believed that as members of those basic units of the State, citizens would no longer be atomized and helpless. Across India, existing village *panchayats* would be built up as units of organised democracy. Provision for the people's committees would be made in the constitution as integral units of the State.

Roy's scheme for decentralised democracy was intended to provide for participatory democracy on a massive scale. The two major aspects of this radical social transformation were institutional renovation and self-transformation of the individual citizen. The second aspect will be considered more thoroughly in Chapter Three. Institutions must be changed, Roy believed, but this was at best only half the formula for social change, as social institutions could be no better than the citizens who set them up. "Every institution," he said, "is as good as the men who work it ... The contention seems "to be that institutions are not made by men, but men are made by institutions! This is the crux of the problem of the modern world."[134]

Self-transformation of the idividual citizen would require education leading to a new psychology or mental attitude of the people. Following Gandhi, he seemed to be convinced that individual citizens were largely responsible when they allowed themselves to be ruled dictatorially. It was due to this mediaeval mentality, he thought, that they were in chains. He cited the case of the Germans who allowed the Nazis to come to power. The problem, according to Roy, was even more acute in India where liberal ideas had not fully penetrated and people had a backward paternalistic mentality .. The purpos e of education in the new decentralized and humanistic society would be to restore in the individual citizen a faith in himself. He would gain confidence in his powers of rational decision. The basis for such a mental transformation would be materialistic, scientific and rational-humanistic.

Within local people's committees, groups of citizens would discuss and plan the affairs of the localities. A few people's committees would be established as a beginning, on a voluntary basis, and later a growing network of these local organizations would emerge through which the electorate could assert its influence. Ultimately, the citizens would "exercise a standing control over the State as a whole."[135]

Conceptually, Roy distinguished between this type of control and the more organic concept of collective control. Roy was not talking about collective control. This was what he sought to avoid. Rather, society, he believed, is the sum of its parts, that is, of the individual citizens. And individual citizens lose their freedom when collectivized. For Roy, Liberalism, Socialism and Communism were all collective systems, in which the individual ego is merged with the collective ego of society. Instead, Roy insisted upon an institutional structure that would maintain the individual moral and intellectual integrity of each and every citizen.[136]

Roy thought that if such institutions could succeed, no party could capture power, and power would reside with the people in the committees. He wrote:

> We shall apply ourselves to the fundamental task of educating the people until the people will no longer allow anybody to capture their power on any plausible pretext. To achieve this, we start to practice the old Platonic principle that education is the foundation of democracy. Believing, on the authority of modern scientific knowledge, that man is essentially rational, we shall endeavor to make all citizens conscious of their rationality. That is the purpose of education. Once democracy will be educated in that sense, scramble for power will no longer be the purpose of politics. Political parties desiring to capture power will no longer be able to sway the people. Politics will become the art of public administration; when every human being can master the art, the state will become identical with society.[137]

It was envisioned that this "resurrection of the individual from the grave of the mass," would take place voluntarily and spread through example. Roy thought that this type of decentralized politics could be practiced anywhere but that it was of particular importance in India. This was because the democratic ideal was just being introduced. In India, such a structure of decentralisation was "the only way to create" an "appreciation" of the democratic way of life and "give to the formalities of parliamentarianism a democratic content."[138]

Further, it would be "irrelevant," Roy thought, to project a time frame for this transformation. Whether it took fifty or a hundred years, the relevant question was "What is the alternative?" And that could only be some form of collectivized dictatorship. But Roy did suggest that by the third election in free India (ten to fifteen years time) a large number of local republics could be establislished which would provide a foundation for building a real democracy.

> The result will be a far-reaching decentralisation of the State. The State will become no more than a clearing house of information, an advisory and administrative machinery to co-

> ordinate and supervise policies formed directly by the people as a whole ... That is how the State will become identical with society.[139]

References

1. D.G. Dalton, "M.N. Roy and Radical Humanism: The Ideology of An Indian Intellectual Elite," in *Elites in South Asia*, eds. Edmund Leach and S.N. Mukherjee (Cambridge: Cambridge Univ. Press, 1970), p. 152.
2. M.N. Roy, M.N. Roy's *Memoirs* (New Delhi: Allied Publishers, 1964), p. 562.
3. *Ibid.*, pp. 568-569.
4. *Ibid.*, pp. 3-4.
5. *Ibid.*, p. 5.
6. *Ibid.*, p. 27.
7. *Ibid.*, pp. 141-147.
8. *Ibid.*, p. 195.
9. *Ibid.*, p. 214.
10. *Ibid.*, p. 355.
11. *Ibid.*, p. 379.
12. *Ibid.*
13. *Ibid.*, p. 382.
14. *Ibid.*, p. 420.
15. *Ibid.*, p. 468.
16. *Ibid.*, p. 575.
17. *Ibid.*, pp. 576-581.
18. *Ibid.*, p. 581.
19. *Ibid.*, p. 584.
20. Jawaharlal Nehru, *An Autobiography* (New Delhi: Allied Publishers, 1962), p. 268.
21. Roy, *Memoirs*, pp. 590-593.
22. *Ibid.*, p. 593. Also see John Patrick Haithcox, *Communism and Nationalism in India* (Princeton, N.J.: Princeton Univ. Press, 197I), p. 237.
23. Haithcox, pp. 247-248.
24. *Ibid.*, pp. 226-248.
25. *Ibid.*, pp. 225-227.
26. *Ibid.*, p. 23l.
27. Roy, *Memories*, p. 599.
28. *Ibid.*, p. 600.
29. *Ibid*, p. 60l.
30. Haithcox, p. 322, footnote.

31. Roy, *Memories*, p. 604.
32. *The Encyclopedia of Philosophy*, Reprint ed. (1972), S.V. "Materialism". by Kieth Campbell.
33. M.N. Roy, Materialism (Calcutta: Renaissance Publications, 1940), pp. 160-161.
34. *Ibid.*, p. 198.
35. *Ibid.*, p. 233.
36. M.N. Roy, *Fragments of A Prisoner's Diary*, 3 Vols. (Dehradun and Calcutta, Renaissance Publications, 1940-43), Vol. 3: *Letters from Jail*, p. 2.
37. *Ibid.*, pp. 18-19.
38. Roy, *Materialism*, p. 1.
39. *Ibid.*, p. 2.
40. *Ibid.*
41. *Ibid.*, Preface to the Second Edition.
42. *Ibid.*, p. 5.
43. *Ibid.*, pp. 53-54.
44. *Ibid.*
45. *Ibid.*, pp. 53-54.
46. *Ibid.*
47. *Ibid.*, pp. 55-56.
48. *Ibid.*, p. 59.
49. *Ibid.*, p. 73.
50. *Ibid.*, pp. 65-66.
51. *Ibid.*, pp. 68-69.
52. *Ibid.*, p. 71.
53. *Ibid.*, p. 74.
54. *Ibid.*, p. 78.
55. *Ibid.*, p. 78.
56. *Ibid.*, p. 96.
57. *Ibid.*, p. 85.
58. *Ibid.*
59. *Ibid.*
60. *Ibid.*, p. 96.
61. *Ibid.*, p. 99.
62. *Ibid.*, p. 103.
63. *Ibid.*, pp. 110-11l.
64. *Ibid.*, pp. 111-112.
65. Sarvepalli Radhakrishnan and Charles A. Moore, eds., *Indian Phiolosophy* (Princeton, N.J.: Princeton Univ. Press, 1957), p. XXII.

66. *Ibid.*, p. xxiii.
67. *Ibid.*, p. xxv.
68. Roy, *Materialism* pp. 217-232.
69. M.N. Roy, *Beyond Communism* (Calcutta: Renaissance Publishers, 1947), p. 64.
70. M.N. Roy, *Politics Power and Parties* (Calcutta: Renaissance Publishers, 1960), p. 212.
71. Roy, Beyond Communism, p. 64.
72. *Ibid.*, pp. 64-65.
73. Roy, *Politics Power and Parties*, p. 212.
74. Roy, *Beyond Communism,* pp. 63-64.
75. *Ibid.*, p. 57.
76. *Ibid.*, p. 56.
77. *Ibid.*, p. 61.
78. *Ibid.*, p. 59.
79. *Ibid.*, pp. 60 -61.
80. *Ibid.*, pp. 61-62.
81. *Ibid.*, p. 53.
82. Roy, *Politics Power and Politics*, pp. 6-8.
83. M.N. Roy, *New Humanism* (Calcutta: Renaissance Publishers, 1947), p. 11.
84. Roy, *Politics Power and Parties*, p. 17.
85. Roy, *Beyond Communism*, p. 106.
86. *Ibid*, p. 103.
87. *Ibid.*, pp. 103-104.
88. M.N. Roy, *Reason, Romanticism and Revolution*, 2 Volumes. (Calcutta: Renaissance Publishers;-1952-1955), 2: 189.
89. *Ibid.*, p. 190.
90. *Ibid.*, p. 200.
91. Shiomo Avineri, "Marx's Vision of Future Society," *Dissent* 20 (Summer 1973): 323-331.
92. *Ibid.*, pp. 323-325.
93. Roy, *Reason, Romanticism and Revolution*, 2: 190-191.
94. *Ibid.*, pp. 193-194.
95. *Ibid.*, pp. 193-194.
96. *Ibid.*, pp. 204-205.
97. *Ibid.*
98. *Ibid.*
99. *Ibid.*, p. 209.
100. *Ibid.*, pp. 208-209.

101. *Ibid.*
102. *Ibid.*
103. *Ibid.*, p. 212.
104. *Ibid.*
105. *Ibid.*, p. 215.
106. *Ibid.*, pp. 216- 217.
107. Karl Marx, *Early Writings*, trans. and ed. T.B. Bottomore (New York: McGaw-Hill, 1964), p. 127.
108. Roy, *Reason, Romanticism and Revolution*, 2: 217- 219.
109. Roy, *New Humanism*, pp. 14-15.
110. *Ibid.*, pp. 15-16.
111. *Ibid.*, p. 2.
112. Roy, *Politics Power and Parties*, pp. 19, 42.
113. Roy, *Reason, Romanticism and Revolution*, 2: 96.
114. *Ibid.*, pp. 68-95.
115. *Ibid.*, pp. 93-95.
116. *Ibid.*
117. *Ibid.*, pp. 102-103.
118. *Ibid.*
119. Roy, *Politics Power and Parties*, p. 39.
120. *Ibid.*, p. 52.
121. *Ibid.*, pp. 213-214.
122. Roy, *New Humanism*, pp. 52-53.
123. Roy, *Politics Power and Parties*, pp. 52-53.
124. *Ibid.*, pp. 42-43.
125. *Ibid.*, pp. 19 - 20 .
126. Roy, *Reason, Romanticism and Revolution*, 2: 67-70.
127. Roy, *Politics Power and Parties*, p. 214.
128. *Ibid.*, p. 182.
129. *Ibid.*, pp. 94, 181-182.
130. *Ibid.*, pp. 181-182.
131. *Ibid.*, p. 183.
132. *Ibid.*, p. 184.
133. *Ibid.*, pp. 62, 93.
134. *Ibid.*, pp. 56-57.
135. *Ibid.*, p. 60.
136. *Ibid.*, p. 27.
137. *Ibid.*, p. 84.
138. *Ibid.*, p. 64.
139. *Ibid.*, pp. 60, 64, 84.

3

M.N. Roy on Radical Humanism

Radical Humanism is the system of philosophy based on M.N. Roy's Twenty-two Theses of Radical Democracy. Roy said that Radical Humanism was Marxism revised in the light of modern knowledge and experience. It involves a proper relationship between means and ends, recognising that the means can never be ethically compromised for the purpose of reaching an ethical end, and that in fact ends and means cannot be analytically separated. It also claims to be a complete system which included a belief in the "totality" of scientific knowledge, and a belief in the rationality and morality of man. It aims at a cultural renaissance which ensures human freedom and is based on philosophical materialism. It also views traditional humanist theories as faulty in that they supposed that man is basically selfish and that he must be subordinated to a metaphysical power to make him good.

Radical Humanism takes an open view of human nature. It holds that there are certain human values which transcend all other considerations. For Roy the development of the human personality is the main purpose of life and this is necessarily bound up with the pursuit of human freedom as nature unfolds. Radical Humanism seeks to build on modern scientific knowledge. In politics, it rejects modern totalitarianism as well as capitalism. It supposes the possibility of a cosmopolitan spiritual community which will also be a rational and moral community. In the Radical Humanist view, man is at the root of society. Man is the measure of all things.[1]

Radical Humanism, also called New Humanism, Materialist Humanism and Scientific Humanism, was elaborated by Roy in his Twenty-two Theses of Radical Democracy, given below in the appendix. It has been defined as follows :

> 'Materialist' or scientific humanism maintains that man and the universe are integrated in a law-governed and self-sufficient cosmic system (thus eliminating any form of transcendentalism); that facts and values are organically related in an evolutionary process; that values are formed in the course of co-ordination between human strivings and knowledge; that the source of all value judgement is the individual striving for multifold self expression and the emotions associated with its fulfilment; That reason (in its scientific and non-esoteric sense) is the universal means to such fulfilment and is thus essential to morality; and that inadequate integrations of human experience, strivings and the process of the universe, when absolutised in habits, institutions and conventions, become the most difficult obstacles in the way of human growth and welfare. It therefore pleads for scientific outlook and enlightenment of the people and maintains that harmony in individual life as well as social organisation (which is so very necessary for human creativeness and welfare) can be truly approximated through dissemination of knowledge and education in cooperative and creative living. The key to human progress is to be found in the quest for freedom and search of truth which are the basic urges of human nature: and the satisfaction of these urges is the source and content of what the Greeks called *agathon* (a generic word covering goodness, beauty and truth)—of human creativeness and welfare. The aspiration of humanism is to develop a cosmopolitan society of free men and women— a society, in which personal life and conduct and social relationships and institutions should be informed with the spirit of individual creativeness and enlightened cooperation.[2]

Human Nature and Freedom

For M.N. Roy, freedom is both, "the cause and the ultimate value or goal of human development."[3] To understand Roy's concept of freedom, one must trace the roots of the diverse influences upon Roy and the evolution of his concept of freedom. Roy's early thinking on human nature and freedom was in accord with the Marxist materialist tradition. Later, his thinking moved closer to the concept of freedom, as seen in the classical Indian philosophical tradition and in some aspects paralleled the thinking of Vivekananda, Aurobindo and Gandhi. Accordingly, Roy came to devalue the material and economic aspects and stress the spiritual aspects. In this section the emergence of Roy's ideas on human nature and freedom will be traced and comparisons will be made with other political thinkers on human nature and freedom.

As a materialist, Roy saw human consciousness as arising out of the material universe. He believed that the universal urge in man for survival manifests itself as the universal urge for freedom, with the emergence of consciousness. Human nature cannot be an "immutable category" as it is subject to an evolutionary process. "To change is human nature," he wrote.[4] Roy approached human nature, then, with an open mind, and argued that if human nature never changed, human progress would have to be abandoned.

The study of human nature was crucial for Roy, as he saw man as "the decisive category of all social sciences."[5] The key to understanding human nature, he thought, was through scientific discovery. The progress of mankind toward freedom from spiritual slavery and toward self-emancipation had, in the past, been stifled because man lacked knowledge of himself. So while the Renaissance held out hope for human emancipation, society again succumbed to spiritual slavery and ignorance because man lacked the scientific knowledge needed to account for himself and his rationality. But in the twentieth century, for the first time in history, science held out the promise that man could know and understand himself materially and rationally. Science could provide the link which would prove that life, human consciousness and volition arose out of dead matter.

For Roy, the three basic aspects of human nature, rationality, morality and freedom, arise from biological evolution. The evolution of man, he believed, could be traced to inorganic matter. And since the physical universe is a law-governed system, it can be assumed that man has the capacity for reason and judgement. This implies that man has the natural capacity to "remake the world in a rational way."[6]

Similiarly, moral judgement and conscience arise materially, as well as instinct and intuition. He believed that even animals demonstrate a rudimentary morality.

> Much emphasis is laid in modern theories on instincts and intuition, on which moral judgement is supposed to be based in preference to man's reason and intelligence. But if we trace the

> biological development of man back beyond the appearance of the human species, you can find rudimentary forms of the power of thinking and reasoning and even moral judgement already in the lower animals. Instinct and intuition are nothing mysterious, but an undifferentiated form of rationalism, which can however teach us a good deal about the working of man's reason.[7]

As a result of grounding morality in the material universe, Roy came to conceptualize the conscience in a reductionistic way. It, came to be viewed in the same manner as the mechanistic biological functions. "Morality," he' wrote, "must be referred back to man's innate rationality. Only then can man be moral, spontaneously and voluntarily." Yet, in actuality, it appears that conscience functions in a rather involuntary way for Roy. It could be argued that he effectively reduced conscience to innate rationality, or to just a higher form of instinct. He went on to argue that:

> [R]eason is the only sanction for morality, which is an appeal to conscience, and conscience, in its turn, is the instinctive awareness of, and reaction to, the environment. In the last analysis, conscience is nothing mystical or mysterious. It is a biological function, as such mechanistic, on the level of consciousness. The innate rationality of man is the only guarantee of a harmonious order.[8]

Roy also argued that "instinct is the motive force of all human actions. This has been established by modern psychology."[9]

From these statements, it becomes clear that in this formulation Roy largely argued away human choice and free will. How can man act conscientiously and with a free will if the conscience is reduced to a mechanistic functioning of man, to biological functions which are innately rational? It seems that in this formulation, Roy has merely reduced conscience to human instinct. One wonders how man can be morally free in this formulation of human nature. Man cannot be immoral because his innate rationality prevents him from choosing that which is immoral. In this way, man becomes a slave to his innate, mechanistic rationality, and thus has no existential moral freedom. If man is rational by definition, and morality arises from rationality, man is also moral by definition. Effectively, the conscience has no function as it is just a conscious manifestation of innate rationality. This may be spontaneous, but involuntarily so rather than voluntarily. This formulation of Roy seems to eliminate completely choice and free will directed by the conscience. This would also be the annihilation of freedom in the existential sense. So, in Roy, the conscience is effectively reduced to innate rationality, a developed pattern of instinct, arising from human nature.

In his view of the evolution of man and freedom, Roy could be accused of embracing biological determinism. But Roy does not see this pattern of biological development as limiting man's freedom in controlling his future. In fact, Roy stated that once man became conscious of his rational essence, he could progress toward true freedom.

> A humanist philosophy starts from the scientifically grounded belief that man is essentially rational and therefore moral. As soon as he becomes conscious of the rational essence and the moral core of his very physical existence, man stands firmly on the way to spiritual freedom. That realistically optimistic view of human nature transforms the ideal of a just and equitable social order from a mere utopia into a practical proposition.[10]

Some critics have noted that Roy's treatment of human nature is oversimplified and reductionistic, that he did not adequately take into account the complexity of human nature and psychology. It is said that he was over-optimistic about man's rationality.[11] In trying to explain Roy's meaning, Ellen Roy wrote, "Let me remove one obvious objection. I do not say man is rational. I say that man, by his nature, is capable of being rational. Rationality is a biological property of man."[12]

It is difficult to understand Roy's actual meaning in regard to will and freedom. He said that man's rationality grows out of the rationality of the material world, the cosmos. But he could not have believed that all men are rational all of the time. One is bothered by his use of the term "determined," in relation to the will and emotions. His cosmology seems to embody a biological determinism. Bhattacharjee has noted that "human will cannot be directly related to the laws of the physical universe." But it "might be conceded that man's emotions, will, ideas etc. are determined... by physical factors and therefore are rational categories." But he believes there needs to be a better analysis of human instincts and emotion. "It is doubtful," he notes, "whether human rationality can be derived from a rational or law governed world ... Law governedness may give rise to a feeling of fatalism in man rather than rationality understood in the above sense." Human rationality, then, must be understood only with reference to man's freedom to choose, according to Bhattacharjee.[13]

The history of mankind, for Roy, is the history of man's struggle for freedom in the unfolding of human personality. He conceptualizes freedom as "the progressive disappearance af all restrictions on the unfolding of the potentialities of individuals, as human beings, and not as cogs in the wheels of a mechanized social organization."[14]

As a Marxist, Roy believed that freedom precluded allegiance to any external forces, whether religious or "neo-religious." In the past, he argued, religion was a powerful force that served to keep man in slavery. He said, "One cannot think freely for himself, and believe at the same time in the religious sense."[15]Today, he noted, secular religions have arisen, such as the political doctrines of Liberalism, Socialism and Communism, centered upon the concept of the social collective, and demanding allegiance to the State. If man is to become free, Roy said, he must regain faith in himself, and renounce all these enslaving dogmas.

> It is absurd to argue that negation of freedom is the road to freedom. The purpose of all rational human endeavor, collective as well as individual, should be the attainment of freedom in ever larger measure, and freedom is real only as individual freedom.[16]

Here it would be useful to note some of the similarities between Roy's concept of human nature and that of the young Marx. Both Roy and Marx rejected a philosophical anthropology, seeing man as a material being. For Marx, man was a part of physical nature, and since man consciously interacted with the world, the whole of physical nature was actually an extension of man. All of Nature, he said, forms a part of human life and nature. "Nature is the inorganic body of man," excluding the human body itself.[17]

Marx saw alienation as a process whereby material objectivity became an alien force to rule over man through economic and social institutions.In this way, man becomes a slave of Nature. The project of freedom, for Marx, was for man to gain control over Nature, which took the form of control over production and his product. Man must ultimately emerge from the "realm of necessity," where he produced unfreely, and out of compulsion, into the "realm of freedom," where he produced freely, i.e. true production. Marx followed the Renaissance concept of work as enjoyment in the realm of freedom. Marx believed that this type of freedom could not be attained in capitalist society. This was because the universal class, the working class, alienated their life-activity under forced labour. Their labour was alienated because they produced out of need alone. Under these conditions, man could not become truly human, a species being engaged in species activity.

Marx viewed man in much the same way as Roy, taking for granted the innate goodness of man, human perfectibility, and the power of human reason. Rather like Roy, Marx saw a continuity in biological evolution running through the animal and human species. For Marx, as for Roy, consciousness and will distinguish man from animals. For Marx, animals are not capable of freedom as they produce only out of need. Man, on the other hand, produces when he is free from physical need and only truly produces in freedom from such need."[18] These qualities distinguish man from animals.

> The animal is one with its life activity. It does not distinguish the activity from itself. It is the activity. But man makes his life activity itself an object of his will and consciousness. He has a conscious life activity. It is not a determination with which he is completely identified. Conscious life activity distinguishes man from the life activity.of animals. Only for this reason is he a species being ... Only for this reason is his activity, free activity. Alienated labour reverses the relationship, in that man because he is a self conscious being makes his life activity, his being, only a means for his existence.[19]

Alienated labour makes life appear as an end in itself, rather than a means to an end which is human freedom or species life. It becomes evident that Marx's notion of freedom embraces much of the classical concept that man can be free and human only in a community. For Marx, species life rather than individual life is the end of species activity. Animals live only to live, but man as a species being lives to be free.

The way in which Roy distinguishes between the animal and human kingdoms is similiar to the way Marx distinguishes between them. For Roy, the major difference is that whereas animals seek to exist, man seeks to exist and, at the same time, to unfold his diverse potentialities. For animals, he sees the struggle for existence as largely mechanical, whereas on the human level, the struggle for existence is purposive. "Man tries to change the environment to suit his purpose." Roy believed that the quest for freedom began with the struggle to conquer Nature, i.e. with the discovery of tools. Roy saw modern technology as an extension of that freedom. It was through "superior intelligence or reason," he believed, that man was able to pursue freedom.[20] So for Roy, as for Marx and Aristotle, life is a means to an end, rather than an end in itself.

For both Roy and Marx, the essence of human nature is human potential, that is, the potential to become free and to become human. In both instances, human consciousness plays a crucial role in the attainment of freedom. Both Roy and Marx rejected a philosophical anthropology, although late in life Roy came to alter his views and to speak of certain constants in human nature. This later spiritual phase will be discussed below. As to Marx, it can be said that human nature is grounded in the potential to become a human being engaged in free creative activity. So man is endowed with a dynamic potential.

For Marx, it is the structure of social organisation which prevents man from developing his full potential as a human being. Roy, on the other hand, put more emphasis on the role of religion and the repressive tyranny of metaphysics, in preventing man from becoming free. What is stable in human nature for Marx is man's potential to become truly human. This is a universalistic view of man. In a similiar way, Roy's view that man has the potential to become free is universalistic.

However, one may point out a significant difference between Marx and Roy in terms of man's freedom in relation to society or the collective. This can be seen most clearly when one comes to understand Roy's final formulation of freedom, as grounded in the Indian tradition, and somewhat similiar to the views of Vivekananda, Sri Aurobindo and Gandhi. Marx takes a more organic and collective view of freedom. For Marx, man can gain freedom only as a member of the collective in a classless and propertyless society. For Roy, on the other hand, man is free primarily as an individual in society, and society is no more than the sum of all the particular individuals that make up the society. "While individuals cannot exist independent of society," Roy wrote, "yet society is no more than integration of individuals, and if you want a good society, you must have good individuals."[21]

The distinction is further illustrated in Roy's concept of the relationship between the individual and the State. He wrote:

> The starting point of the humanist approach to political problems is that the relation between the individual and the state, between man and society, between freedom and organisation, cannot be solved unless man, the individual, and his freedom, is given at least equally important place in these political equations. Until now, political thinking has placed all emphasis on the interests of the State, everything is justified.[22]

M.N. Roy's concept of freedom led him to envision a future free society of individuals which would ultimately embrace all mankind. Such a society would be cosmopolitan, transcending the nation-state and resulting in a world government of free spiritual individuals.

Roy defined freedom as "the progressive elimination of all the factors, physical, social and psychological which obstruct the unfolding of man's rational, moral and creative potentialities." The individual in a free society, he believed, must not only enjoy economic self- sufficiency and security, but also be free from cultural regimentation. "The sum total of freedom actually enjoyed by its members is the measure of the liberating or progressive significance of any social order." Individual freedom cannot be dismissed as an empty abstraction" and "freedom is real only as individual freedom."[23]

So it is clear that Roy came to stress the goal of the spiritually free individual in the good society. He said that "group morality" cannot really guarantee against the abuse of power. And, since "values operate through individuals," the "only way to guarantee the greatest good to the greatest number" is to ensure a "government composed of spiritually free individuals accountab1e... to their respective consciences."[24] These individuals in the executive power of the State must be free not only from vested interests, but also from the "vagaries of the collective ego."

Roy's concern for a society of spiritually free individuals stems from his final formulation of the idea of freedom. That this ultimate formulation is grounded in and flows from traditional Indian thought on spiritual freedom has been illustrated. The concept in Indian thought is that of *Mukti* or *Moksha*. In relation to Roy's final formulation of freedom, we may trace its evolution through at least three stages.

Dennis Dalton has examined the evolution of Roy's thought on freedom and noted the close parallels between Roy's concept of freedom and that embraced by Sri Aurobindo, Vivekananda and Gandhi. First, Roy, along with Gandhi asserted that freedom meant more than political independence. But while Marxists mainly stressed the need for economic rights and responsibilities, the Gandhians emphasized the "moral aspect of freedom." The concept of freedom which dominated the Indian nationalist tradition was that of political independence as well as "self-rule or self-control," that is, *swaraj*. Aurobindo distinguished between "internal" (moral) and "external" (political and economic) freedom. Also, according to Vivekananda, "one may gain political and social independence, but if one is a slave to his passions and desires, he cannot feel the pure joy of real freedom."[25]

In 1937, Roy's concept of freedom was closer to that of Marx than to Gandhi's conception. He saw political independence and the radical transformation, economic, social and political, of Indian society as an end. This transformation was largely seen in economic and social terms. The emphasis was upon material concerns such as the distribution of wealth, leaving aside the spiritual aspects of freedom. Later, Roy's conception of spiritual freedom "appears and co-exists for a decade with his materialist view of freedom." It was only during the radical humanist period, beginning in 1946, however, that spiritual freedom became paramount. In New Orientation Roy called for a "new philosophy of freedom."

He pointed out that the Radical Democratic Party must not be a party of the "economic man" but rather a "party of moral men, moved by the ideal of human freedom." He believed that "ethical values are greater than economic interests" and that "spiritual freedom is the ultimate value of his system."[26]

Dalton observed that Roy conceived of spiritual freedom in two ways. First "he posits spiritual freedom as not only the ultimate value of radical humanism in its hierarchy of values, but also as the key motivating force of human action." Roy said, "the urge for spiritual freedom, though it has remained largely in the subconscious, has been the lever of the entire human development ever since the birth of the species." This notion of spiritual freedom as a final cause was familiar to Sri Aurobindo, Vivekananda and Gandhi. For Vivekananda, spiritual freedom was identified with the Hindu conception of *Mukti* or *Moksha*. According to Vivekananda, "freedom is the one goal of all nature ... everything is struggling towards that goal." Secondly, Roy conceived of spiritual freedom as a "prerequisite for social and political freedom." Roy came to argue that "spiritual liberation is the condition for social and political liberation. Radical humanism is the message of that liberation." So Roy came to believe that "the burning problem of our time is the problem of moral transformation."[27]

In comparing Roy's ideas on freedom to those of Sri Aurobindo, Vivekananda and Gandhi, it must be kept in mind, however, that Roy did not base his beliefs upon the system of Vedanta as the others did. He insisted that freedom be grounded in a materialist philosophy to the end. But Dalton argues that "Roy's materialism had no real logical relation to his ethical or political ideas." He believes that Roy's "appropriation of some aspects of materialist philosophy to justify in his own mind his appeals to rationalism and modern science" did not succeed. He concluded that "the consequence was an incongruous conglomeration of scientism, irrationalism and moralism that vitiates the claim of radical humanism to being a system of philosophy."[28]

Roy certainly departed from the Marxist view that freedom is dependent upon the economic base, and in this respect, he moved closer to the traditional Indian position. Roy, like Gandhi, came to see spiritual freedom as a prerequisite for social and economic freedom. For Aristotle, on the other hand, the economic base, i.e. "household goods" which provided economic freedom, were a prerequisite for the good life of the philosopher engaged in contemplation *(eudaimon)*.[29] For Marx, economic freedom, in the form of the development and common ownership of the economic base and the ultimate abolition of property rights was a prequisite for the loss of alienation and the spiritual development of man. For Marx, the realm of freedom emerges only when the realm of necessity (unfree production) is effectively conquered. Marx believed that man could maximize his freedom to the extent that he could produce freely. But for Roy, economic sufficiency is not the precondition for freedom.[30]

Bhattacharjee argued that Roy's concept of freedom was "narrow and negative." This was because Roy saw freedom as the removal of all barriers to the unfolding of the latent potentialities in man, and these are not "diverse" in character, but "biologically inherent."[31] Bhattacharjee contended that Roy ignored the positive social aspects of freedom, as defined in the social sphere by such thinkers as Harold Laski and T.H. Green. He noted that Roy came to denigrate the concept of positive freedom in the social sphere because of his disillusionment with the social experiment in the USSR under Stalin.

While it is true that Roy departed from the Hegelian concept of the realization of positive freedom through the State, the crucial distinction really lies in the vehicle for positive social change. This concerns the level of analysis for social change. For Roy, the unit of analysis for change is the individual rather than the structure of the society as a whole.

Roy, then, pleaded that the individual must first change as a prequisite to changing the whole society. In this way, the moral and spiritual values of the society will be renovated. These values must come from within the individual and as they spiral outward, they will, in turn, change the structure and functions of institutions in society. It can be argued that this is also a positive view of freedom. Roy sought to enhance the worth and dignity of the individual, and saw that the Marxian structural approach runs the risk of the "eclipse of the individual" and of ethics.[32]

Bhattacharjee also criticized Roy for assuming that the quest for freedom leads to the search for truth, and that the discovery of truth, through science, will promote freedom and morality. Bhattacharjee pointed out that there is no guarantee that scientific truth will lead to the search for and progress toward morality and the rationalisation of society. It is an empirical fact, he pointed out, that man often uses this type of knowledge to harm society and himself, and may ultimately use it to destroy civilization.[33] Roy's optimism can be traced to his nineteenth century belief in the inevitability of progress grounded in scientific discovery and the application of scientific knowledge through technology to advance the cause of freedom.

It can be argued that Roy's rejection of Marxism was premature and based more upon the practice and result of actually existing socialism, e.g. Stalinism, than upon the ideas in the "writings of Marx and Engels. The critique of Marxism in Roy's writings leaves one with the impression that Marx envisioned human liberation as taking place through the political sphere, that is, through political emancipation in which the individual ego is absorbed in the collective ego of the State. But there is reason to question this interpretation of Marx.

There is no evidence that Roy was familiar with the writings of the young Marx. Had he been able to consider Marx's writings on the relationship between political emancipation and human emancipation, as set forth in Marx's early writings, it is unlikely that he would have criticized Marx quite so harshly.

Marx's view of the relationship between political emancipation and human emancipation emerges from his essay "On the Jewish Question." In this work, it is clear that Marx did not believe at the time of its writing that man could emancipate himself through the political apparatus of the State. "A State may be free without man himself being free," Marx wrote. "By emancipating himself politically, man emancipates himself in a devious way, through an intermediary, however necessary this intermediary may be ... The State is the intermediary between man and human liberty."[34] Marx argued that:

> Human emancipation will only be complete when the real, individual man has absorbed into himself the abstract citizen; when as an individual man in his everyday life, in his work, and in his relationships, he has become a species being; and when he has recognised and organised his own powers as social powers so that he no longer separates this social power from himself as political power.[35]

It is noteworthy that, for Marx, man becomes a species being "as an individual man," and not through the merging of his ego into the collective ego.

In fact, Marx believed that human emancipation must ultimately take place in the sphere of civil society, as did Roy, Gandhi and Jayaprakash Narayan. Marx saw that "political emancipation is just the final form of human emancipation within the framework of the prevailing social order."[36] Political emancipation just gives sway to egotistical concerns, which in turn, produce more alienation. The liberal political system allows such elements as wealth, religion, education, occupation and private property to manifest themselves.[37] "Political emancipation is a reduction of man, on the one hand to a member of civil society, an independent and egoistic individual, and on the other hand, to a citizen, to a moral person."[38]

So Marx realized, as did Roy and Gandhi, that man could not be "moral" when the State dictated morality, e.g. within the framework of a State religion. Although the State attains universality of thought in this way, this has little to do with the true emancipation of humanity, Marx thought. In the State, with political emancipation, man has a "double existence. He lives in the political community, where he regards himself as a communal being, and in civil society where he acts simply as a private individual, treats other men as means, and becomes the plaything of alien powers."[39] In the State man appears to be "universal" but this is an "imaginary sovereignty," and "unreal universality." In the State there is a conflict between the "general interest" and the "private interest," between the "political state" and "civil society."[40] That man is politically emancipated from religion in the State is just "an expression of the fact that man is separated from the community, from himself and from other men."[41]

Science, Rationality and Consciousness

Science, for Roy was the source of knowledge of the universe and as such the basis for all human progress. "Science," he said, "is as old as the human race... It is as old as philosophy itself."[42] Science begins with. the desire to know. "The word itself means knowledge."[43]

Man, he thought, was

> ...born with the spirit of enquiry into what could be called the metaphysical ... The original habit of man to assume supernatural causes of natural phenomena was a manifestation of scientific spirit, the essence of which is the belief that everything has a cause, something cannot come out of nothing.[44]

In discussing the relationship between science and philosophy, Roy argued that they are not two different things.[45] His position was rather that philosophy, in the past, dealt with those problems that science was unable to address, due to insufficient knowledge of the material world. Consequently,

> ...the philosophical consequences of modern science is to abolish completely the distinction between science and philosophy. The problems reserved for philosophy, of time, space, substance and causality, have come within the jurisdiction of scientific

> investigation, and have been at last solved ... Science is the method of acquiring knowledge; philosophy is systematisation and coordination of the knowledge already acquired.[46]

Roy believed that man sought knowledge about the universe in order to "live more satisfactorily," that is to increase his control over nature.[47] Early scientists attempted to explain the physical world by "reducing natural phenomenon to a unitary physical existence." In this respect, he refers to the materialists Kanada and Kapila in India and Thales and Heraclitos in Greece.[48] Historically, lack of knowledge led to-the creation of a pantheon of gods, but human curiosity produced a theology, i.e. "a science of God himself." The rise of spiri tualism, for Roy, merely demonstrated man's ultimate and undiminished desire to know.[49]

But ultimately, the accumulation of knowledge enabled man to explain natural phenomena, including himself, in terms of physics, freeing him from the necessity of creating gods.[50] The "iconoclastic nature of science" means that the old gods must be destroyed. "Scientific humanism," he said, "seeks to explain man through science. He will no longer remain a mystery as in old humanism." When it is possible to explain how "man arose out of the background of the physical universe, we can revive the old humanist doctrine that man is the center and creator of all things, moving on to humanist, radical democracy."[51]

For Roy, the acquisition of scientific knowledge was purely physical, having nothing to do with the transcendental. He wrote:

> The biological functions, which are the foundation of all knowledge, are purely mechanical reactions. Nothing supernatural enters into the process of acquiring knowledge. There is brain, a biological mechanism, and physical objects surrounding us ... mind again is nothing but the function of a physical entity called brain ... Our knowledg e is nothing more mysterious than the sum total of such impressions caught by the retina of our eyes as well as by other sense organs, and stored in our brain.[52]

Roy argued that politics could not be separated from science and philosophy. "Politics," he wrote, "as a branch of social science, is also a science."[53] And he observed that:

> [S]ience has given confidence to a growing number of human beings that they possess the power to remake the world ... Political principles are not abstract conceptions; They are determined by concrete conditions affecting the daily life of man organised in society. On the other hand, they are expressions of those

> conditions. Therefore, political principles are empirical conceptions, and have only pragmatic value. They affect us intimately as the concrete conditions of our social existence. We feel the necessity of changing them, when- ever the preventing social conditions affect us adversely.[54]

This strictly materialist and empirical basis for political views stemmed largely from Roy's Marxist views.

That he had yet to envision what was to become the supreme value of his political philosophy, spiritual freedom, is evident in his statement that "politics cannot be spiritualised. Spiritual or moral politics is often the refuge for cheats and humbugs."[55]

Political values, Roy believed in 1940, must be derived empirically on a scientific basis.

> Just as general philosophy co-ordinates knowledge acquired in all the various departments of science, similarly, political philosophy must co-ordinate the knowledge acquired in the various departments of the social activities of human beings.[56]

> The social and economic base in Marxism, Roy noted, is ... nothing but a philosophical approach to politics, a scientific mode of solving social problems. It is only our conception of philosophy, of philosophy as the science of sciences; it is the sum total of the entire human knowledge which makes sense out of politics ...There are laws governing human life, as they govern the physical universe ... Therefore the problems of politics can be approached as scientific problems.[57]

For Roy, such a scientific view of politics includes both the idea that (1) the evolution of society is a determined process[58] and (2) that man is free to remake the world through the application of scientific knowledge.[59] The "mystics," Roy said, attempt to prove that

> social behaviour is not guided by any law, that the evolution of society is not a determined process, that politics is not a branch of science, that principles of politics are not to be readjusted to the necessities of human existence, and that human society need not undergo revolutions from time to time.[60]

But he was optimistic that

> science has given confidence to a growing number of human beings that they possess the power to remake the world ... To prevent them from doing that, .. you must tell them that they are automatons, that they are mere slaves of fate ... Science today enables philosophy to rescue herself from this state of prostitution.[61]

A scientific view leads to the conviction that "man makes the world in which he lives," and that he has the power to make it over and over again whenever necessary. One who is to be a revolutionary, Roy believed, must embrace this view. He wrote:

> A revolutionary is one who...[believes that] ... the world can be remade better than it is today ... by human efforts...who starts with the knowledge that the world has been remade time and again, and that the process of remaking the world takes place of necessity ... One cannot be a revolutionary without possessing scientific knowledge. One must be a scientist to be a true revolutionary.[62]

And, "Freedom from dogma," he claimed, "is the specific feature of scientific thought."[63]

In 1946, Roy seemed to be seeking beyond the material sphere for the guiding principles of his political philosophy. He pointed out that even though politics is a branch of social science, "it is difficult to practice politics scientifically."[64] The "one guiding principle of all scientific investigation is that no proposition should be given credit of being scientific unless it can be stated in mathematical terms." But "where emotions are concerned, science must not claim a high degree of probability for its presuppositions." And since emotion cannot be measured mathematically, "it is difficult to lay down rigid laws of political practice ... "He observed that modern politics had become a matter of emotion, with the swaying of the public by unprincipled demagogues. This dampened the hope for a scientific politics in the near future.[65] Although Roy never lost faith in the intrinsic rationality of man, he became more concerned about the ability of modern politicians to exploit man's emotions at the expense of rationality.

In terms of his faith in the rationality of man, M.N. Roy may be truly said to be a child of the Enlightenment. "The Enlightenment" was necessary to "secularize the laws of nature." Roy's admiration for the philosophical principles of the Enlightenment can be seen from his characterization of this period in *Reason, Romanticism and Revolution*. In the eighteenth century, he noted, rationalism broke away from its metaphysical tradition ..." There was great expansion of scientific knowledge and there arose

> ... a prevailing belief that reason was applicable to human affairs, and that, rationally regulated, they would lead to universal good ... Not only was man capable of solving all the riddles of the universe, of penetrating deeper and deeper into the secrets of

> nature; freed from ignorance, prejudices and superstitions, human intelligence could also find the ways and means for a rational, and therefore harmonious, regulation of social relations.[66]

Roy perceived human rationality as the basis for Radical Humanism or New Humanism. The conception of a humanist consciousness involved the development of man's inherent rationality.

> A humanist says; I must act as a rational and moral human being; as such I appeal to the innate reason and morality of my fellow human beings. And I shall appeal to them not only by precept, but by my behaviour. If my behaviour appeals to them, they will realise that it is my philosophy which appeals to them. Thus, as a social being, a humanist can attain his ideal every day of his life.[67]

The political approach of the humanist "results from his attitude to his fellow beings, from this confidence in the innate, potential, rationality and morality of all human beings."[68] According to Roy, it was only through reason that a "government of the people" could be established. He was convinced that people would "ultimately respond to the appeal to their reason rather than to any other appeal."[69] He believed the loss of faith in the rationality of the common man was a basis for elitism. With the division of society into economic classes, the "society was horizontally divided between the elite and the masses." The average man "moved only by emotional appeal" could not be "intellectual and rational." Consequently, "only the elites were considered fit to rule." But Roy argued that, "we must return to direct democracy where every individual has the opportunity of influencing the affairs of society."[70] We must maintain, he said, "that every single human being is potentially capable of developing his creative powers, his intelligence, his discrimination, as much as any other human being. Scientific humanism can make that assertion." That is the "starting point for humanist political practice."[71]

Consciousness, as life itself, for Roy, arises out of the physical universe. "Even the most primitive form of life, the amoeba," he wrote, "possesses a primitive form of consciousness. But to acquire the knowledge of various phenomena is the privilege of ... human beings ... In a sense, knowledge is a higher form of consciousness."[72] Similiarly, " ... conscience ... is not a mystic inner voice nor a divine presentiment, but a biological heritage— an emergent novelty of the process of evolution."[73]

Furthermore,

> Rationalism is the mental reflex of physical causality ... Causality is reason in nature. If nature were irrational, that is to say, if

> causality were not an objective reality, an ontological category, rationalist thought would be impossible. Intelligence is a biological function, and, as such, is a part of physical nature. Reason is born of intelligence. It is the consciousness of causality in nature ... Reason derives its authority from the objective physical laws, which, in the last analysis, are but generalised statements of causal relations.[74]

The fundamental difference between the physical universe and human nature, for Roy, is that "the physical universe is law-governed, the laws being inherent in itself, whereas, man possesses will and can choose."[75] This is because "between the world of man and the world of animate matter, there lies a world of biological evolution. It is through the intervening biological world that human will is related to the laws of the physical universe." And for Roy, "it is the reason in man which harmonises the play of human will with the law-governedness of the physical universe."[76]

Roy sought to reconcile freedom of will and determinism of natural law. He said, "man can control destiny, provided that he progressively rises to the realisation of his participation in the rational process of nature."[77] Roy asserted that will is not the "antithesis" of physical law. Yet, he seemed to believe that will can defy a physical Law.[78] Generally, "it is reason which harmonises human will with the law-governedness of the physical universe." But this can be interpreted to mean that will can be "playful" and thus "antithetical to physical law."[79]

B.S. Sharma has argued that Roy's cosmology is a restatement of Engel's ideas, relying in the evidence of natural sciences, rather than the principle of the dialectic.

> Life, with its free will, originated as a novelty in the context of the physical universe governed by deterministic laws. While Engels could explain the novelty in dialectical terms, Roy cannot give an adequate account of how the capacity of matter to produce life operates. His only explanation is this: in as much as the entire process of biological evolution takes place in the context of the world of dead matter, human will cannot be an antithesis to the law-governedness of the physical universe.[80]

The ultimate consequence of Roy's cosmology of man is inescapably, a narrow, simplistic, deterministic and reductionistic view of man. Bhattacharjee pointed out that "Roy oversimplified the problem of human nature." The "dynamism of the human mind has not been fully taken into consideration."[81] Roy's account cannot adequately account for irrationality. For Roy, irrationality seems to be foreign to human nature. He did not adequately account for emotion in man and its function as a basis for irrational behaviour. Further, since will and conscience are seen as arising from the physical universe, these dimensions of human nature are reduced to the point of being superfluous. The ideal, for Roy, is that will and emotion would be reconciled with reason. But since reason is grounded in the "law-governedness of the physical universe," this essentially makes the will subject to the physical determinism he sees in the cosmos. Conscience is also grounded in the physical universe. Thus there is no escaping the fact that in this cosmological scheme, man is trapped in a deterministic way and bound to the physical sphere. Also, "rationality is not a metaphysical category but a biological one."[82] In such a cosmology, one wonders how the rebellious spirit of man would be released. Man is bound to the physical sphere in the same way that Roy saw man as bound to the rule of a deity in theology.

Perhaps part of the problem is how Roy derives his values. They arise either "*sui generis*" (in nature) or empirically. Roy believed that the categories of natural law are vacuous. Ultimately, Roy can only remedy this weakness in his cosmology by falling back on the notion of spiritual freedom in traditional Indian thought.

There is a rational teleology in Roy, similiar to that in William Godwin and other thinkers influenced by the Enlightenment. This slowly unfolding human rationality and potentiality in history also transforms the nature of man and consequently the nature of society. This logically leads to a sort of necessitarianism, as in Godwin. Godwin argued that every action of man is a result of necessity, and that only sometime in the future would human rationality evolve to the point where anarchic society, in which each individual would rule himself, could be ushered in. Until this time, he thought, political controls and sanctions would be required.

For Roy, man evolved from the lower life forms, and developed a human consciousness. In the state of lower evolution, Roy saw man as Hobbesian, concerned primarily with self preservation. He believed man's values correspond to the level of human evolution, that is, to his level of consciousness. Increasing rationality in man led to the origin of society and the acceptance of social obligations.[83] Man is transformed from the realm of self preservation with egotistical values, to the realm of humanistic consciousness with universalistic values by the unfolding of his human potentiality, his rationality, in the search for freedom. Roy believed that this potentiality has been unfolding throughout history, and that through it man would establish Radical Humanism.

Sharma has pointed out that "human nature, according to the philosophy of New Humanism, is determined more by physical and biological rather than by social and environmental Factors."[84] Roy was convinced that the rational element in human nature would result in a harmonious future society. He saw Radical Humanism as a vehicle for the emergence of man into that future society.

Rationality, in the unfolding of human potential and freedom, also became a source of values for Roy. Moral instinct was identified with the urge for freedom. Roy said "man is moral because he is rational and the universe is a moral order governed by laws inherent in itself." Consequently, "we need a humanistic ethics" based on a "naturalistic rationalism," and built on a "mechanistic cosmology and a physical-realist ontology."[85] But this raises questions concerning moral obligation, as Sharma has pointed out. "If all human actions are merely the satisfaction of this urge, there is no point in asking people to be good, when they have to be so in any case, in pursuance of their urge for freedom."[86]

Critics have pointed out that "Roy's connotation of reason is imprecise." It is both, "a faculty of individual personality and the law of the universe." This results in a "confusion of fact and value." Roy has also been criticised for having "no theory of perception to explain how the mind is related to the external world."[87]

New Humanism, for Roy, was

> a set of principles which have relevance to all branches of man's life and social existence and show a way towards their reorganisation. They are principles which can inspire mankind to take things in their own hand and shape their social world according to their reason and needs.[88]

Man being essentially rational, he "can think for himself, that he has created his world and that he can remake it according to his own decision rationally arrived at."[89] "The purpose of all social endeavor," Roy said, "should be to make man increasingly conscious of his innate rationality."[90] This could be done through education[91] or through science.[92] The failure of parliamentary democracy, he thought, was due to its "failure to explain man himself."[93] Much of the crisis in modern society," Roy believed, could be traced to the fact that human affairs were no longer controlled by "individual reason and judgement." He wrote:

> In the case of perhaps ninety-five percent of human beings, the individual personality is eclipsed, unconscious, and inoperative ... Reason and discrimination are at a discount in public life because these can be exercised only by individuals, and the

> individual itself is at a discount. In consequence, a small minority of self willed and often self-appointed men at the helm of affairs manage to guide everything according to their own proclivities or fixed ideas, irrespective of the enormous volume of reason that could be brought to bear on world affairs if the potential rationality of all human beings could assert itself in an intelligently expressed public opinion.[94]

Radical Self-Transformation and Social Change

Roy came to see and abhor the mystifications surrounding the modern State. Reliance upon the organised and centralised power of the State, due to the Hegelian conception of freedom had, he believed, greatly diminished the faith of the individual in himself. Roy came to believe that freedom, which was freedom for the collective only, and which placed the interests of the collective above those of the individual, ceased to be moral because it led to an ever greater concentration of power and a greater diminution of individual moral freedom. As morality came to be defined in utilitarian terms, individual morality, that is, true morality, withered away.

Consequently, Roy, following Gandhi, came to place the hope for the future on the individual. The irrational organisational structures of society, he believed, could be broken down and social and economic ills remedied only when individuals began to transform themselves. This degree of reliance upon the individual was a departure from orthodox Marxism. Although for Marx individuals make history and change the world, their consciousness is shaped by social and economic forces subject to a historical teleology. This suggests that the root of the problem of social change, the object of the revolutionary, must be to transform the structure of society which will, in turn lead to the transformation of the individual into a rational and human individual. As we have seen, for Roy, on the other hand, consciousness arose from the biological evolution of man and his naturally emerging rationality. So factors other than the social and economic structure of society accounted for man's consciousness. This premise led Roy to focus upon individual moral self-transformation, rather than upon violent revolution for the renovation of society. He wrote that "gradualism is the quickest tempo of social change ..."[95] He envisioned the future transformation of Indian society as taking place in this way.

Social change, based on individual self-transformation, was grounded in the principles of Radical Humanism. Roy wrote:

> The fundamental principle of New Humanism is to revive the old idea of the sovereignty of the human individual. According to it, every political organisation or social and economic institution must be judged by its ability to help the development of the individual human people who live under those institutions.[96]

For Roy, social change based upon individual self- transformation was the heart of Radicalism.

> Any effort for a reorganisation of society must begin from the unit of society—from the root, so to say. Such an effort to develop a new philosophy of revolution, on the basis of the entire stock of human heritage, and then to elaborate the theory and formulate the principles and practice of political action and economic reconstruction, .. can be called Radicalism. Radicalism thinks in terms neither of nation nor of class; its concern is man; it conceives freedom as freedom of the individual.[97]

Since society was to be transformed gradually over a period of time by enlightened individuals, Roy thought that education was a pivotal factor in the emergence of enlightened individuals. The twentieth thesis of his Principles of Radical Democracy states that:

> In the last analysis, education of the citizen is the condition for such a reorganisation of society as will be conducive to common progess and prosperity without encroaching upon the freedom of the individual. The Radical Democratic state will be the school for the political and civic education of the citizen. Its structure and function will enable detached individuals to come to the forefront of public affairs. Manned with such individuals, the state machinery will cease to be the instrument in the hands of any particular class to coerce others. Only spiritually free individuals in power can smash all chains of slavery and usher in freedom for all.

As opposed to government education intended to "create mental conformism," the new education would be an education

> not imparted with the purpose of maintaining any given status quo, but with the sole purpose of making the individuals of a community conscious of their potentialities, help them think rationally and judge for themselves, and promote their critical faculties by applying it to all problems confronting them.[98]

Roy thought that in a "backward" country, government education could not raise the intellectual level of the people.[99] Under Radical Humanism, people would "remember their critical faculties which governments naturally fear." With such education, man would appear as the "highest culmination of the entire process of evolution."[100]

Roy believed that a "cosmopolitan commonwealth of free individuals was a possibility.[101] It would be a spiritual community, not limited by the boundaries of national States. He thought that the radical perspective of the future was that national States would "gradually disappear under the impact of cosmopolitan Humanism," leading to "one world," or a world government.[102]

It is clear, that Roy envisioned peaceful and constitutional social change, and given the emerging potential of man there was no necessity for violent revolution. "Gradualism" would, in the final analysis, provide the surest and swiftest progression to a free and democratic society. But Roy was ambiguous with respect to historicism, that is, as to the driving force of social change. While Roy wanted to avoid the deterministic historicism embodied in orthodox Marxism, he ultimately smuggled this determinism back into his scheme of social change. He could never fully free himself from it, because it was entailed in the basic presuppositions of his cosmology of man and the universe. Sharma has pointed out that revolution is a determinist process for Roy, as for Marx, because "free will itself is an evolute of the determined process of nature."[103] In 1942, Roy wrote:

> [J]ust as the rise of the temperature of a volume of water creates a commotion affecting the entire volume, just so does a human community experience a commotion whenever new forces are generated within its structures. The commotion develops and culminates according to its law which is only an extension of the law governing all of physical processes."[104]

This view embodies a physical determinism which makes social change subject to physical laws of the material universe. Such a view necessarily limits man's freedom to change history, and introduces into Roy's system a type of determinism analogous to that in Marxism. As Sharma pointed out, "Roy considers the process of social evolution as part of the physical world and consequently the laws governing the physical world are seen to also govern social evolution."[105] The ambiguity in Roy is seen in another statement: "Social phenomena are of course, determined very largely by the intentions of men; but there are historical factors which operate independently of the intentions of politicians and parties."[106]

In a Radical Humanist democracy, Roy believed, "decentralisation will prevent centralisation of power, and the function of the State will be reduced to coordination of the activities of the autonomous social institutions."[107] Party politics would be abolished to help individuals think for themselves.[108] Such a society would rely upon local initiative and cooperation rather than rule from the top.

Unlike Gandhi, Roy emphasized the need to increase industrialisation and the standard of living on a wide scale. He believed that the further development of technology advanced the humanist quest for freedom. In 1949, he said "there is no purpose in politics unless it increases the welfare and happiness of men" and "that it is men alone who can bring it about, not impersonal forces and factors."[109] In outlining the parameters of a future cooperative society in India, he decided that the "supreme need of the country [was] to raise the standard of living of the masses."[110] He wrote, "A balanced and beneficial economic development of any country should be guided by two considerations: 1. the basic purpose of national economy is to provide food, shelter and clothing for the people; and 2. one must cut the coat according to the cloth available."[111] Accordingly, Roy thought that it was a mistake for the Government of India to neglect agricultural development and emphasize the development of heavy industry. Such a policy came about, not through economic rationality, but because "the agricultural economy came to be regarded as the result of colonial subjugation."[112] He warned that "a substantial increase in agricultural production is the basic condition for any real development of the country." He also feared that agricultural mechanization would aggravate the population problem and create mass unemployment.[113]

Roy believed that India's material needs could be met by establishing an economic system based on decentralized and cooperatively owned units of production interlinked and with overall planning of production and distribution. He thought there would be no problem in overcoming the "small minority" who might "place selfish interests above the general welfare." Peasants would be encouraged to organise cooperative communities in which land and capital would be held in common. In this way,

> the desired agrarian revolution will take place inexpensively as well as non-violently. The theoretical issue of private ownership verses nationalisation of land will be solved in practice to the general benefit and all-round satisfaction. Non-productive ownership will automatically disappear in a cooperative society, which will make room for individual ownership of the produce of one's labour.[114]

Not only agriculture, but "allied industries" would "be developed on the basis of regional cooperative societies." Surplus capital from these industries would in turn be used to establish large scale industries and mining industry, also to be held cooperatively. Newly formed capital would "not be the means of exploitation," but would "perform the social function of stimulating production for the use of the community and raising the general standard of living."[115]

Establishing a system of interlinked cooperative units would rationalize the economy, eliminate exploitation, and ensure compelling reasons for support from existing entrepreneurs.

> In the context of this new type of economic organisation, the theoretical controversy about the merits or demerits of nationalisation and private ownership will be meaningless. A co-operative system embracing the entire national economy will by its very structure eliminate exploitation of labour for private profit; but at the same time, nobody will be expropriated or otherwise injured. Privately owned industries, which had grown up previous to the development of the new system, will remain during the transition period. Thereafter, they will also have the freedom to exist, further develop and compete with the new system ... There will be no coercion; the anarchic system will break down because of the impossibility to compete with a non-profit-making economy sustained by co-operative efforts of practically the entire society.[116]

In contrast to presently existing state controlled economies, which "breed corruption and inefficiency" and have "resulted in economic regimentation and eclipse of liberty," a truly socialized economy, Roy thought, would be democratic.[117]

> Democratisation of the economic life will make a reality of political democracy, at the same time, the evils of collectivism—negation of individual freedom, regimentation and bureaucratic control—will be avoided. The function of government will be limited to the administration of State only as the political organisation of society. The function of the government will be to maintain law and order and coordinate the activities of various autonomous institutions concerned respectively with the diverse aspects of social life.[118]

The heart of Radical Democracy would consist of sovereign local people's committees, which would perform the functions of local government. The whole electorate would come together in local conventions and choose a candidate among themselves. This would ensure the accountability of the elected officials.[119] The local committees would send delegates to sub-divisional and district people's committees, but control of the entire state machinery would remain vested in the local people's committees.[120]

Economic reform would provide that the land and mineral resources be the "collective property of the people." The constitution would provide for a guaranteed minimum wage, social security and free education up to age fourteen.[121] Industrial and agricultural enterprises would be publicly owned and the net income treated as public revenue.[122] The resulting system would include the best elements of both the Western parliamentary and Soviet political systems.[123] Roy suggested that the system would initially be run on an experimental basis, as it could not be pre-determined how those institutions would function.

Radical Democracy would be grounded in the Materialist world view that the world is made by man himself, that "human life is an end in itself," and that "man is the measure of all things."[124] The State would be democratic, pluralistic and "identical with the entire society." "In the free state visualised by us as a practical possibility," Roy wrote, "detached individuals, the modern version of philosopher kings, will be at the helm of public affairs...Spiritually free men cannot be corrupted by power."[125]

References

1. Sada Nand Talwar, Political Ideas of M.N. Roy (Delhi: Khosla Publishing House, 1978), pp. 101-121.
2. Ellen Roy and Sibnarayan Ray, *In Man's Own Image* (Calcutta: Renaissance Publishers, 1945) p. 7.
3. D.G. Dalton, "M.N. Roy and Radical Humanism: The Ideology of an Indian Intellectual Elite," in *Elites in South Asia*, eds. Edmund Leach and S.N. Mukherjee (Cambridge: Cambridge-Univ. Press, 1970), p. 161.
4. M.N. Roy, *Reason Romanticism and Revolution*, 2 Vols. (Calcutta: Renaissance Publishers, 1952-1955) 2: 18.
5. M.N. Roy, *Politics Power and Parties* (Calcutta: Renaissance Publishers, 1960), p. 134.
6. *Ibid.*, p. 138.
7. *Ibid.*, p. 137.
8. M.N. Roy, *New Humanism* (Calcutta: Renaissance Publishers, 1947, p. 11.

9. M.N. Roy, *Fragments of a Prisoner's Diary*, 3 Vols. (Dehradun and Calcutta, Renaissance Publishers, 1940-43), Vol. 1: *The Memoirs of a Cat*, p. 44.
10. Roy, *Politics Power and Parties*, pp. 81-82.
11. G.P. Bhattacharjee, *Evolution of Political Philosophy of M.N. Roy* (Calcutta: Minerva, 1971), pp. 110-111.
12. Talwar, p. 16.
13. Bhattacharjee, p. 114.
14. Talwar, p. 114.
15. Roy, *Memoirs of a Cat*, p. 29.
16. Roy, *New Humanism*, pp. 53-54.
17. Karl Marx, *Early Writings*, trans. and ed. T.B. Bottomore (New York: McGraw-Hill, 1964), p. 126.
18. *Ibid.*, p. 128.
19. *Ibid.*, p. 126.
20. Bhattacharjee, p. 116.
21. Roy, *Politics Power and Parties*, p. 141.
22. *Ibid.*, p. 120.
23. Roy, *New Humanism*, pp. 52-53.
24. *Ibid.*, pp. 58-59.
25. Dalton, p. 159.
26. *Ibid.*
27. *Ibid.*, p. 161.
28. *Ibid.*, p. 162.
29. Aristotle, *The Politics of Aristotle*, trans. and ed. Ernest Barker (London: Oxford Univ. Press, 1979), pp. 18-19. Eudaimon is happiness attained by an individual through his own efforts. Aee Aristotle, *Nicomachean Ethics*, trans. Martin Ostwald (Indianopolis: Bobs-Merrill, 1962), p. 307.
30. Bhattacharjee, p. 115.
31. *Ibid.*, pp. 114-117.
32. *Ibid.*
33. *Ibid.*, pp. 118-119.
34. Marx, p. 11.
35. *Ibid.*, p. 31.
36. *Ibid.*
37. *Ibid.*, p. 12.
38. *Ibid.*, p. 31.
39. *Ibid.*, p. 13.
40. *Ibid.*, p. 15.

41. *Ibid.*, p. 15.
42. M.N. Roy, Scientific Politics (Calcutta: Renaissance Publishers, 1942), pp. 22.
43. *Ibid.*, p. 27.
44. *Ibid.*, pp. 24, 28.
45. *Ibid.*, p. 24.
46. *Ibid.*, pp. 35, 50-51.
47. *Ibid.*, p. 47.
48. *Ibid.*, pp. 31-32.
49. *Ibid.*, pp. 32-33.
50. *Ibid.*, p. 50.
51. Roy, *Politics Power and Parties*, p. 115.
52. Roy, Scientific Politics, pp. 35-36.
53. M.N. Roy, *New Orientation* (Calcutta: Renaissance Publishers, 1946), p.15, Scientific Politics, pp. 17, 52.
54. Roy, Scientific Politics, p. 39.
55. *Ibid.*, p. 52.
56. Roy, *Scientific Politics*, pp. 55-56.
57. *Ibid.*
58. *Ibid.*, p. 52.
59. *Ibid.*, p. 53.
60. *Ibid.*, p. 52.
61. *Ibid.*, p. 53.
62. *Ibid.*, p. 38.
63. *Ibid.*, p. iii.
64. Roy, *New Orientation*, p. 15.
65. Roy, *Scientific Politics*, p. 65.
66. Roy, *Reason, Romanticism and Revolution*, 1: 224.
67. Roy, *Politics Power and Parties*, p. 127.
68. *Ibid.*
69. *Ibid.*, p. 140.
70. *Ibid.*, p. 117.
71. *Ibid.*, pp. 117-118.
72. Roy, *Scientific Politics*, p. 36.
73. Roy, *Reason, Romanticism and Revolution*, 2: 263.
74. Quoted in Bhattacharjee, p. 110.
75. B.S. Sharma, *The Political Philosophy of M.N. Roy* (Delhi: National Publishing House, 1965), p. 6.
76. *Ibid.*
77. *Ibid.*, p. 55.

78. *Ibid.*, p. 73.
79. *Ibid.*
80. *Ibid.*
81. Bhattacharjee, pp. 110-111.
82. Roy, *Politics Power and Politics*, p. 44.
83. *Sharma*, p. 68.
84. *Ibid.*, p. 107.
85. Roy, *Politics Power and Parties*, p. 45.
86. Sharma, p. 76.
87. *Ibid.*, pp. 119-121.
88. Roy, *Politics Power and Parties*, p. 140.
89. *Ibid.*, pp. 138-139.
90. Roy, *New Humanism*, pp. 48-49.
91. Sharma, pp. 120-121.
92. Bhattacharjee, p. 107
93. Roy, *Politics Power and Parties*, p. 116.
94. *Ibid.*, pp. 130-131.
95. *Ibid.*, p. 83.
96. *Ibid.*, p. 168.
97. Roy, *New Humanism*, pp. 49-50.
98. Roy, *Politics Power and Parties*, p. 59.
99. *Ibid.*, p. 119.
100. *Ibid.*, p. 178.
101. Roy, *New Humanism*, p. 50.
102. *Ibid.*
103. Sharma, p. 104.
104. Roy, *Scientific Politics*, p. 269.
105. Sharma, p. 69.
106. Roy, *Politics Power and Politics*, p. 190.
107. *Ibid.*, p. 185.
108. *Ibid.*, pp. 97-98. Roy decried the existence of the Party to the extent that he urged the members of the Radical Democratic Party to disband the party. Under Roy's guidance, the party was dissolved with the hope of transforming it into a "broad and comprehensive social movement for the spread of education and freedom."
109. *Ibid.*, p. 114.
110. M.N. Roy, *Radical Humanism* (Calcutta: Renaissance Publishers, 1952), p. 48.
111. *Ibid.*, p. 45.
112. *Ibid.*, p. 46.

113. *Ibid.*
114. *Ibid.*, p. 52.
115. *Ibid.*, p. 53.
116. *Ibid.*, pp. 53-54.
117. *Ibid.*, pp. 44-45.
118. *Ibid.*, p. 55.
119. Roy, *Politics Power and Parties*, p. 166.
120. M.N. Roy, *Constitution of Free India: A Draft* (Delhi: The Radical Democratic Party: 1944), p. 42.
121. *Ibid.*, pp. 11-14.
122. *Ibid.*, p. 37.
123. Roy, *Politics Power and Parties*, p. 79.
124. *Ibid.*, p. 189.
125. *Ibid.*, p. 81.

4

J.P. Narayan on Democratic Socialism

The political thinking and writings of Jayaprakash Narayan (J.P.) contributed significantly to twentieth century Indian political thought. J.P.'s ideas concerning the transformation of Indian society evolved over an extended period, during which he was an active participant in Indian politics, first in the Indian Nationalist Movement, and later in the campaign to establish Gandhian Democracy. The evolution of the political thought of J.P. paralleled, in many ways, that of M.N. Roy.

Jayaprakash Narayan was born on October 11, 1902 in Sitabdiara Village in the Saran District of Bihar. He was a member of the Kayastha caste, which constituted the most educated community in the region.[1] His father was a government employee and intermediate landlord between the Maharaja of Dumaraon and the peasant cultivators. Jayaprakash attended the collegiate school at Patna matriculating in 1918 and earning a District Merit Scholarship to Patna College.[2]

During this period, J.P. came under the influence of the Bengal terrorists, drawing inspiration from the doctrine of immortality in the Bhagavad Gita.[3] He was further radicalised by the Rowlatt Act and the Massacre at Julianwala Bagh in Amritsar in 1919. Consequently, in 1921 he refused to take his university exams, vowing to no longer attend a British institution.[4]

J.P. was married in 1920. His father-in-law was a lawyer active in Gandhi's Champaran campaign to help landless labourers.

In 1922 he was invited by a friend to come to the United States to study. His wife Prabhavati declined to accompany him, choosing instead to live at Sabarmati Ashram in his absence.

In the United States, J.P. studied at the University of California in Berkeley and at the University of Wisconsin. At Ohio State University, J.P. was influenced by M.N. Roy's India in Transition as well as the works of Marx, Lenin, Trotsky, Plekhanov and Rosa Luxemberg.[5] He also read M.N. Roy's paper, New Masses and the Communist Partys Daily Worker.[6] As a result, J.P. became a convert to Marxism, seeing socialism as the necessary basis for individual and societal perfection.

After receiving his M.A. Degree from Ohio State University, J.P. returned to India in 1929 when his mother became seriously ill. There he met Mahatma Gandhi and Jawaharlal Nehru shortly after his arrival. Gandhi urged him to take a vow of sexual abstinence and devote his talents to the Nationalist Movement.[7]

J.P. found that

Nehru agreed with him that socialism was the best course for the future. At this time, he was interested in becoming a college lecturer but was diverted from these plans when Nehru asked him to serve as the secretary for the Labour Research Department of the Congress at Allahabad.[8] He attended the Congress Conference at Lahore in December and January, 1929-30. His work in the trade union movement included attempts to achieve the introduction of labour laws.[9]

When large numbers of Congressmen were arrested in 1932, J.P. set up an underground office in Bombay, becoming the Acting General Secretary of the All India Congress Committee. He was arrested and jailed in 1933.[10] In Nasik Jail, J.P. joined with others to lay plans for a socialist party in India. Among the planners were Asoka Mehta, Ram Manohar Lohia, Minoo Masani, Yusuf Meherally and Achyut Patwardhan. J.P.'s confinement ended in April 1934.[11] In May he organized a convention to launch the Bihar Congress Socialist Party. He was elected General Secretary with Acharya Narendra Deva as President of the Party.

In 1934, J.P. along with Minoo Masani helped to organize the Congress Socialist Party, becoming General Secretary. At this time the Comintern shifted its policy toward the Nationalists, calling for a national front. J.P. was still skeptical of many Congressmen and proposed that the Socialists form a united front with the Communist Party. In 1936, he visited M.N. Roy to gain his cooperation and support.[12] J.P. was also elected to the fifteen member Congress Working Committee.[13]

From 1936 to 1939, the Communists were admitted to the Congress Socialist Party. But their attempt to capture the Party eventually led to their expulsion from the Party.

In the early 1940's, J.P. was active in the Quit India Movement. During the previous period, J.P. had been influenced against Communism by the Moscow State trials, his personal experience with Communists and his readings, including Eugene Lyon's Assignment in Utopia, Arthur Koestler's Darkness At Noon and John Dewey's account of his probe into the murder of Leon Trotsky. J.P. was arrested and imprisoned for nine months in 1940 and again in the Lahore Fort from 1944 to 1946.[14]

After the death of Mahatma Gandhi in 1948, J.P. rejected historical materialism and became increasingly suspicious of party and power politics. Just before M.N. Roy's death in 1954, J.P. visited him to discuss the idea of partyless democracy but Roy was too ill to discuss his ideas.[15]

When the Indian National Congress became a political Party, the Congress Socialist Party separated from the Congress, becoming the Socialist Party. The strength of the Party was badly damaged, however, by its poor showing in the 1952 elections.

J.P.'s thinking during this period increasingly emphasized the spiritual regeneration of public life in India and he moved closer to the ideas of Mahatma Gandhi and Vinoba Bhave. In February 1953, J.P., J.B. Kripalani and Narendra Deva met with Nehru and discussed the possible cooperation between the People's (Praja) Socialist Party and the Congress in the Land Gift (Bhoodan) Movement. But in 1953, the Praja Socialist Party rejected this course and in 1954 collapsed. In 1952, J.P. joined Vinoba Bhave's Bhoodan Movement at the age of fifty.[16]

In July 1952, J.P. underwent a fast after which he renounced the philosophy of dialectical materialism. A visit to Mongroth village in Uttar Pradesh where the population of the village had promised to donate all the land to the village commons, resulted in J.P.'s dedication to the establishment of *Gramdan*. He began walking from village to village actively seeking land donations in the Gaya District of Bihar. He saw this movement as a viable alternative to the violent pattern of social change advocated by Marxism. He now decided that goodness must come from within, and was not necessarily conditioned by the external environment.[17]

In 1954, J.P. set up an Ashram in Sokhodeora primarily for the purpose of training Sarvodaya workers. The Ashram was to establish a perfect community through which the inhabitants would be purified. The spiritual gains made through living in the community would be diffused throughout society through devoted social service.

In the late 1950's, J.P. became active in the Gram Panchayat movement in the Government sponsored effort to re-establish these local institutions, in a three tier structure. He was appointed as the head of the Panchayati Raj portfolio. J.P.'s most important theoretical writing was accomplished during the 1950's and 1960's after his final denunciation of materialist Marxism.

In the 1970's, J.P. reentered politics as he actively led student protest movements against Congress Ministries in Gujarat and Bihar. These movements led to the declaration of Emergency Rule by Prime Minister Indira Gandhi in June 1975, and J.P. was once again imprisoned.

J.P. was active in the defeat of the Ruling Congress Party in the national elections of March 1977 and the establishment of the Janata Government. J.P. died on October 8, 1979.

Marxism and Nationalism

Similiar to M.N. Roy and Mahatma Gandhi, J.P. was not an "armchair radical," but actively participated in the Indian Nationalist Movement and the struggle to establish socialism and later Gandhian Democracy. He once remarked that " ... socialism is ninety percent practice and ten percent theory."[18] His political thinking evolved through and was shaped, consequently, by his experiences and observations over his lifetime. His early thinking was firmly grounded in the central tenets of orthodox Marxism, but when he began to observe the gap between the claims of Marxism and the actual results in the USSR, he came to acknowledge that many of these assumptions must be thoroughly questioned, and in the last analysis, rejected. He came to see that the reconstruction of Indian society would require much trial and error. In regard to how wealth might be distributed in India, he wrote in 1953, "In the sphere of technique the last word has not been said. We are all going through the stage of experimentation and it is worthwhile that we experiment in this sphere of technique also."[19] Consequently, he shunned the study for the dusty village. Ultimately, his thought was shaped by the Indian peasants and workers, as well as the thinking of socialists and academics. In the end, he rejected the entire body of conventional wisdom concerning the transition to socialism, and its nature and basis. Similiar to Gandhi, and to some extent, Roy, he eventually rejected a narrow political solution to the transformation of society, seeing the root of the problem as ethical, and its solution dependent upon the potential for the radical transformation of human nature and motivation.

J.P. was closer to Gandhi than to Roy, in the sense that he saw freedom as positive, believing that the transformation of society must be based upon the organic whole and involve self-sacrifice and service to the community. Whereas Roy persisted in the conviction that increased abundance of material goods and the further development of the means of production were bound up with human emancipation, J.P. perceived the inherent flaw in the desire for ever greater levels of material consumption. J.P., like Gandhi, was ultimately convinced that simplicity in lifestyle and moderation in consumption were integral aspects of a mature moral society.

According to Bimal Prasad, "the beacons of light illuminating J.P.'s life were the ideals of freedom and equality. His entire life can be described as a quest for revolution which would usher in a sociopolitical order enshrining these ideals." J.P. was greatly influenced by the three main currents of thought in contemporary India: Marxism, Gandhism and Democracy.[20]

J.P. derived the ideals of equality and brotherhood from Marx. From his study of Marx, he became convinced that political freedom was not enough, and that equality was needed along with the "end of exploitation, poverty and hunger."[21] What attracted J.P. to Marxism was its universalistic appeal and the promise held out to the down trodden and wretched of the earth for political and human emancipation. Its aura of systematic scientific rationality appealled to J.P. the intellectual and J.P. the aspiring young revolutionary. He saw the Marxian way as the path of liberation—the solution to India's political, economic, social and spiritual bondage.

J.P. was a nationalist as well as a Marxist. Consequently, when the Communist international changed its policy, in 1928, under Stalin, and stopped supporting indigenous movements such as the Indian Nationalist Movement, J.P. perceived the policy as a "perverted application of the principles of Marxism to the Indian situation."[22] As a nationalist, J.P. believed that the freedom struggle in India was paramount and that the Indian National Congress was the most important organisation engaged in the struggle. He was disgusted that the Communists in India attacked the "bourgeois nationalism" of the Congress and called Gandhi a "lackey of Indian capitalists and not a sincere freedom fighter." It seemed to him that Comintern policy on nationalist movements in colonial countries was isolating Communists from the national movements.[23] But the Comintern believed the task at hand was to build up local party organisations.[24]

J.P. became the acting General Secretary of the Indian National Congress in 1932. His analysis of the freedom struggle convinced him that the struggle for independence and socialism should be combined. Consequently, he envisioned a socialist party which would be free from the control of the Comintern and function within the framework of the nationalist movement. He also considered that this would "keep the nationalist movement on the path of struggle and away from constitutionalism."[25] In addition, the socialists in the Congress hoped to attract peasants and workers to join the ranks of the nationalist movement and help orientate its programme toward a socialist reconstruction of Indian Society. With these considerations in mind, J.P. founded the Congress Socialist Party in 1934, serving as the General Secretary. The architects of the party could, he believed, more correctly apply Marxism to the Indian situation than the Communists.[26]

The founders of the party "shared a common well being." Their view was basically Marxist-Leninist in its interpretation of Indian and international political economy. They saw the faltering world capitalist system as doomed. They agreed with the Marx-Engels interpretation of history, in the Communist Manifesto, as universal class struggle. They fully accepted the Marxian theory of surplus value, which was at the root of capitalist exploitation, as elaborately laid out in Capital. And they adopted, uncritically, Lenin's theory that the Imperialist structure of the world economic order represented the highest stage of capitalism. They envisioned the rationalization of the Indian economic system through State ownership of the primary means of production and State planning for the establishment of a sound foundation for socialism. Progressive elimination of the contradictions arising historically could be systematically carried out.[27] They looked to the USSR for the model of the future Indian society: J.P. was prepared to copy the Soviet experiment in detail, but calculated that the transformation should proceed at a slower pace, employ encouragement and promotion, avoid coercion, where possible, and utilize the abundant supply of labour in the subcontinent before relying on mechanization.[28]

In 1934, J.P. elaborated his understanding of socialism in an essay entitled, "Socialism: A Science of Society." He wrote:

> The ideas which socialists preach are ... based on a scientific analysis and understanding of the social process: they are based, in short, on a science of society—a science which has withstood the criticism of at least half a century and has steadily gained in prestige and influence, until it has come to be looked upon by millions of people the world over as their only guide and savior.[29]

Replying to criticism of the socialists, embodied in a resolution adopted by the Congress Working Committee on Bombay in 1934, that the socialists in the Congress "talk of the necessity of class war," J.P. elaborated his ideas about the nature of social organization. It is clear that he considered the fundamental unit of social analysis to be class, which he conceived as universalistic throughout history. Following Marx, he traced the origin of class to the economic sphere, i.e., the production process and the relationship of individuals to the means of production. Consequently, he saw class war as endemic to historical society, in no way created by the socialist, but rather discovered by him as a scientist with insight into the fundamental nature of social organisation. It is only the socialist, who understands the basis of class war, according to J.P., who can point the way toward a new society free from this evil. "Classes or class struggles," he wrote,

> are not created by political parties. If anything political parties are the result of classes and the conflict of classes. A class, in the sense the term is used in socialist literature, comes into being independently of individual wills and desires. In every known form of social organisation, excepting the most primitive forms, men have been marked off into classes, depending upon the part they played in the process of production and the relationship they have to the instruments and materials thereof. The formation of classes carried with it the corollary of definition of rights, privileges and duties. In every known form of society there have been classes of privilege and power and others of toil and subjection. It is here that the source of class war has lain and not in the theories of the socialists. Class war existed before man discovered it and raised it into a first-class sociological doctrine. Therefore, it is meaningless to speak of socialists preaching class war. Class war is there. What the socialists preach is that we must fight on the side of the oppressed. In fact, if there is anyone who desires to end class war it is the socialist. He says, however, that it is possible to do so only after classes have been abolished. A classless society, i.e., a society of producers alone, can be a society which is free from class war. [30]

J.P. further elaborated his conception of socialism in 1936 in *Why Socialism*. It is clear that at this point in the evolution of his thought, he saw the fundamental problem of establishing a socialist society as the transformation and rationalisation of the economic base. Once the power to control the means of production had come into the hands of the socialists, J.P. believed, the root cause of inequality would vanish and the opportunity for every person to develop his full potential would be realized. "Socialism ... is a system of social reconstruction." It involves "the reorganisation of the whole economic and social life of the country: its farms, factories, schools, etc. ... It follows, therefore that those who desire to construct a socialist society ... must control the machinery of the state."[31]

J.P. rejected biology as the fundamental source of inequality in society. Clearly, there are differences in innate capacities, he said, and the socialist readily admits to this. But there is little relationship between ability and wealth, he argued. Inheritance accrues to the heir regardless of mental or physical prowess. And while "it is true that the businessman must have ability, others should also gain wealth through their ability." But often,

> ...the businessman's laboratory alone seems to be productive of wealth. The evil of inequalities was never said to lie ... in the fact that only a few are gifted by nature to become great poets and scientists ... The source of the socialists protest is that many potential Tagores are denied the opportunity for self-development ... In our modern world, where property has became a universal sanction, it is the unequal distribution of property that is the core of the social problem.[32]

In orthodox Marxist fashion, J.P. viewed material wealth as illegitimate in capitalist society. Following classical economic doctrine, embodied in the labour theory of value of Locke, he pointed out that "the source of wealth is nature and the agency which creates it is human labour. This is the rock bottom of all economics." Accumulation becomes possible when man can "produce more than he needs for his subsistence." It follows that if everyone were "free to work for himself, own his tools and have free access to nature, then every able bodied person would be able to accumulate wealth." J.P. pointed out that in the case of the Indian peasant, it is easy for him to produce more than is necessary for him to live, but he no longer has use of all that which he produces. He lives in poverty in the midst of great wealth. "The poverty of the people," J.P. stressed, "is due to the fact that the means of production ... are no longer in .their hands.. there is nothing they can do except sell their labour to others ... If the means of production were freely available to each individual, there would be no poverty."[33]

J.P. emphasized that since labour is the source of all value, great wealth cannot be achieved except by the accumulation of surplus value "produced by employment" and by the "monopoly of some part of nature such as land." This, he noted, "is the true secret of the inequality of wealth and the true meaning of exploitation." History shows that no group would allow themselves to be exploited through wage labour, except through "compulsion." "Where the open frontier existed so that anyone could clear the jungle and cultivate his own plot, no one worked for another, except for mutual benefit." But "a group of people arose practically everywhere who established an exclusive ownership over nature, particularly over land, and subjugated others to slavery and serfdom." Then, the invention of steam power made possible the industrial revolution and the mass "exploitation of workers."

> The whole game of capitalist business consists in the attempt ... to appropriate as large a share of the surplus wealth as possible. Herein lies the secret of all capitalist competition and all the subtle and complicated business practices taught in the universities ...[34]

This is obviously a rehearsal of the theses set forth by Marx in the first volume of Capital, in terms of contemporary Indian conditions. So it was through Western economic and political thought that J.P. first came to a systematic conceptualization of Indian society. Based upon his analysis, he posited two theoretical solutions to the problem.

The first solution would be to "reconstitute society in such a way that every individual may be free to work for himself." But this solution is not viable, he said, since it would "result in a low standard of living" and would require "a dictatorship of the small producer." The second solution would be the "socialist solution," that is,

> to abolish private ownership of the means of production and to establish over them the ownership of the whole community ... The abolition of private and establishment of social ownership over the means of production mean the eradication of economic exploitation, the ending of economic inequalities, in other words, the removal of the basic curse of the present society ... Social ownership means that all wealth is held in common and shared equitably, the basis of distribution being, initially, the amount and character of work done and, finally the need of the individual.[35]

J.P.'s enthusiasm for and uncritical embrace of the orthodox socialist solution largely stemmed from his ignorance of the actual situation in the Soviet Union. At this point, he saw Marxism and Socialism as synonomous and interchangeable terms. "Today," he wrote, "it is possible to say that there is only one type, one theory of socialism Marxism."[36] His praise for "the great Russian experiment in socialist planning" was evident in chapter II of *Why Socialism*.

> Socialism is opening a new page in history ... What this may mean to ...masses of men and women ... may best be seen by turning to Russia, where a faith and a spirit have been awakened for which neither the sky nor the sea, the wind nor river remains unconquerable. To think that only a few years back this country was one of darkest despair and most oriental lethargy! [Socialism] releases the hidden springs of initiative and creativity, in making it possible for humanity to mold its growth.[37]

J.P. attributed to prejudice the view that the Soviet Union is "bureaucratic and corrupt" and that it has "killed initiative."

In 1936, J.P. set forth the basic objectives of the Congress Socialist Party. Broadly speaking, these were the achievements of complete political independence from British rule and the establishment of a socialist society. Specifically, the socialists aimed to transfer power to the producing masses through a State controlled and planned economy, and by socialisation of the principle industries. The State would establish a monopoly of foreign trade. Princes, landlords and "other exploiters" would be appropriated without compensation, and land distributed to the peasants. Co-operatives would be established for production, distribution and credit, and cooperative and collective farming encouraged. Debts owed by peasants and workers would be liquidated, and the right to work guaranteed. The socialists advocated adult franchise and elimination of discrimination based on religion, caste and sex. The "so-called" public debt of India would be repudiated. "To everyone according to his needs and from everyone according to his capacity" would ultimately become the basis of distribution and production of economic goods.[38]

J.P.'s assumption that the CSP objectives could be smoothly implemented in India resulted in large part from misinformation about the Soviet Union, and an uncritical acceptance of the central tenets of Marxist-Leninist thought. First, he accepted the assumption that nationalisation of the means of production would effectively transfer power to the masses. "We know the secret of power— economic domination. When those who toil become masters of the economic order," he wrote, "they will naturally have power."[39] It is evident that the basis for this assertion was J.P.'s belief that democratic worker control existed in the Soviet Union, and that producers participated in the planning and decision making process. He lacked an understanding of the actual elitist bureaucratic system then emerging in the USSR. There, he believed, "every unit of production and distribution take part in planning." The "men at the top coordinate, fit things together, guide and direct." He noted that "Russia seems most anxious to avoid centralization of economic control." And, he attributed "administrative freedom and full creative initiative" to autonomous geographical units.[40]

Further, J.P. accepted the claim that production was planned "in accordance with the needs of the people." He explained that "the essentials of economic planning" are, that "production, distribution and saving (in the form of state investments) are properly adjusted and that all these march along a road carefully laid out in advance ... in accordance with the needs of the people." It was not until later that J.P. began to see more clearly the contradiction between consumption and saving (investment) which is inherent in the construction of the industrial infrastructure by the State in an industrially underdeveloped country. It was Trotsky who in the USSR, realized and pointed out to the other members of the Politburo that a period of "primitive socialist accumulation" was unavoidable for rapid industrialisation by the state. It was only later that J.P. would appreciate this contradiction and its potential to reinforce elitist control at the expense of broad sections of the proletariat.[41]

J.P. also accepted the utilitarian maxim that measured the progress of socialism in terms of material production and which assumed that the full potential of human nature would emerge spontaneously, once the socio-economic transformation was underway. "Russia alone," he wrote, "has kept her head high, has made steady progress in production and in raising the standard of living, .. providing full employment for all ... The economic organisation of a country is the key to its entire life."[42]

J.P. had little doubt in 1936 that socialism was the natural social system for India. Identifying imperialism and nascent capitalism in the subcontinent with British colonialism, he believed that the rationalization of society in the direction of a socialist pattern would follow naturally upon political independence from British rule. The fundamental obstacles in India, he believed, were external and imposed by a foreign power, rather than internally bound up with Indian society and tradition. The Indian social and economic institutions which were averse to socialism, such as feudalism, communalism and zamindari (the feudal system of land tenure), were, he believed, decaying and decripit, and would easily be·pushed aside by the, gathering momentum of the nationalist revolution. As for emerging capitalism, without British sponsorship, it would wither and die.

> If we acquire sufficient power to achieve complete independence, we shall have power to do almost anything in this country. There is no power or party in India stronger than Independence, and if we humble the latter there will be no one to challenge our will. The princes and the landlords, who may seem rather formidable today, propped up by British force, would wither away at our first touch: The capitalists, perhaps a little stronger, would also be powerless to check us.[43]

Socialist planning, J.P. believed, was not only superior to the capitalist anarchic economic system, but 'was also superior to capitalist planning which Roosevelt was instituting in the United States. The goal of socialist planning, he said, is to "run the economic machine in the interests of the whole society" but capitalist planning aims to "keep profits flowing to the capitalists."[44] Private ownership of the means of production must be abolished, "destroying vested interests."

In socialist India, the government would establish departments to run industries and set production quotas, with worker representatives participating. Rationing would ensure the needs of the poor while workers, "no longer wage slaves, would become ... the masters of the factories." Worker unions would have a "decisive hand" in running mills, and ensuring "higher wages, better housing, shorter working hours, schools, maternity houses, parks, museums and libraries." Workers would be "transplanted to a new world of freedom, of initiative, of power, of opportunities for cultural advancement" while former owners would become workers too.[45]

Individualistic, small businesses would become integrated into cooperatives as small shops would be "enemies of socialism." J.P. supposed at this point that if the economic base was cleansed of opportunistic potential and reconstructed in such a way as to thwart any 'temptation to take advantage of others, reformation of the human sphere would automatically follow. Later, he severely criticized socialists for making such glib assumptions. The old economic applecart must first be upset because "as long as the social relationships inherent" in existing economic institutions last, "exploitation and injustice last, no matter how well meaning human units in these relationships are." J.P. insisted that economic structures must be broken down so that they no longer impede the flowering of human nature.[46]

In the agricultural sphere too, J.P. considered socialism to be the most appropriate system for India in 1936. "There is not the least doubt in our mind," he wrote, "that socialism alone can save Indian agriculture from ruin and bankruptcy; can alone make the peasant prosperous and progressive; can alone make the nation strong and powerful." He was not dismayed by the predominately agrarian character of the subcontinent. "It is possible to build up socialism anywhere no matter how backward the place may be," he argued, although he supposed this would "lower the pace of socialist reconstruction."[47] Vested interests must first be cleared away in the countryside-everything "that leads in any manner whatsoever to the exploitation of the tiller of the soil." Agrarian depts would be liquidated, landholdings pooled, 'and cooperative credit and marketing systems as well as subsidiary industries would be established.

In the long run, such a renovation of the village economic structure would be less catastrophic, thought J.P., than following the capitalist route in the attempt to make small proprietors self-sufficient. And he saw the socialist solution as advantageous to the peasant because there would be less economic risk, he would gain culturally and ethically, and the new society would restore features of traditional society. It would strengthen the nation, making integrated planning possible."[48] And while in industry, forcible socialization would be necessary, the peasant could be gradually coaxed through "education, propaganda, demonstration, subsidy and preferential taxation, into seeing the advantages of socialism."[49]

J.P. bolstered his vision by attempting to sanctify it through finding parallel patterns in the Hindu tradition. First, he noted, "landlordism was never a feature of Hindu Polity ... The tiller of the soil paid a fixed share to the king and there we were no middlemen." Concerning village cooperative farming, he argued that while "it finds no mention in the Manusmriti, .. it is indisputable that there were long periods. of Indian history where a form of village existed ... in which common tenure of land and sometimes also common tillage were recognized and practiced."

> The socialist aim follows in spirit and lines the old system—except that the socialist village, instead of being a closed circle, a closed economic unit, would be an actively cooperating unit in a larger economic system. [Socialism] would transform the village from its present mean position to one of prosperity and culture unknown in any age of Indian history.[50]

J.P. felt that the fear of machine production disrupting the quality of village life and ushering in urbanization was ungrounded. First of all, he said, the "so-called self-sufficient village" does not presently exist.

Acknowledging that cities are "monsters of human habitation," he denied that socialism would lead to the replication of such cities. On the contrary, he pleaded, socialism has as its aim "the harmonious and well balanced *growth of the whole society.* " J.P. continued:

> [While] it is true that the socialist hugs machinery, .. to him machinery is not an instrument of exploitation ... Machines to us mean friends of labour—things that relieve human toil and increase its productivity.[51]
>
> The assumption that machinery will inevitably create monstrosities·of cities and rural unemployment by disrupting village economies is wrong. Machines if used for private benefit by a handful of people who own them, will undoubtedly produce these and worse results. But that society as a whole, making use of these efficient and powerful, instruments of production for the good of the entire population will also encounter these same results is too absurd a proposition to be accepted.[52]

In 1936, J.P. took sharp issue with the economic ideas of Mahatma Gandhi, concerning the future of Indian society. Convinced that his Marxist analysis was scientific and therefore correct, J.P. criticized Gandhi's ideas as "dangerous" and wrote a critique of Gandhi's approach which included comments concerning socialism.[53] J.P.'s criticism of Gandhi was sparked by an interview of Gandhi by the zamindars of Uttar Pradesh at Kanpur.

When Gandhi was asked how the CSP policy which "threatens the extinction of private property" would affect Congress policy, he replied that

> I shall be no party to dispossessing the propertied classes of their private property without just cause. My objective is to reach your hearts and convert you so that you may hold all your private property in trust and use if for your tenants and use it primarily for their welfare.[54]

Gandhi expressed his opinion that if a referendum was held, the people of India would not vote for the wholesale expropriation of the propertied classes." He also issued a stern warning to the landlords stressing their social responsibilities as holders of the nation's wealth.

> I am working for the cooperation and coordination of capital and labour and of the landlord and tenant ... But I must utter a note of warning. I have always told the millowners that they are not exclusive owners of the mills and workmen are equal sharers in the ownership. In the same way I would tell you that the ownership of your land belongs as much to the ryots as to you; and you may not squander your gains in luxurious or extravagant living, but must use them for the well being of the ryots. Once you make your ryots experience a sense of kinship with you and

> a sense of security that their interests will never suffer at your hands, you may be sure that there cannot be a clash between you and them and no class war. A class war is foreign to the essential genius of India which is capable of evolving communism broadbased on the fundamental rights of all on equal justice. The Ramarajya of my dreams ensures the rights alike of the prince and the pauper ... Supposing that there is an attempt to unjustly deprive you of your property you will find me fighting on your side.[55]

Gandhi also expressed his faith to the zamindars that "an indigenous socialism of the purest type" could evolve in India and pointed out that the essential difference between his conception of socialism and that of the West.

> The socialism and the communism of the West are based on certain conceptions which are fundamentally different from ours. One of such conceptions is their belief in the essential selfishness of human nature. I do not subscribe to it for I know that the essential difference between man and brute is that the former can respond to the call of the spirit in him, can rise superior to the passions that he owes in common with the brute and, therefore, is superior to the selfishness and violence which belongs to the brute nature and not to the immortal spirit of man. That is the fundamental conception of Hinduism ... Our socialism or communism should therefore, be based on non-violence, and on the harmonious cooperation of labour and capital, the landlord and peasant.[56]

Reversing the formula of the socialists, Gandhi saw the root of the problem as moral rather than political and "his solution was based on his faith" in human nature. He believed that while the State, an instrument of coercion, could never be made moral, the landlords, who often badly mistreated their tenants, could reform themselves. In that instance only, could the nation's wealth be used equitably and justly. "All of your fears," he told the landlords,

> are those of a guilty conscience. Wipe out the injustices that you may have been guilty of ... Once you turn a new leaf in the relations between the zamindars and the ryots, you will find us on your side jealously guarding your private rights and property ... The nation cannot own property except by vesting it in individuals. It simply assures its just and equitable use and prevents misuse; and I do not think you can have any possible objection to holding your property for the benefit of the ryots.[57]

J.P. sharply criticized Gandhi for his remarks. He argued that there was nothing particularly Indian about Gandhi's views. In fact the idea of a "synthesis of contending forces in society" and the "theory of trusteeship" are the "commonest ideas of the West preached by smug bourgeois professors, thinkers and churchmen," he said. J.P. noted that William Godwin's Political Justice taught the theory of trusteeship and the concept is known as "reformism: in socialist society. As such, "reformism is interested not in securing social justice, but in covering up the ugly fissures of society."[58]

J.P. also found it reprehensible that Gandhi's Ramarajya would have paupers.

> It does not occur to Gandhi to ask why only a few are in the position of princes, landlords and capitalists, while the remaining are paupers ... It accepts the established order with its low and high classes. Its only concern is to improve the conduct of the higher classes toward the lower. Not daring to ask where the landlords and capitalists' wealth comes from, it asks them in its compassion, to act as trustees of the poor and to use their wealth for the welfare of the latter.[59]

J.P. charged that Gandhi had "sanctified theft," and given tacit approval to violence. Further, he said, Gandhi's position is contradictory.

> If the property that is in the hands of the wealthy is not theirs, no one has any justification in encouraging them to keep it ... If, on the other hand, it is theirs, earned rightfully by them, no one has any cause to ask them to give it away to others."

And then on a Marxian note, J.P. concluded that

> The problem is not one of morality or ethics. It is a problem of scientific analysis of property and the method of its production and distribution ... Karl Marx did the greatest service to humanity when he undertook the analysis of capitalist property and proved that it was based on the exploitation of labour ...[60]

J.P. viewed Gandhi's reliance upon changing human hearts as inadequate, because there is no guarantee that acquired virtues would be inherited. And all this transformation must be carried out in an "atmosphere of individualism and private property."[61]

The basic assumption underlying J.P.'s criticism of Gandhi's attempt to reform India by changing the hearts of the landlords was that human characteristics are determined by a definite mode of production and must have a class character. This is the view of historical materialism, and logically precludes the idea of an essential human nature as the phrase is normally used. According to J.P.'s thinking in 1936, there is little hope that human nature can change unless the mode of production is first transformed.

J.P argued that Gandhi was wrong about Western socialism and communism being "based on the essential selfishness of human nature." He wrote:

> Nothing could be further from the truth. Had socialists taken such a low view of human nature, they would never have dared to proclaim as their ideal, a society based on the pursuit of common welfare. Has it not been the most persistent argument against socialism that it assumes an impossible refinement of man's nature? Quite the contrary to what Gandhiji thinks, the socialist has an unlimited faith in human nature and it is one of the major items of his constructive programme to remould it.[62]

Neither J.P. nor Gandhi were entirely correct in their assertions about human nature. Both were viewing the concept of human nature within different conceptual frameworks. Essentially, and logically, both were correct from their different presuppositions and viewpoints. Raghavan Iyer points out that

> whether one chooses on optimistic conception or a pessimistic view of human nature, is logically independent of the choice between an open and a closed view of human nature, or again, of the choice between the acceptance and the rejection of the perfectability of man, or finally, the degree of power and autonomy that is granted to man in relation to ... his material and social environment.[63]

Concerning the socialist view of human nature, Mihailo Markovic states that: "Future-oriented theorists radically opposed to the injustices of the existing society, tend to be very optimistic in their conceptions of human nature."[64] As a humanist, Marx viewed man as a being of praxis who changes both nature and himself.

Markovic points out that "Marx did not develop a systematic theory of human nature." But "he showed how human nature can be construed as a dynamic, historical concept without lapsing into relativism. It must include both universal invariants and constituents that vary from epoch to epoch." This gives human nature a historical dimension. Secondly, Marx showed that "a human individual is at the same time a unique person, concerned with self-affirmation and objectification of his subjective powers, and a social being ... " Marx wrote, "It is above all necessary to avoid postulating society once again as an abstraction over against the individual as a social being."

> Third, Marx gave new life to Aristotle's distinction between actuality and potentiality. No matter how degraded and alienated actual human existence might be, man always preserves a potential for emancipation and creativity. Fourth, Marx specified the conditions under which human potentiality is crippled and wasted; The division of labour, private property, capital, state oppression, false ideological consciousness. Their abolition is a necessary condition of universal emancipation.[65]

The normative concept of human nature in Marx is completely optimistic. Markovic points out that "negative human characteristics are interpreted as mere facticity, as transient features likely to disappear when the unfavorable conditions which produced them are removed." But "rather than qualifing the positive as the essence, and negative as the facticity, one has to recognize the conflict of general human dispositions in the essence itself." Markovic goes on to point out that "the concept of human nature lacks an inner dialectic. Since it is a historical concept, and its development cannot be determined by external causes, the source of man's self creation must be in the inner contradictions of human nature."[66] "It is interesting that Gandhi's conception does involve an inner dialectic between good and evil, whereas for Marx, according to dialectical materialism, there is no inner dialectic."

Iyer pointed out that Marx did not see what a theory of human nature must involve.[67] He "failed to formulate a clear conception of human nature." Marx "attempted to answer questions about human nature in early philosophical works, but entirely ignored them in his later works, in which Marxism as a system was elaborated."[68]

This analysis of Marx's thinking about man helps to understand the basic division among Marxists and non- Marxists on the issue of human nature. It also allows one to see why Gandhi might have perceived the socialist view of human nature as "selfish" and how his own view of human nature is in some respects closer to that of humanist Marxists.

Of the two major divisions among Marxists concerning human nature, the official ideology largely dismisses the concept of human nature on the basis that it is "incompatible with the base and superstructure model and the theory of class struggle." According to historical materialism, human characteristics are determined by a definite mode of production and must have a class character.[69]

Humanists, on the other hand, reject "rigid determinism" and "the view is adopted that the emancipation and self-realization of man as a being of free and creative activity (praxis) is not necessary but only possible." "Both freedom and creativity" as well as "aggressiveness and destructiveness ... are all recognized as constituents of actually existing human nature. The potential for praxis is the ideal end which gives a sense of direction to human self-creation in history."[70]

That J.P. was expounding a crude form of Marxism which largely ignored Marx's early normative view of human nature and extracts out the concept of human nature in accord with historical materialism, is seen in his reply to Gandhi. J.P. wrote:

> The socialist's denial of the philosophy of change-of-heart does not spring from his lack of faith in human nature, but from his understanding of human psychology—the relation between behaviour and environment. He believes that it is the social environment which shapes human behaviour ... A capitalist exploits labour not because he is vicious, but because that is what [bourgeois] society ... wants him to do ... The socialist, therefore, believes that if the behaviour of whole groups and classes has to be changed, a change should be effected in social organisation itself. For example if the capitalist class has to be prevented from exploiting labour, the organisation of society must be so altered as to make that exploitation impossible ... Human nature responds not to the so called spirit that is said to be in all of us, but to the environment.[71]

That is, human behaviour would be reformed through a reliance upon structural barriers to immorality, rather than upon the will, which is seen as essentially impotent to bring about such a change. This view entails a cynical and distrustful view of the individual and leads to the view that elitist leadership is necessary for the reform of society by, for example, a vanguard party. And similar to Hobbes, it views genuine altruism, i.e. disinterested behaviour, as highly improbable in the world as we know it. It makes Gandhian radical self-transformation impossible.

J.P. believed that:

> when the environment encourages ... the exploitation of man by man, it is too much to expect that moral precept will do more than touch the heart of a stray individual or so. It cannot transform society.[72]

For J.P., the revolutionary will transform society from the top, after seizing State power.

> The socialist wants ... first to change the social environment and acquire full power over the state in order to be in possession of the means of propaganda and education. He creates the

> predisposing environment and thus uses systematic methods of education ... How does he change the environment? By organising the exploited and oppressed for the overthrow of the established order and the seizure of power. Then he proceeds to build on the new foundation.[73]

For Gandhi, on the other hand, the State could never be the mechanism for the moral transformation of society.

It can be argued, then, that Gandhi was essentially correct in characterising the socialist's view of human nature as selfish. They accept the "facticity" of selfishness in human nature in the capitalist historical epoch, largely as a result of a reductionistic and deterministic view of human behaviour and psychology. For Marx, man could become a species being only in the "realm of freedom" after the elimination of the fundamental sources of alienation in society. Further, the concept of class is rooted in the conviction that men act largely in Hobbesian self-interest, rather than altruistically in bourgeois society. J.P. doubted that Gandhi could ever convince most landlords and capitalists to act in an altruistic fashion. Self-interest was seen to coincide with class interest. Marx argued that bourgeois society turns men into egotists, in the *Economic and Philosophical Manuscripts*. This egotism is a perversion of man's species nature, but nevertheless, it is a fact for him, that men cannot act otherwise within bourgeois society. Self-interest becomes the driving force of history for Marx, which ultimately overcomes the class contradictions of bourgeois society, and brings about the classless society. Consequently, in the Marxist system, and according to dialectical materialism, the individual ceases to be an egotist only with the structural transformation of society.

Gandhi, on the other hand, subscribed to a view of human nature which included an inner dialectic between good and evil. This dialectic was not materialist or historical but transpiring within each individual, who either sank to the depths of human degradation or triumphed over evil. Gandhi said, "Human nature will find itself only when it fully realizes that to become human it has ceased to be bestial or brutal." He believed "Man must choose either of the two courses, the upward or the downward, but as he has the brute in him he will more easily choose the downward course than the upward ..." He also said that "the essential difference between man and the brute is that the former can respond to the call of spirit in him, can rise superior to the passions, to selfishness and violence, which belong to brute nature and not to the immortal nature of man."[74] Gandhi had a frankly optimistic view of human nature.[75]

Many non-Marxian socialists, such as Edward Bellamy, embraced an optimistic view of human nature. Bellamy "accepted the complexity, richness, and creativity of human nature, its capacity for self-expression as well as self-transcendence."[76] The essential difference between Gandhi and most socialist thinkers, is the way human nature is viewed in relation to the material structure of society. For Gandhi, the individual could sink or swim, regardless of his environment. Most socialists, on the other hand, see the need for the structural transformation of society, as did Bellamy in *Looking Backward*. Iyer points out the contradiction that exists between believing in the infinite potential of human nature, on the one hand, and "external organisation and formal regulation" on the other, embodied in most social theories since the enlightenment.[77] This is the contradiction seen in both Bellamy and J.P.

In 1936, J.P. essentially subscribed to the view expressed by Lenin in *What is to be Done*. He thought that the workers and peasants must be led by the revolutionary intellectual. J.P. attached little weight to Gandhi's suggestion that the Indian people would not vote for the expropriation of private property. "What value," he wrote, "would [the social scientist] attach to the opinion of backward, ignorant oppressed masses? All the problems of society would have disappeared immediately if the masses really knew what was good for them.[78] J.P. concluded that

> Gandhism may be a well-intentioned doctrine—but a dangerous doctrine. It is dangerous because it hushes up real issues and sets out to remove the evils of society by pious wishes. It then deceives the masses and encourages the upper classes to continue their domination.[79]

J.P. drafted a resolution, later defeated by the Congress which urged Congress to remove support from Gandhi's spinning, weaving and "Hindu orientated" removal of untouchability programmes. He also asked Congress to admit that the best method of achieving complete independence was through the organisation of the workers and peasants on the basis of their economic class interests. J.P. wrote:

> We do not believe that *charka* and *khadi* will resuscitate the 700,000 villages of India, nor remove the grinding poverty of the masses. We do not believe that regular spinning or the use of khadi or products of village handicrafts will in any way make the Congress members better fitted for continuing the struggle for freedom in an intenser form as contemplated by the working committee.[80]

In 1943, J.P. clarified his position on non-violence. He noted that "Gandhiji is in no event prepared to depart from non-violence. With him it is a question of principle."[81] But he was not prepared to totally denounce the use of violence in every situation. He thought that non-violence, if used on a large scale would "make violence unnecessary," but said, "I should not allow cowardice, clothed in Shastric subtleties, to block the development of this revolution and lead to failure." The objective was a "total revolution of the masses," and at this time, he still doubted that it could be carried out in a non-violent way.[82]

With the intensification of the Nationalist Revolution in 1942, J.P. began to shift the way he viewed the revolution, from the Leninist pattern to a more indigenous pattern in which the Gandhian programme of *swaraj* for the villages and greater decentralisation was envisioned.

Democratic Socialism

By 1944, J.P. had softened his stand toward Marxist orthodoxy and the way in which the rational transformation of society must occur. He had not only become considerably disillusioned with the quality of life in the Soviet Union but had also become pessimistic about a purely material base for human motivation and action. He began to question Marxist assumptions that the economic sphere constituted the basis for all of human behaviour. He began to express his concern that society be not only prosperous but also made up of "good men." He became more concerned with values and more doubtful that desirable values would arise spontaneously out of the rationalized economic and social structures of society. He began to look toward the "ideal" as a source of inspiration for societal values. And he came to value the contribution to society of both the "materialist" and the "idealist."

J.P. also began to trace the roots of his emerging value system to the classical Indian tradition, including its religious aspects. More and more he questioned the Marxian conceptual framework which had largely shaped his thought since his student days. J.P. came to accept the Gandhian path of the humanist reformation of society. He agreed with Gandhi that non-violent means is the just path, but still felt that immoral acts might be necessary to bring about a necessary revolution in history.

Further, J.P. no longer saw Indian society in terms of class conflict but perceived elements which transcended the narrow boundaries of class, caste, tribe, religion, community and political persuasion. He began to see that there are elements of cultural heritage which all Indians shared as a cohesive force in Indian society. He expressed concern for what "character and type of men" should make up the society of free India, and criticized the assumption of many socialists that good men would emerge automatically from society. He wrote:

> In laying the foundations of the Indian nation and the future free society of India, it is not sufficient to pay attention to the material aspects of India alone. The human aspect ... is perhaps even more important than that of material well being.[83]

He criticized socialists for neglecting values in their plans for socialist society:

> We socialists ... have always conceived of man in a socialist society as an educated, developed, dutiful, good member of society ... We believed complacently that when economic life had been socialized and acquisitiveness and exploitation removed from society, man in the course of the social progress would evolve automatically into a paragon of virtues. But recent experiences have shown that there is as much need of fixing targets and assuring planned progress toward them in the field of character building of a nation as in the economic field ... To neglect character would be one sided development.[84]

J.P.'s thinking on the relationship between values and social action, at this point, was inconsistent. He argued that an "a priori" standard of values—of morality and immorality is needed for the revolutionary socialist. Yet, he still suggested that at times it may be necessary to violate the moral code in bringing about the revolution. This does not make the actions moral but perhaps necessary. He believed that a source for idealist values could be found in the Indian tradition, but remained basically apologetic in his attitude toward the socialist revolutionary's inconsistent application of values.

J.P. argued that in order to "create good men" the nation should "discover and establish basic values of life." These would serve as the "cornerstone of education, the common platform of all political parties and the matrix of our economic life."[85] Religious freedom would be ensured, while allowing both the "idealist" and the "materialist" to participate in the project of character building. He wrote that "Socialists must fix a priori the moral standards and concepts of their society, modifying and developing them as social progress goes apace."[86]

J.P. argued that a socialist morality could be established which would be "superior to all moral codes." Whereas Marx showed that "moral codes are usually psychological devices for the preservation of the rights and privileges and enjoyments of the dominant classes in society," socialist morality would be "free from the taint of being a handmaiden to class oppression."[87]

Yet, J.P., in 1944, was not fully prepared to accept Gandhi's argument that the ends can never justify the means. "I am not prepared to reject the use, within limits, of immoral means for moral purposes—if for nothing else, because I do not possess the requisite moral strength to do otherwise." He believed that killing, deceiving or lying to the enemy remained immoral even though the socialist fathers considered them to be "of inevitable necessity" and "thereby permissible" in the class war. "Even the most uncompromising revolutionary socialist must consider lying and killing as immoral to be resorted to only for the sake of the revolution."[88] So it is clear that at this point, J.P. still believed that immoral means could be used for the virtuous end of a socialist revolution.

J.P. was taking an ambivalent stance, since if revolutionary why not consider them moral in terms of the final end? But at this time, J.P. had come to doubt that morality would emerge out of the revolution unless there were established a priori standards of conduct. He felt that the Soviet Union had given a warning that those who use violence in the revolution are willing to continue its use after the revolution.[89]

J.P. suggested that a source of common values for the future Indian society should be based on the Indian cultural tradition, as these arise from a "common history and a common geography." It seems that after the Quit India movement that J.P.'s nationalism had begun to triumph over his Marxism. He found a "very large and essential unity that characterized ... Indians."[90] so that nationalism, grounded in a common history and geography seems to transcend class for J.P. Values arise from cultural tradition—they are no longer located in class and class consciousness for him.

In 1946, J.P. outlined his plans for the democratic socialist transformation of Indian society. It is clear that his ideas had changed considerably since 1936. He had gained a much greater appreciation for the contribution to be made by the common people in building up units of self government on the local level. He had moved much closer to Gandhi's position on the decentralization of the political structure of Indian society, largely adopting Gandhi's constructive programme. J.P.'s thinking seems to have been in a transition stage between adopting patterns from existing socialism in the Soviet Union and relying upon Indian tradition for inspiration. But it is clear that J.P. was gravitating toward the Gandhian model.

In 1946, the Congress Socialist Party programme of constructive action included "the atomization and dislocation of imperialism" while building up local and regional Swaraj governments which would ultimately coalesce to form the Free Republic of India. These governments would launch non-cooperation with the British, launch industrial strikes, encourage peasants to take over zamindari lands, fight against the tyranny of feudal princes and aid the struggle of Congress ministries within the administrative system. In addition, constructive programs would be launched in the villages to carry out educational and cultural work, health drives, survey work, trade union activities, and to establish student service centers and self help programs.[91]

The objective of the CSP in the village was the establishment of a *gram raj*. A *gram raj* is a self governing village, not merely a *panchayat*, the local governing council. The *gram raj* was to be built up by the villagers themselves, through their own initiative. J.P. wrote:

> The gram rajs as I conceive them would make foreign rule unnecessary, would become the centers of struggle and resistance during a revolution and would constitute the bricks with which the structure the free Indian Republic could be built.[92]

Constructive work would lay the foundation for cooperative farming and industries in the village.

J.P. further elaborated his thinking on democratic socialism in 1946 in "My Picture of Socialism." This essay reveals that J.P.'s theoretical perspective was, in several aspects, similiar to that of M.N. Roy in 1946. J.P. believed that essentially, Marxism was not dogmatic but scientific.

> Marxism is a science of society and a scientific method of social change that includes social revolution. As such there can be no room for dogmatism or fundamentalism in Marxist thought ... In science there is no such thing as final truth. Science progresses by the progressive elimination of untruth from human knowledge. If Marxism is a science, Marx could not have expounded ultimate truths, but only made approximations to them. Today with a vastly developed store of human knowledge and vastly greater experience and observation of capitalist society, we are in a position to make for nearer approximations to the truth than Marx. The unending merit of Marx is that he gave us a method to understand and change history, even as Darwn gave us a method of understanding life.[93]

It is clear that, like Roy, J.P. believed that Marxism was essentially changing and dynamic, rather than dogmatic; that greater knowledge enabled the use of Marxist methodology to greater advantage today, and finally that Marxism could be used to understand and change history.

There are two stages to socialism, J.P. wrote, the transition stage and socialism itself.[94] The transition stage in India, he believed, involved first, the achievement of a "free Indian democracy," and secondly, the transition from that democracy to socialism. J.P. believed that if democracy could be established in India, the CSP could come to power and establish socialism through the ballot. He preferred the democratic path and pointed out that Marx did not rule out the possibility that workers in democratic countries such as America and Britain might obtain their objectives by peaceful means.[95]

The essentially intransigent problem in India, however, was in establishing that democratic society, he argued. J.P. saw three major barriers to such a society in 1947: communalism (as a result of Muslim League activity), feudalism (the princely order) and imperialism (British rule). He did not believe the British would leave India without a fight and saw feudalism as deeply entrenched and difficult to remove democratically. Consequently, he wrote, "I see a major revolution intervening on our road to socialism." The revolution would be nationalistic, demanding that the British quit India, but go beyond in asking for land to the tiller and a people's government.

> I have stated clearly that in a full and untramelled democracy I shall adopt democratic means to achieve socialism. But as we are faced with undemocratic forces which have to be defeated and destroyed before socialism can be ushered in, I conceive a period of trouble and turmoil, a revolutionary phase of the transition, a phase in which not only the democratic revolution should be completed, but also considerable progress made toward socialism. A state and society emerging from such a revolution, should then be able to pass in a democratic manner into full socialism.[96]

But J.P. suggested an alternate scenario based upon his perception of the changing nature of the Congress organisation. He pointed out that the "dominant sections" of the Congress are "guided by capitalistic ideas" and exploit the name of Gandhi. Their declarations of social policy, he argued, "are merely tactical moves to placate the masses in order not to lose their support."[97] In the past, the Congress served the people, but "in this form, the Congress is ... becoming defunct ... it is changing into a purely parliamentary party." J.B. Kripalani had just resigned from the Congress. J.P. noted that "vested interests are growing, there is a rising tide of selfish politics ... politicians are ready to mouth any ism to become popular." The "middle class character" of Congress, he believed had led to "moral decay." He feared that such selfish interests would "thwart socialism" and later when the organisation tried to free itself from vested interests, it would be too late. Congress would find that it had become a "bourgeois party." J.P. began to consider an independent path for the socialists.[98] He feared that there might be no revolution at all, and that the country would find itself "saddled with undemocratic rule." In that case, there would have to be a revolution "based on an alignment of classes" and organised by a socialist party, independent of the Congress.

J.P. began to appreciate that imperialism was only one factor among several with which the forces of freedom would have to deal. He began to attach more weight to the indigenous forces—communalism, feudalism and capitalism, which threatened the establishment of a democratic India and a peaceful transition to democratic socialism.

J.P. outlined several aspects of his vision for the future of socialism in India. In the agriculural sphere, socialism would be established in two stages, first the co-operative stage and secondly, the collective stage. The zamindari system would be abolished and land parcelled out to individuals in holdings of between five and thirty acres. There would be no absentee ownership and the unit of agricultural economy would be the village. As in Roy's Draft Constitution scheme, legal ownership of land would rest with the village as a whole, while peasants would have "proprietary rights" over the land settled with them. In practice, the overall village productive operation would be cooperative with the peasant's proprietary right restricted to the right to receive produce from the collective in proportion to the size of his holdings. J.P. implied that the discrepancy in the size of holdings would gradually be narrowed down over time. There would be no free market in land as the peasant could sell land only to the gram panchayat, Wages would be paid in kind. J.P. believed that this program could be carried out in the village with a "wise mixture of coercion and persuasion."[99]

Basically, three types of industrial units would be established. First, large industries owned and managed by federal or provincial governments. Secondly, small scale cooperative industries, and finally industries owned by a municipality or the community. J.P. calculated that such "dispersed ownership" would prevent the State from becoming totalitarian.[100]

In his vision for a future socialist India, J.P. rejected the idea of a dictatorship of the proletariat. He said "socialist India must be democratic." Proletarian parties would be allowed with "only the rulling class and their political and economic institutions" suppressed. People would be free to form voluntary organisations for political purposes and there would be independent organs of the working class such as trade unions. Over all, an "economic and political democracy" would be established. "Man will be free," he said.[101]

When the Indian National Congress transformed itself into a political party in 1947, J.P. and the CSP separated from the Congress to form the Socialist Party, an independent party. At this time, J.P. still believed in the role of the party in the establishment of socialism. He envisioned the Socialist Party becoming truly "the party of the peasants and the workers." He was still thinking in terms of a mass organisation of socialists led by a party.[102] He still said the role of the Party as "convincing the people" and "converting them to socialism."[103]

But as many socialists were prone to do, J.P. underestimated the viability of the capitalist system and its ability to effect structural transformations in the economy so as to survive. Underestimating the force of the rising middle classes, he wrote, " ... the frontiers of capitalism are receding; and those of socialism and communism are advancing ... Capitalism is old and discredited. The chances of socialism are brighter today than they were thirty years ago."[104]

The swift moving events in India during 1947 and 1948 affected J.P. deeply and moved him closer to the Gandhian perspective with regard to the transformation of Indian society. And while still appreciating the Marxist perspective, J.P. found himself thoroughly disillusioned with Marxism in practice. He re-evaluated his position with regard to means and ends, coming to fully accept Gandhi's perspective. Rethinking the relationship between the central assumptions of Liberalism and Marxism-Leninism and society in practice, he gravitated toward a critique of both liberal democracy and Marxism.

After Gandhi's assassination in 1948, J.P. wrote:

> The greatest thing [Mahatma Gandhi] taught us was that evil means can never lead to good ends and that fair ends require fair means. Some of us may have been sceptical of this truth, but recent world events and events at home have convinced me that nothing but good means will enable us to reach the base of a good society, which is socialism.[105]

J.P. had come to abhor the state of affairs in the Soviet Union. Nazism and Stalinism, he said, had led "to the eclipse of moral values from social life." But J.P. still believed that there was room for moral values in Marxism and that "for the achievement of socialism, a strict regard for means is of the highest importance."

> If by socialism we mean a form of society in which the material needs of every individual are satisfied and also in which the individual is a cultured and civilized being .., then I am absolutely clear that we will never reach this goal except by strict adherence to certain human values and standards of conduct. It is too often believed that all would be well only if there were no exploitation in society and everyone was well fed and housed. But a society of well-fed and clothed and housed brutes is a far cry from socialism.[106]

By 1948, J.P. began to question the utility of power politics in bringing about the good society. Power politics, he now argued, leads to the idea that the end justifies the means. The role of the State was also questioned. "The theory that all politics are power politics," he wrote, "has the necessarily underlying basis—that the State is the only instrument of social good." He perceived that "depending upon the State for every effort at social change and development" in the Congress, was a dangerous trend. He began to question whether it was necessary to capture State power to bring about desired social change. Following Gandhi, he began to argue that "constructive workers should cut themselves off from the parliamentary machine and function independently..." He began to view the State as a subsidiary force which must be controlled by society, not the other way around. Such a democratic socialist society would be established, he believed, through constructive work, and would correspond with the democratic ideal of both Marx and Gandhi. In this way, the State would wither away.[107]

J.P. described the democratic socialist phase of his political evolution as a "half-way house between Marxism and Gandhism."[108] He arrived at this perspective when he became convinced that the Soviet elitist political system was "the end product of the socio economic system that was set up there."[109] This period was also characterized by his questioning the theory of violence in Marxism. He adopted the view that in society where change could be brought about democratically, it would be counter-revolutionary to resort to violence. Secondly, he argued that socialism could not exist or be created in the absence of democratic freedom. Finally, he rejected the dictatorship of the proletariat, which, he saw, meant the dictatorship of a bureaucratic oligarchy. Yet, he remained concerned with the capture of power, during this period, believing that it was necessary to hold power to establish democratic socialism.

The conceptual barriers to J.P.'s evolution to the final phase of his political thinking were removed during a fast at Poona in 1952. His further questioning of the philosophical conceptual foundations of Marxism led to a "final break" with Marxism. This irreversible liberation from the Marxian conceptual framework led him to construct a more systematic critique of Marxism and Western socialism and finally to his decision to withdraw from party and power politics in 1954. He determined to devote the rest of his life to the *bhoodan* or land-gift and Sarvodaya movements.[110] Finally, in 1957, he resigned from the Praja Socialist Party, elaborating his conviction that Marxism and Western socialism could not lead to the moral society. His embrace of Indian socialism or *Sarvodaya* and dedication of his life to its cause (*jeevandan*), marked the beginning of the final phase of his political thinking.

Critique of Marxism and Western Socialism

In 1957, J.P. denounced Marxism and Western socialism, developing a critique of these perspectives and explaining the basis for his embrace of the Gandhian philosophy of social change through *Sarvodaya*. The hope for socialism, he now believed, was its transformation into *Sarvodaya*.

J.P. questioned the central tenets of Marxism and socialism by developing a sharp critique of the "axioms" of socialist society. First, a central assumption of Marxist orthodoxy is the assumption that if certain changes are made in the social structure and its foundation it would be possible to build up a socialist society. The "means of production" are supposed to govern the "relations of production." Looking at the United States and the Soviet Union, J.P. said, the means of production "from the technological view" are not different. Yet entirely different relations of production result.[111] But he left this point fairly undeveloped, failing to go on to analyze the specific differences. Generally he referred to the Soviet economic system as "state capitalism." Logically, it would seem that Marx would be vindicated on this point, if, in fact, mechanization and centralization had led to capitalistic relations of production in both societies. The point he was making, it seems, was that the nature of the overall superstructure in both societies assumes a vastly different form.

Secondly, J.P. addressed the gap between theory and practice in socialist society. Marx, he noted, conceived of the "noble ideal of a stateless and classless society." Yet the actual situation in existing socialist society was a bitter power struggle under an oligarchic political structure. This ongoing power struggle, he believed, demoralized the party and corrupted the original ideals of the socialists.[112]

An even more serious charge made by J.P., was that Marxism is based on amoralism.[113] This leads, he said, to the doctrine that the end justifies the means. This amoralism, he charged, fails to take into account the question of good and evil. Lacking a moral standard of values, the question of good and evil was seen as relative. This, he believed, led to attempts at one-sided development of society. Historically, Marxists were concerned only with reconstructing the material structure of society. But,

> [I]f you are engaged only in shaping the environment in which the individual man lives—the social, economic and political environment— and if you are neglecting the individual, I am sure you will find that all these elements that go to constitute the nature of man as he is today will vitiate all your efforts all your attempts at social reconstruction.[114]

J.P. wished to point out that the political transformation of society must involve both structural change and moral change based on a non-relativistic standard of values. To focus on structural change only, as he accused many Marxists and socialists of being guilty of, was one-sided development. Equally futile, he thought, was one-sided development in the opposite direction in which one totally concentrates upon human nature. The historical example of this was Buddhism, he said. While Buddha taught that man may be free from misery by controlling his passion, he forgot that human history was a product of both human nature and social circumstances.

The amoralism, he came to associate with Marxism and socialism in practice led J.P. to adopt Gandhi's perspective that the ends can never justify the means.

> Marxism as a philosophy of action is amoral. In Marxism any means are good means provided they serve the ends of the social revolution.

In fact, he pointed out, politicians have always practiced amoralism. "That the end justifies the means is the basis of political action everywhere."[115] In practice, then, it was necessary to apply what Dr. Ram Manohar Lohia called the "test of immediacy."

> We must see that what we are doing squares up with what we intend to do in the ultimate stage. If ... we indulge in activities which contradict these ideals, .. on which the new society will ultimately be based, there is no rational ground for supposing that we will, by some dialectical contrivance, ultimately arrive at that goal."[116]

J.P. also came to reject the idea that the class struggle based on self-interest would lead to socialism. He came to see the basic contradiction underlying this assumption.

> So far the dynamics of social change has been the conflict of self interests ... Labour actuated by self interest wishes to create a different social order in which it is assumed selfishness will not rule the lives of men. Here you have a fundamental contradiction. As the Hindi proverb says, you cannot plant a thorn tree and expect it to bear mangoes.[117]

Instead, he argued that the true basis for socialist society would be a moral individual who would "voluntarily limit his wants and his freedom in the interest of his fellow human beings." He redefined socialist society as "one in which the individual is prepared voluntarily to subordinate his own interest to the larger interest of society."[118] The essential characteristic would be "self-control." "What is needed is not a system of dynamics based on conflict of interests, but one that is based on the values of the society that we all wish to create."[119]

J.P. broke with Marxism when he decided that materialism could never be a basis for morality.

> If man and his consciousness and the society and culture which he has built up are mere manifestations of matter—how so ever dialectically active—I can see no reason why in such a society anyone should try to be ... generous, kind, unselfish .. What incentive can there be for moral behavior?[120]

This meant that Marxism was internally inconsistent in its theory of action. It meant that when "philosophical materialists" struggle for noble causes, their action was not consistent with their philosophy." This difficulty could be avoided, he said, if man was seen as an "automaton," but then man would have no "choice of action and no freedom of will." But, "the whole Marxian theory of revolutionary leadership is based on the assumption of free will."[121]

Similiarly, he argued, the Marxian approach to consciousness is faulty. Seeing consciousness as arising out of matter, Marxists attempt to understand it in the same manner, that is, scientifically and objectively. This, he believed was the source of Marxist amoralism. But consciousness, he decided, is ultimately subjective and can only be subjectively experienced. Finally, consciousness arises from the spiritual aspect of man rather than the material, and the root of morality is in the ultimate spiritual experience of self-realization.

> A great debate has raged in philosophy whether matter came first or consciousness. The point is that no matter which came first, there are today modes of existence that may be described

> as matter and consciousness. The mistake Marxism made was to assume that consciousness (whatever its origin) could be understood in the same manner as matter. It did not realize that the laws of matter cannot be applied to the realm of consciousness. The study of matter is an objective exploration, whereas that of consciousness is a subjective exploration. The study of matter, the objective exploration science in short, is necessarily amoral.[122]

It is only in the "ultimate spiritual experience" that the subjective and the objective merge.

> The root of morality lies in the endeavour of man to realize his Self. For one who has experienced this unity, the practice of morality becomes as natural and effortless as the drawing of breath.[123]

It is clear that this perspective places J.P. once again in the mainstream of the Indian philosophical tradition. Self-realization, a basically spiritual experience, became for him the source of moral values for the just society.

J.P. further criticized socialists and Marxists for failing to discover a political framework consistent with the Marxist ideals of freedom, equality and brotherhood. It was clear, he argued, that the so-called dictatorship of the proletariat must ultimately evolve into an elitist oligarchy—a bureaucratic one party dictatorship. Secondly, he questioned whether democratic socialism in Europe was sufficiently decentralized in structure to allow scope for the democratic partipation of the people. He thought that the Yugoslav experiment to create people's participation through people's committees and workers councils in a no-property state was a commendable effort but feared that "a democracy within a one-party dictatorship" would be created.[124] He saw the developments in Sweden using small scale and non-state co-perative enterprises as more hopeful.[125]

The fundamental problem of political structure, J.P. came to see, was that of decentralization. The ideal structure which he sought in democratic socialism, he ultimately found in Gandhi's conception of *Sarvodaya*.

> Some years back it became clear to me that socialism as we understand it today cannot take mankind to the sublime goals of freedom, equality, brotherhood and peace ... I am persuaded that unless socialism is transformed into *Sarvodaya*, these goals would remain beyond its reach ... [126]

J.P. also charged that Marxists and socialists had failed to envision an economic structure compatible with the ideals of Marxism. At the root of the problem, he thought was the dependence upon nationalization, which inevitably led, as in the Soviet Union, to centralization, bureaucratization, lack of industrial democracy, and lack of worker participation. The relations of production in the Soviet Union, he believed, were not socialistic but capitalistic. It would be impossible, he thought, to "graft on to this system a democratic, decentralized political superstructure." His thinking evolved toward the Gandhian conception of small-scale communally owned industries. He envisioned "dispersed ownership" at different levels, rather than concentrated ownership in the hands of the central government.[127] Ownership would be in municipal corporations, villages, and other cooperative units.

A related failure of socialism, J.P. concluded had been the prevailing attitude toward the peasant, and he warned that such an attitude would fail in Asia. Marxists and socialists pinned their hopes on the revolutionary consciousness of an industrial proletariat, while taking a cynical view of the peasants. Marx described the rural existence of the nineteenth century as "idiocy." Many socialists saw the solution to the problem in first distributing land to the peasants to gain their support, and then instituting collectivization. But for peasants who were emotionally attached to their land, this was not a viable solution for J.P. Instead, the peasants would voluntarily form village cooperatives so that there could be "villagization of land." Land ownership would be communal, but rights of proprietorship maintained.

At the same time, J.P. realized that voluntary and democratic development would not proceed as rapidly as, for example, that under Stalin. A dictatorship could accelerate capital formation by forcing meager consumption upon the peasants. But without force, the pace would be slower and involve other than satisfaction of greater and greater material wants. He concluded that rapid industrial development, as in the Soviet Union, would require a dictatorship, but that such a pattern of development had little to do with progressing toward the moral society.[128]

Finally, J.P. rejected Marxist and socialist techniques of struggle. As a democratic socialist, J.P. rejected the inevitability of violent class struggle, arguing that democratic institutions should be utilized in the struggle for socialism. But after several years experience working in the *bhoodan* or land-gift movement with Vinoba Bhave, he came to believe that techniques for social change should be based on Gandhian non-violent mass action. In 1953 he wrote:

> ... if we are able to move hundreds and thousands of landless people and make them peacefully squat on the lands which are

> owned by landlords but which are tilled by the landless labourers and which should rightfully belong to them and thereby offer resistance to the powers that be, no matter whether there are arrests, baton charges and shootings, then there is reason to believe that no power would be able to overcome that force.[129]

At this time, J.P. was thinking of such a revolutionary mass movement for the capture of power by the socialists.

In 1956, J.P. no longer perceived the necessity for the capture of State power. Such social change cannot be imposed from above, he decided, but must come about voluntarily.

> All of us agree that socialism is a way of life, an attitude of mind, a certain ethical behaviour. What is not so universally recognized is that such a way of life, attitude, behaviour, cannot be imposed from above by dictates of the government ... What is needed is a socialist movement, a mass movement of human reconstruction ... Such a movement obviously will be non-political in the sense that its aim will not be the capture of the state, because the state will be irrelevant to its purpose, namely the remaking of man.[130]

"No State," he said, "can force the individual to adopt the ideal 'from each according to his capacity and to each according to his needs.'" It should be willingly accepted by the community and we can start practicing it now.[131]

J.P. agreed that it would be possible for wealth to be distributed to the poor, by the State, but that the end result would not be a moral society. New forms of inequality would arise. Following Gandhi, he said that "if the poor accepted the new philosophy [Of sharing] and practiced it in their own lives ... on a mass scale, the rich could not be far behind."[132] The best way to distribute wealth, he concluded, was voluntarily. "Sharing of wealth is real and full socialism."

But the following year, in 1957, he abandoned democratic socialism, coming to the conclusion that socialism should be converted into *Sarvodaya* by setting up a decentralized and cooperative pattern of the organisation of society. This would include much experimentation and most of the necessary innovations would come from Indians themselves, although something, he thought, might be learned from Sweden. It would be an indigenous type of transformation, appropriate to the social context and cultural heritage of the subcontinent. *Sarvodaya* would come about primarily through the Gandhian technique of social revolution and reconstruction through the *bhoodan, gramdan* and *gram raj* movements.[133]

References

1. Allan and Wendy Scarfe, *J.P., His Biography* (New Delhi: Orient Longman, 1975), p. 23.
2. *Ibid.*, p. 30.
3. *Ibid.*, p. 32.
4. *Ibid.*, p. 43.
5. *Ibid.*, p. 55.
6. *Ibid.*, p. 65.
7. *Ibid.*, pp. 71-72.
8. *Ibid.*, p. 73.
9. *Ibid.*, p. 76.
10. *Ibid.*, pp. 83-86.
11. *Ibid.*, p. 94.
12. John Patrick Haithcox, *Conununism and Nationalism in India* (Princeton, N.J.: Princeton, Univ. Press, 1971), pp . 225 - 227.
13. Scarfe, pp. 96-104.
14. *Ibid.*, p. 122.
15. Haithcox, p. 322, footnote.
16. Scarfe, p. 262.
17. *Ibid.*, pp. 226-284.
18. Jayaprakash Narayan, "The Ideological Problems of Socialism" in *Revolutionary's Quoted*. Bimal Prasad (Delhi: Oxford Univ. Press, 1980) p. 158.
19. *Ibid.*, p. 171.
20. Bimal Prasad, ed., *A Revolutionary's Quest* (Delhi: Oxford Univ. Press, 1980), p. ix.
21. *Ibid.*, p. xi.
22. *Ibid.*, p. xiii.
23. Scarfe, p. 93.
24. Prasad, p. xiii.
25. *Ibid.*, p. xiv.
26. *Ibid.* Manohar Lohia, N.G. Goray and The founders of the CSP included Ram Asoka Mehta, Minoo Masani, Yusef Mahrally and Achyat Patwardhan. Also see Scarfe, pp. 88-89.
27. Scarfe, pp. 88-89.
28. *Ibid.*, p. 92.
29. Jayaprakash Narayan, "Socialism: A Science of Society," in *Revolutionary's Quest*, pp. 3-4.
30. *Ibid.*, pp. 4-5.

31. Jayaprakash Narayan, "The Foundations of Socialism," in *Revolutionary's Quest*, pp. 6-7.
32. *Ibid.*, pp. 7-9.
33. *Ibid.*, pp. 9-11.
34. *Ibid.*, p. 13.
35. *Ibid.*, pp. 14-15.
36. *Ibid.*, p. 6.
37. Jayaprakash Narayan, "The Objectives of the Congress Socialist Party," in *Revolutionary's Quest*, p. 20.
38. *Ibid.*, pp. 16-18.
39. *Ibid.*, p. 19.
40. *Ibid.*, p. 20.
41. *Ibid.*
42. *Ibid.*
43. *Ibid.*, p. 34.
44. *Ibid.*, p. 21.
45. *Ibid.*, p. 27.
46. *Ibid.*, p. 25.
47. *Ibid.*, p. 26.
48. *Ibid.*, pp. 27-28.
49. *Ibid.*, pp. 29-30.
50. *Ibid.*, p. 30.
51. *Ibid.*, p. 311
52. *Ibid.*
53. Jayaprakash Narayan, "The Gandhian Alternative," in *Revolutionary's Quest*, p. 51.
54. *Ibid.*, p. 35
55. *Ibid.*, p. 36.
56. *Ibid.*, pp. 36-37.
57. *Ibid.*, p. 37.
58. *Ibid.*, pp. 38-39.
59. *Ibid.*, p. 39.
60. *Ibid.*, p. 41.
61. *Ibid.*, pp. 42-43.
62. *Ibid.*, p. 43.
63. Raghavan Iyer, "The Moral and Political Thought of Mahatma Gandhi" (New York) Oxford Univ. Press, 1973), pp. 88-89.
64. A Dictionary of Marxist Thought, 1983 ed., s.v. "Human Nature," by Mihailo Markovic, p. 215.
65. *Ibid.*, pp. 215-216.

66. *Ibid.*
67. Raghavan Iyer, *parapolitics* (New York: Oxford Univ. Press, 1979), p. 52.
68. Iyer, *Moral and Political Thought of Mahatma Gandhi*, p. 88.
69. A Dictionary of Marxist Thought, p. 216.
70. *Ibid.*, pp. 216-217.
71. Narayan, "The Gandhian Alternative," in *Revolutionary's Quest*, p. 44.
72. *Ibid.*
73. *Ibid.*
74. Iyer, *Moral and Political Thought of Mahatma Gandhi*, pp. 90-91.
75. *Ibid.*, p. 95.
76. Iyer, *Parapolitics*, p. 312.
77. *Ibid.*, p. 313.
78. Narayan, "The Gandhian Alternative," in *Revolutionary's Quest*, p. 45.
79. *Ibid.*, p. 51.
80. Scarfe, p. 104.
81. Jayaprakash, Narayan, "To All Fighters for Freedom, I," in *Revolutionary's Quest*, p. 78.
82. *Ibid.*
83. Jayaprakash Narayan, "The Bricks of Society," in *Revolutionary's Quest*, p. 115.
84. *Ibid.*
85. *Ibid.*, pp. 116-117.
86. *Ibid.*
87. *Ibid.*
88. *Ibid.*
89. *Ibid.*, p. 118.
90. *Ibid.*
91. Jayaprakash Narayan, "To All Fighters for Freedom, III," in *Revolutionary's Quest*, pp. 105-107.
92. *Ibid.*, p. 109.
93. Jayaprakash Narayan, "My Picture of Socialism," in *Revolutionary's Quest*, p. 120.
94. *Ibid.*
95. Jayaprakash Narayan, "The Transition to Socialism," in *Revolutionary's Quest*, p. 127.
96. *Ibid.*, p. 132.
97. *Ibid.*, p. 131.

98. Jayaprakash Narayan, "The Socialists and the Congress," in *Revolutionary's Quest*, pp. 136-137.
99. Narayan, "My Picture of Socialism," in *Revolutionary's Quest*, p. 123.
100. *Ibid.*, p. 124.
101. *Ibid.*, pp. 124-126.
102. Jayaprakash Narayan, "The Structure of the Socialist Party," in *Revolutionary's Quest*, pp. 149-151.
103. *Ibid.*, p. 154.
104. *Ibid.*, p. 153.
105. Jayaprakash Narayan, "Ends and Means," in *Revolutionary's Quest*, p.139.
106. *Ibid.*, pp. 142-143.
107. *Ibid.*, pp. 141-142.
108. Jayaprakash Narayan, "From Socialism to Sarvodaya," in *Revolutionary's Quest*, p. 190.
109. *Ibid.*
110. *Ibid.*, p. 192.
111. Jayaprakash Narayan, "The Ideological Problems of Socialism," in *Revolutionary's Quest*, pp. 158-159.
112. *Ibid.*, pp. 159-160.
113. *Ibid.*, p. 160.
114. *Ibid.*
115. Narayan, "From Socialism to Sarvodaya," in *Revolutionary's Quest*, p. 190.
116. Narayan, "The Ideological Problems of Socialism," in *Revolutionary's Quest*, p. 161.
117. Jayaprakash Narayan, "New Dynamics of Social Change," in *Revolutionary's Quest*, p. 175.
118. *Ibid.*
119. *Ibid.*, pp. 175-176 .
120. Narayan, "From Socialism to Sarvodaya," in *Revolutionary's Quest*, pp. 192-193.
121. *Ibid.*, p. 193.
122. *Ibid.*
123. *Ibid.*, p. 194.
124. Narayan, "The Ideological Problems of Socialism," in *Revolutionary's Quest*, pp. 162-164.
125. Narayan, "From Socialism to Sarvodaya," in *Revolutionary's Quest*, p. 191.

126. *Ibid.*, p. 192.
127. Narayan, "The Ideological Problems of Socialism," in *Revolutionary's Quest*, pp. 165-160.
128. *Ibid.*
129. *Ibid.*, pp. 169-170.
130. Narayan, "New Dynamics of Social Change," in *Revolutionary's Quest*, pp. 174-175.
131. *Ibid.*
132. *Ibid.*
133. Narayan, "From Socialism to Sarvodaya," in *Revolutionary's Quest*, p. 191.

5

J.P. Narayan on Sarvodaya

While Jayaprakash Narayan moved closer to Gandhian political thought in the late 1950's, his actions in the political sphere continued to be somewhat inconsistent. He never quite conformed to the traditional image of the saint in Indian politics. Even though he renounced all personal ambition as a politician, his actions suggest, particularly after 1973, that he never quite gave up participation in the political process, even in the realm of party politics. His leadership in the Gujarat and Bihar protest movements in 1974 and 1975 contributed significantly to the rise of the opposition Janata Party which successfully challenged the Ruling Congress Party in 1977.

Even while claiming that he had no interest in party politics, J.P. continued to argue that it was "absolutely necessary to have a strong opposition party" in order "to run parliamentary democracy successfully in India."[1] He feared that a one party dictatorship might lead to the demise of the parliamentary system and set a bad example for other nations in Asia. While severely criticizing parliamentary democracy, he saw it as superior to dictatorships, even when it assumed a largely dictatorial form.[2] Consequently, he argued that there was no inconsistency in working for non-party democracy and at the same time working for the success of parliamentary democracy.

In spite of his reluctance to completely abandon the sphere of party politics, J.P. effectively played the role of a Socratic gadfly in relation to the Congress Party and leftist political groups, addressing the broader moral issues of social and political transformation. Neither his close associates in the Socialist and Communist Parties nor the Congress policymakers were spared his sharp criticism of the direction of Indian polity after independence. He quarrelled with Nehru over development policy and warned those in power that they had drifted far from the Gandhian vision of free Indian society. His association with Vinoba Bhave and his work in the *Bhoodan* Movement convinced him that the establishment of local village republics through the *Gramdan* system could lay the foundation for the realization of *Sarvodaya*, a democratic, partyless, decentralized and non-violent socialist pattern of society concerned with universal human welfare and the realization of human potential. A mass movement was necessary for the realization of *Sarvodaya* and this presented a dilemma.

Mobilization from above would smack of elitism and result in a political structure opposite to that envisioned by *Sarvodaya*. Political mobilization through party politics would further fragment and destroy whatever unity remained in the villages. Yet most villagers remained apathetic, lacking the education and civic orientation needed for the establishment of functioning democratic village republics. Only a mass movement, then, of the type envisioned by Gandhi could bring vision of revolutionary change to the villages. Time was an important factor also as the task would prove more difficult once politicization along party, caste and communal lines became institutionalized. Vested interests were becoming entrenched, and increasingly channeled through the party system.

Essentially, there were two competing visions as to the future of Indian society. It is clear that those at the helm of the State and in charge of planning envisioned the industrialization of Indian society, along lines similiar to that in the Soviet Union. This vision viewed the village as either historically obsolete or only useful as a temporary structure for funneling rural development inputs. Development programmes would be run largely from urban centers and the architects would be urban economists. In actuality, early planning perilously neglected rural development, giving priority to the development of heavy industry. Theodore Roszak observed that:

> Economists, for all their purported objectivity, are the most narrowly ethnocentric of people. Since they are universally urban intellectuals who understand little of rural ways, they easily come to regard the land and all that lives and grows upon it, as nothing more than another factor of production. Hence, it seems to them no loss, but indeed a gain to turn all the world's farming

> into high-yield agri-industry, to depopulate the rural areas, and to crowd the cities to the chronic breakdown of crisis.[3]

The other vision was the broader and more utopian notion of decentralist economics.

> It is the tradition we might call anarchism, if we mean by that much abused word a libertarian political economy that distinguishes itself from orthodox socialism and capitalism by insisting that the scale of organization must be treated as an independent and primary problem.[4]

It was the vision of a "nobler economics that is not afraid to discuss spirit and conscience, moral purpose and the meaning of life, an economics that aims to educate and devote people...[5] Indeed, Schumacher suggested that "the biggest single decision that any country in the position of India has to take is the choice of technology."[6]

For J.P., the immediate struggle,.. is not a riot of one class against another, but rather the struggle for a humanist pattern of society, which would restore the individual to the place of primary importance in society, embrace rationality, cooperation, harmony, science and intellectual and spiritual freedom. Individuals would become subjects rather than objects in history. The struggle would be waged against both, centuries of historical inertia and imperialism, and the atomization of society through industrialization, urbanization and the politics of class interests. He believed it was necessary to emphasize the problems and fallacies of parliamentary democracy as well as statist and oligarchical socialism and communism.

There were parochial and romantic elements in J.P.'s vision for the new society, but in large, it was also a universalistic vision. With roots in the village, J.P. felt a pull toward the rural life and saw urban life as essentially alienating. There was thus an element of the agrarian ideology, associating morality with the simplified village lifestyle. Finally, J.P. found sanction for the restoration of the self-sufficient and self-governing village republic in classical Indian tradition. Unlike Gandhi, whose convictions and actions were largely grounded in moral beliefs, even when defeat seemed certain, J.P.'s beliefs and convictions were more easily influenced by empirical evidence. His observations of the working of industrial society, both in the West and in the Soviet Union, and of the two different patterns of political rule, convinced him that a centralized pattern of development in India would result in disaster. Although there was a spiritual element in his search for a better pattern of organization for society in Indian tradition, again, he did not approach the solution with a mystical faith but sought contemporary evidence that a decentralized pattern of society was workable in India. He advocated experimentation also. His tour of Europe, including Sweden and Yugoslavia, convinced him that decentralization and development were possible and more democratic than other patterns of rule in modern society. There was an element of impatience in J.P. as a social reformer. He wanted to find the correct path for development and get on with the task.

As vested interests became more entrenched after independence, and a political elite became established, enjoying the perquisites of office and losing sight of India's dusty villages, J.P. despaired of hope that parliamentary democracy, under the leadership of the Congress Party, could transform India into an egalitarian and democratic society.

Critique of Parliamentary Democracy and the State

At the heart of J.P.'s critique of parliamentary democracy, the party and the State, is the fundamental distinction made by Vinoba Bhave between *rajniti*, party and power politics, and *lokniti*, non-party and non-power politics. In "From Socialism to Sarvodaya," J.P. stated that it became clear to him that power politics could never lead to the goals of "equality, freedom, brotherhood and peace."[7]

The major objections which J.P. had to parliamentary democracy were: it is contrary to the nature of human society and the social nature of man; its basic principles are unsound; it is a foreign transplant not rooted in Indian soil; people in India do not understand it; it does not contribute to a true community; it is built upon an improper economic foundation; it emphasizes rights rather than responsibility; it looks to elitist party rule; it does not produce individuals, but alienates individuals from themselves; it leads to the creation of a mass society, large scale exploitative industrialization, urbanization, uncurbed materialistic desires for more and more consumption, and the atomization of society.

J.P.'s conviction that parliamentary democracy was contrary to the nature of human society and the social nature of man was derived from the Spanish political philosopher Salvador de Madariaga. Madariaga argued that the concept of the State based upon an "arithmetical, mineral or inorganic sum of individuals," has this quality.[8]

In 1959 in "A Plea for the Reconstruction of Indian Polity, J.P. wrote,

> Man is a social animal and is endowed with a social nature. Further, the relation of the individual to society is not like that of the grain of sand to the sand dune. The relationship is rather like

> that of the living cell to the living organism. Man always lives in organic relationship with other men. It is the totality of these living relationships that constitutes society. Society is not a mere sum of individuals.[9]

On the other hand,

> Modern Western democracy is based on a negation of the societal nature of man and the true nature of human society as an inorganic mass of separate grains of individuals; the conception is that of an atomized society ... the ... procession of democracy rests on the arithmetic of votes.[10]

In 1962 in Communitarian Society and Panchayati Raj, J.P. distinguished between the organic or communitarian view of society which "puts man in his natural milieu as a responsible member of a responsible community" and "treats man not as a particle of sand in an inorganic heap, but as a living cell in a larger organic entity," from Western society where society is "atomized" and "political democracy is reduced to counting of heads."[11]

J.P. argued that the principles of parliamentary democracy are unsound. At times he spoke of the mistique of elections as "sham democracy." In 1936 he wrote:

> It is with the appearance of the ballot box and the party system-of government that the fiction of democracy came into being. These two institutions were supposed to have conferred power on the whole people, equally on the humblest and the highest. But the economic order which weighs the scales too heavily on the side of the propertied interests, makes of this democracy a mockery. The rich have their great resources, their huge election funds, their great newspapers, their schools and colleges.
> And the poor? Well, they can have their dole or ... starve. The right to exercise the vote in these conditions means little to the workers.[12]

Later in a statement which appeared elitist, but was meant to decry the lack of preparation of the many millions in India for the process of voting, he questioned the rationale behind the concept of one individual having one vote.

> [E]ven the basic principles of this parliamentary democracy are not sound. Everyone has one vote, one vote to everyone. What is the sense of it, will you please, tell me? Pundit Nehru has one vote and Pundit Nehru's chaprasi, also has one vote ... The most eminent philosopher has one vote and the fool in the village

> also has one vote ... The stupidity of this, of giving a vote, an equal vote, to everyone to decide the fate of the country—that is one of the dearest ideas of democracy. But to me it does not make sense.[13]

"Parliamentary democracy," he pointed out, "assumes that the voters understand the programmes and policies of different parties and cast their votes understandingly."[14]

But in fact, "even the limited choice" placed before the electorate were by and large incomprehensible to it."[15]

J.P. also questioned the principle of decision making by majority. Even if the majority rule, he pointed out, the minority must be forced to comply. But in a multi-party system, such as in India, even the majority did not rule but rather a minority. Moreover, in the cabinet system, he argued, the system works on the basis of leadership. "In effect, democracy boils down to the dictatorship of one man. Especially, if you have a powerful person at the helm ... the entire cabinet, the parliament, and the people, accept his views and you have the dictatorship of one man."[16]

Further, parliamentary democracy was a foreign transplant, not rooted in Indian soil. J.P. argued that:

> While borrowing has been a common means of social development, no borrowed institution can thrive unless it is properly acclimatized and integrated. Every institution of society grows out of its own peculiar soil and is nourished and nurtred by its own unique climate and environment.[17]

In 1957, he argued that the "implantation of any idea or institution that is not adopted to the native sail or grafted upon the roots of our own life will not bear fruit or contribute to the organic and healthy growth of the body politic."[18] The British had "paid no regards to India's own political patterns—ancient or contemporary," and neither had the fathers of the Indian Constitution.[19]

J.P. believed that most people in India did not really understand parliamentary democracy. "Present Indian democracy is the product of the conflict of politically and economically conscious elements in Indian society with British imperialism." The Indian masses, he observed, "did not struggle to establish these institutions" nor did they "struggle for the right to vote ... Vast numbers of them do not appreciate the value of that right nor understand how to use it. This makes democracy, based on adult franchise, unreal and insubstantial."[20] In Towards A New Society, he wrote, "this kind of party system, this kind of election, they do not understand. It has not come out of them ... An analysis of the present political situation would show that parliamentary democracy is not suited to India."[21]

J.P. also concluded that since parliamentary democracy emphasizes party rather than community, it cannot lead to the establishment of true communities. Writing on the concept of organic society, he pointed out that the problem goes beyond that of decentralization. He noted a fundamental difference between Western society and the organic or communitarian view. The economic structure or base of Western society, that is, a "certain form of industrialization" and resulting atomization of society is reflected in the political institutions of that society, e.g. in "political parties built around competing power groups." The organic view, on the other hand, "puts man in his natural milieu as a responsible member of a responsible community.[22]

> Now, a community in order to be real, that is, in order that it might be infused with the sense of a community, must emphasise in its internal life such ethical values as adjustment, conciliation, harmony and cooperation. Without these there can be no community. The community can never be at war with itself; one part of it fighting the other ... and the majority ruling over the minority. Such a kind of political battle is possible only in the mass society where there is no community. This does not mean that within the community there can be no difference of opinion or interests. But they must be adjusted together and harmonised so that the community and its individual members live and grow and evolve materially and spiritually. The job is to discover the political and economic institutions and processes that can accomplish this task.[23]

With respect to the economic foundation of Western society, J.P. felt that modern industrialism created a spirit of economism in which human values became subordinated to so called economic progress. This led to the disintegration of society and the alienation of persons.[24] The aim of the community, he thought, should be the welfare of all its members, not individual profit. There should be cooperative sharing. "The economy .. must ... be subordinate to, and subserve the aim of a balanced development of human life ... It cannot be an economy of unlimited wants."

There was also an ecological element in this plea as J.P. said that the community "must think of future generations" It should "try its best to return to nature what it takes from it .. The economy of the community is in cooperative harmony with nature ..." The community must not engage in destructive warfare with nature. [25] J. P. saw that Western Democracy, ... is really "elected oligarchy."[26] In 1957 he wrote:

> The party system with the corroding and corrupting struggle for power inherent in it, disturbed me more and more. I saw how parties backed by finance, organization and the means of propaganda could impose themselves on the people, how people's rule became in effect party rule; how party rule in turn became the rule of a caucus or coterie ...
>
> The party system as I saw it was emasculating the people ... All that parties were concerned with was to capture power for themselves so as to rule over people ... This to me did not spell freedom. . ."[27]

Finally, the mass party became a "sort of state within the State.[28] And the inherent tendency toward centralization and bureaucratization in parliamentary democracy leads to the "autocracy of the bureaucrat."[29]

J.P. denied that the individuality of the person would be submerged in the organic society of his conception.

> It is exactly in the mass society, which falsely proclaims the sovereignty of the individual, that the individual is alienated from himself. and becomes a nameless digit, which the political and economic masters manipulate for power and profit and glory ... It is only in the community, in which the sense of community has developed, that the individual is a distinct personality living with other personalities, and has the possibility to develop to the highest being ...[30]

Finally, J.P. questioned the utility of the State itself. He saw the State as a "Juggernaut," and concluded that a non-violent social revolution could not come about by constitutional means. In 1964, he wrote, "I do not think it would be possible in the next fifty years for the State ... to provide for social security in every village."[31] "In the very nature of things the government by itself can never succeed in banishing poverty, making democracy work, bringing about a socio-economic revolution and establishing social and economic justice."[32]

Ultimately, the State should wither away. In 1957, J.P. wrote,

"I. .. feel strongly that human freedom can be fully and wholly realized in a stateless society ... I am sure that it is one of the noblest goals of social endeavor to insure that the powers and functions and spheres of the State are reduced as far as possible ..."[33] Disillusioned with both Western socialism and the parliamentary system, J.P. sought a substitute in Gandhi's constructive approach toward selfrule- - in his concept of *Sarvodaya.*

Partyless Democracy, Communitarianism and Indian Socialism

Convinced of the inability of Western socialism and parliamentary democracy to produce a moral society, J.P. turned to Indian tradition in search of a system of values upon which to build Indian social and economic polity. The principles "enunciated and practised" in the ancient Indian polity, he believed, would "be in line with the natural course of social evolution" and "more valid from the point of view of social science that any other."[34] He suggested that "India was perhaps the earliest home of democracy" as "Kings in the earlier times were elected by and subject to the Kshatriya autocracy." He noted that local institutions provided a "stable, democratic basis for Indian polity," and that the democracy of the village communities continued into the British period. The distinguishing marks of ancient polity were "community, self-development and self-regulation of communal life."[35]

The community in ancient India, according to J.P., took two forms. First, the territorial community, that is, the village, township, kingdom or republic, and the functional or occupational community, the varna. The four varnas, Brahmin or priest, Kshatriya or warrior-ruler, Vaishya or trader-artisan, and Sudra or labourer, had a theoretical as well as a practical form and basis. "Each varna was self-determining and yet integrated with and responsible to the territorial community" and there was a "remarkable self-determining pattern of a complex ethico-socio-economic life."[36]

J.P. argued that the "two fundamental truths" of the varna order of society are that human beings have different aptitudes and that every individual should be enabled to pursue and develop his or her natural gifts and inclinations. J.P. saw these principles as the scientific basis for the reorganisation of society.

In 1959, Indian cultural tradition was seen by J.P. as a basis for Indian consciousness, rather than class or class interest. In strongly nationalistic tones, he spoke of institutions that have acquired a: certain:character that is "uniquely Indian" and a "way of life cast in an Indian mould." An attitude of mind has grown," he said, "that again operates in a peculiarly Indian framework."[37] Even with the foreign invasions and administrations, "the hidden springs of Indian life have been powerful enough to reassert themselves and pierce through the over-lain layers of foreign institutions and ways of life."[38]

J.P. identified this reassertion of Indian consciousness with historical spiritual revivalism. He pointed out that the 'age of saints,' *Sant-Yuga* ... represented just such a reassertion during the period of Muslim domination. Nanak, Kabir, Tulsi, Tukaram, Ramdas and the other saints of that time endeavored to dig up the buried treasure from under the debris of a shattered civilization. Likewise, during the British period, the line of spiritual teachers from Raja Ram Mohun Roy to Mohandas Karamchand Gandhi represented the rebirth of India and the reassertion of her vital springs of life."

The ancient and enduring Indian village was idealized as a pillar of moral strength preserving the most noble values and communal solidarity. Through many upheavals, the village community stood like a rock, carrying on its life and running its affairs in its appointed manner ... Much that remained in India of lasting value and merit is attributed ... to this stability of Indian society provided by the ancient village organizations."[39]

For J.P., this ancient tradition of democracy in the village provides the most sure basis for the future of Indian society.

> The self-governing village communities were the foundation stones of ancient Indian polity.
>
> Their strength came from within and not from without. Their authority rested not on rights and powers granted by a central authority, but on the willing consent of the families that constituted them.[40]

Gandhi's inspiration for the rejuvination of the Indian villages, then, was largely adopted by J. P. He came to see the wisdom in Gandhi's desire to see the Indian National Congress transform itself into a *Lok Sevak Sangh* or People's Service Organization after independence. Future polity, he believed, must be a people's politics (*lokniti*), as the Indian freedom movement had been, rather than a politics of the state (*rajniti*).

Gandhi's vision for the uplift of the villages and their transformation into model communities was based upon the concept of *Sarvodaya*, meaning the social good, public interest or universal welfare. Raghavan Iyer pointed out that "His concept of *Satya*, with *ahimsa* as the means, determined his doctrine of Satyagraha or active resistance to authority, while the concept of *ahimsa*, with *Satya* as the common end, enabled him to formulate his doctrine of *Sarvodaya* or non-violent socialism."[41]

There were three major facets of Gandhi's programme: Gramdan, *Gram Sankalpa* or *Gram Shavalamban* and *Gram Swaraj*. As explained by J.P. :

> Gramdan represents a revolution in the mind, a revolution in the values, a revolution in the attitude towards property and other things— pooling of resources, sharing not only of land, but also of labour, skill, intelligence, money ... Those who have skills, those who have knowledge, will place these at the disposal of

> the village community. Those who have nothing but labour power would contribute labour power.
> Those who have bullocks, ploughs, or other things, would do the same ... The old Marxian slogan of 'from each according to his capacity and to each according to his needs' would then be realised.[42]

The resources of the village would be "communalized" and placed at the disposal of the entire community.

Gram Swavalamban signified the concept of village self-sufficiency; Gandhi and J.P. realized that a way must be found to increase production in the village and to increase gainful employment. It would need to employ simple means of technology and be labour intensive. The alternative would be the further disintegration of the village community through urban migration. " ... We think there are certain ways men should live together to preserve their humanity,"[43] J.P. wrote , "We think one way of doing it is to live in small communities, to have smaller units of production." It would be essential, he believed, for individuals to limit their wants and be willing to share resources if society was to become democratic.[43]

Gram Swaraj was the concept of village self-government. J.P. thought that such decentralized units would make political parties unnecessary and useless. "If Gramdan removes these conflicts and makes the community a homogeneous community and a human community, then there would be no need of parties there. It would be possible for the villagers to adjust their differences of opinion and come to unanimous decisions, or nearly unanimous decisions," he argued.[44]

Underlying the non-violent approach to social change was the conviction that in essence the fundamental revolution involved moral rather than political change. In "A Plea for the Reconstruction of Indian Polity," J.P. explained that the State itself was grounded in and arose because individuals failed to become moral individuals. Lacking individual dharma, there could be no *Gram Dharma* and this made necessary an instrument of coercion, the modern State.

> The most difficult question that democracy faces today is how to resolve the following dilemma: When there is liberty, it leads to abuse and necessitates state interference, and when there is state interference it leads to curtailment of liberty. How then to preserve liberty and prevent its abuse? There are no political means by which the dilemma can be resolved, there are only

> moral means. The obverse side of the medal of liberty is responsibility. If the individual is not prepared to take social responsibility, if he uses liberty for self aggrandisement and neglects or hurts the interests of others, some form of Statism becomes inevitable ... The only democratic answer to Statism and totalitarianism is trusteeshp.[45]

> The test of human evolution for me became man's ability to live in amity, justice and cooperation with his fellow men without outward restraints of any kind. That is why I have considered the human and social problem to be at bottom a moral problem.[46]

The concept of dharma signifies duty, righteousness, moral law; social and personal morality; natural law and natural obligation. In Indian thought, "dharma helped to knit the political into a cosmic whole, a gradually ascending hierarchy of ends reflected in successive phases of the life of everyman."[47] Aurobindo explained that:

> It was a marked feature of the Indian mind that it sought to attach a spiritual meaning and a religious sanction to all, even to the most external social and political circumstances of its life, imposing on all classes an ideal, not, of rights and powers but of duties, a rule of their action and an ideal way and temperament, character, spirit in action, a dharma with a spiritual significance.[48]

For Asoka, the notion of dharma allowed diverse individuals to "fuse their religious and political concerns in a non-sectarian 'secular' state in which all religions were respected."[49] For Gandhi, *dharma* signified the Kantian concept of a universal categorical imperitive of duty. "Men must perform their dharma for its own sake if dharma is to have any meaning at all."[50] Gandhi's individualism was derived from the concept of dharma, and each individual, he thought, must discover his own *dharma*.[51] *Dharma* for Gandhi also implied non-violent means or the social goal of *ahimsa*.[52]

The concept of *dharma* became the moral basis for J.P.'s vision for the transformation of Indian society through Sarvodaya. He wrote:

> If I were to redefine *dharma* today, I would redefine it in the sense of the identification of the individual with other human beings, till we identify ourselves with the entire human community—the world community of human beings—and we become world citizens. In the development of human society—as in the development of the individual ... it is this value of spirituality that has to be placed in the position of control ... Material values are also important—we must have our bread to

> eat. But the bread must be not only for us, it must be also for others. If we are concerned with our own bread, then that is materialism. If we are concerned with other people's bread, then that is spiritualism.[53]

As the Brihadaranyaka Upanishad conceives dharma as "the sovereign power ruling over kshatriya or temporal power," so J.P. argued that science and technology must be subordinated to moral values.[54]

Those volunteers who went to the villages to work for *Sarvodaya*, and who were joined by J.P. in the 1950's were inspired to work for rural uplift by Gandhi during the Nationalist Movement. In March 1948 at Gandhi's *asharam* at Sevagram near Wardha, his workers met and formed the Sarvodaya Samaj. This organization was to function as

> a free and voluntary body with an obligation to strive towards the uplift of all in the world, using truth and nonviolence as a means to this end. Their aim was to create a social order in which there would be no distinction of class or creed, nor exploitation of any kind. It was fundamental that means be employed to achieve these ends.[55]

In 1951, Vinoba Bhave, a follower of Gandhi, hit upon a method by which he believed non-violent socialism in the village might come about. After a prayer meeting in a village in Nalganda District, forty untouchable families begged him for land to enable them to earn a living. Bhave appealed for gifts of land and received 100 acres from one wealthy landowner. This inspired him to launch a campaign of "Bhoomidan-Yogni," the worship of God through sacrifice of land.[56] This was the origin of Bhoodan.

On April 18, 1951, Bhave launched his *Bhoodan* Movement in Eastern Hyderabad state, in the Telengana area where mobilization of the peasants by the Communists had been carried out. Bhave encouraged all landowners, both large landowners and poor peasants to donate one-sixth of their land to the village community—as a token of Bhave's share as a "sixth son of the family."[57] In this way, Bhave believed the foundation could be laid for a gram swaraj or true village community, in a voluntary and non-violent way.

J.P. became involved in the *Bhoodan* movement in 1952, after a meeting in Mongroth village in Hamirpur district of Bihar, in which the entire population of the village expressed their willingness to donate all their land for communal sharing. From this point on, J.P. began to advocate Bhoodan and Gramdan and work in the villages of Bihar to establish Gramdan as a first step toward *Sarvodaya*. This also indicated to him that there was no longer a need for political parties. Shortly after this, J.P. renounced Marxism and later severed his leadership in the Socialist Party.

In 1954, at a conference of *Sarvodaya* workers at Bodh Gaya, J.P. made a speech in which he took a vow of *jeevandan*, that is, a pledge to devote his whole life to Vinoba Bhave's campaign and to renounce participation in party and power politics.[58] J.P. saw in *Bhoodan* the germ of total agrarian revolution" and called it "the Revolution Beautiful." A week of work in the Gaya District of Bihar resulted in gifts of nearly seven thousand acres of land.[59] In Bhave's campaign, he saw a practical application of Gandhi's social philosophy. He wrote:

> In the beautiful revolution of gramdan, ownership was not abolished by force of any kind, but freely surrendered to the community. The outward social change 'was as accomplished by inward change. It was an example of what Gandhiji meant by a double revolution. In place of social tensions, conflicts and tyrannies, there were freedom and mutual goodwill and accord, making it possible for an unprecedented output of free collective initiative and endeavor.[60]

Gandhi's vision of trusteeship, it was thought, could be reached through Sampattidan, a programme of converting not only land but the proprietorship of all property to the larger community. J.P. emphasized that laying the foundation for *Sarvodaya* involved a "two pronged method." It first required persuasion. A revolution in ideas and values and secondly a programme of self help and self government through which individuals in small communities would learn to manage their own affairs and cooperate together, must be devised.[61] This revolution would be morally superior to both revolutions made by violence and to those made by law. A non-violent means would be consistent with a non-violent end. Where violent revolutions destroy the old society in one sweep and "build the new brick by brick," in a non-violent revolution change of the old and construction of the new proceed side by side and step by step.

> [B]ecause the non-violent method relies on persuasion and conversion, because it aims to begin at the bottom, because non-violent revolutionaries are not themselves engaged in any struggle for power, because their whole attempt is to enable and help the people to help themselves to stand on their legs and to manage their affairs through their ground-level institutions, because of all this the non-violent method is far more likely to put power in the hands, of the people than either the violent or the constitutional method.[62]

Since decisions would be made by consensus in the village assembly, rather than by voting, this method of solving local problems would serve to solidify the community and to minimize differences, rather than to magnify them as in a party system.[63] It would create an:

> ... identity of interests; a feeling of unity in the midst of diversity; a sense of freedom within the framework of accepted social responsibilities; differentiation of functions converging to the single goal of the good of the community and its members. Caste, class, race, religion, politics—all these divide men into different, often conflicting groups. The community brings them together, unites them and harmonizes their interests ... Production and consumption are not two contraposed sides of an economic bargain manipulated by distinct agencies, but an integrated process serving a single and direct purpose.[64]

J.P. reaffirmed his belief that since man is a product of both nature and culture, there must be a harmonious blending of the two elements. This, he argued, would be possible in relatively small communities. He adopted Aldous Huxley's notion that the individual's psychological needs cannot be fulfilled unless three conditions are met. First, the individual must have a "fair measure of personal independence and personal responsiblity within and toward a self-governing group." Secondly, "work must possess a certain aesthetic value and human significance." Third, the individual should be "related to his natural environment in some organic, rooted and symbiotic way."[65]

J.P. disagreed with those who argued that there was an inherent logic in science. and technology toward the breakup of the village community and the appearance of mass society and large scale industrialization. Persons, he thought, determined the nature of society, rather than science and technology. He said:

> Science and centralized large-scale production and large conglomerates of human habitations are thought to go necessarily together. Nothing could be more absurd. Science is of two kinds: (a) pure science and (b) applied science. I would call pure science alone science, and the other technology. [66]

Large scale production came into being, he argued, because first it was more profitable and the "money-makers were the dominant class in society." Secondly, the governments; preferred large scale production because it was necessary for making war and it helped them concentrate great power in their hands.

"Poor science," he said, "had no say in the matter." On the other hand, science could have been applied to the goals of "peace, goodwill, cooperation, freedom and brotherhood" rather than the "aims of power, profit and war."[67] "Science has turned the whole world into a neighbourhood, but man has created a civilization that has turned even neighbours into strangers."[68] But in the communitarian society, he believed, the "false and unscientific" dichotomy between urban and rural life could be overcome. Society would be agro-industrial with a balance between agriculture and industry. This arrangement would be natural since both are essential for human life and development.[69]

Finally, *Sarvodaya* would embody Gandhi's goal and conception." In this structure individuals would stand at the center of ever widening circles—an oceanic circle whose center would be the individual. The individual would be a world citizen and in such a structure, nation states would have no place.[70]

Primary communities, villages or sections of urban areas would come together to form regional communities and these would in turn form district communities. Collectively, district communities would form provincial communities (*Pranta Sabhas*) and together these would form the national community (*Rashtra Sabha*). Similiarly, a world community might also come into being.[71]

J.P. and others participated in the establishment of several *gramdan* villages and were successful in establishing legislation to legalize such institutional arrangements. The Gandhian workers for village reconstruction, the Sarva Seva Sangh moved beyond land gifts or *bhoodan* to the second phase, the establishment of *gramdan* villages. The following phase would have established *Gram Swaraj* or community self government. A *gramdan* village was to establish a *Gram Kosh* to which everyone joining the *gramdan* had to contribute a portion of his or her income, produce or labour. Proprietors of land were required to donate one-twentieth of their land for distribution among the landless. Legal title to the land was surrendered to the gram sabha or village community. Right of possession (except the donated, area) was retained, along with the right of usufruct (except for the contribution to the *gram kosh*) and the right of inheritance. Land could be sold only to the *gram* and with the permission of the gram sabha. The *gram kosh* was to be used to help the village destitute and for development of the village according to the plans and decisions of the *gram sabha*.[72]

The Bihar Gramdan Act provided that seventy-five percent of the people in the village must give their consent and joining landowners must represent fifty-one percent of the land in the village to establish a *gramdan* village. If sufficient *gramdan* programmes could be established in a district, the entire district could be converted into a gram district, and also this could happen on a state and on a national level.[73]

In general, the process of *Gramdan* involved three stages:

> (i) prapti in which the people are persuaded to join *gramdan* and, voluntarily, to transfer the ownership of their land to the village council. (ii) pushti-in which the village implements the primary conditions of *Gramdan*, such as the redistribution of the one-twentieth part of donated land among the landless. (iii) nirman-The stage in which, through the *Gram Sabha*, resources are mobilized and a programme of reconstruction and development of the village begins.[74]

Planning would be carried out on the sub-district regional level (e.g. the development block), and would be tailored to the needs of the primary communities within that region. It was also envisioned that worker associations would come into existence, federated into an economic council and analogous to historical varna organizations.[75] Selection of the panchayat, or the executive of primary communities would also be done through consensus, rather than by election contests and voting. *Gram Panchayats* would come together to choose the *Panchayat Samati* on the regional level and the *Zilla Parishad* on the district level. Contrary to the structure later established in the *Panchayati Raj* system, the *panchayat* councils would extend to the state assembly and also form the *Lok Sabha* on the national level. At the provincial level, there would be no ministers or Chief Minister and on the national level, no Prime Minister as "the office of Prime Minister leads to the hero cult" and "smacks of the gunpowder of *totalitarianism*"[76] There would be a president of the *Rashtra Sabha*, the highest level of the panchayat organization, and political parties would be kept out of the local bodies at least up to the district level.[77]

In 1959, J.P. believed that:

> If the responsibility were really thrown upon the people so that they could see clearly that their suffering was due to the fact that they had chosen the wrong type of people to manage their affairs, the relationship between the people, their representatives and civil servants would be so intimate and direct that it should not take so long for the people to remedy the situation.[78]

The moral qualities and mental attitudes most needed for communitarian society, J.P. believed, were a concern for truth, aversion to violence, love of liberty and the courage to resist oppression and tyranny, a spirit of cooperation, readiness to adjust self-interest to the larger interest, respect for others opinions and tolerance, readiness to take responsibility, belief in the fundamental equality of man and faith in the educability of human nature.[79]

Like M.N. Roy, J.P. emphasized the role of education, pointing out that "the task of preparing the very soil in which the plant of democracy may take root and grow is not a political but an educative task."[80] Education could not be left up to the State. Rather, its values must be inculcated through the society:

> The prevailing social ethics, the family, the religious and educational authorities and institutions, the example that the elite set in their own lives, the organs of public opinion— all these have to combine to create the necessary moral climate for democracy to thrive.[81]

The establishment of panchayats or village governments through the *Panchayati Raj* programme began in the 1950's. This programme was an attempt by the Government of India to go part way toward institutionalizing Gandhian thinking on decentralized rural development. *Panchayati Raj* was an attempt by the Indian Government to revive the historical village institutions, and relegate to the villages a degree of local decision making. Previous efforts to revive the panchayats had been made by the British, but for the most part, they remained dormant. *Panchayati Raj* established local bodies on three levels: the *Panchayat*, on the village level, the *Panchayati Samati* on the regional level, and the *Zilla Parishad* on the district level. They did not extend up to the state and national level as envisioned by J.P.

J.P. thought the system, as established, was certain to fail as it produced a hybrid, grafted onto the parliamentary system of rule, in which government, including planning was largely centralized. By 1957, it was reported by the *Mehta Commission* that those units of *Panchayati Raj* which had been established were functioning poorly.

In 1961, J.P. charged that the real initiative of the government in establishing Panchayati Raj was not to establish a true pattern of participatory democracy, but rather to get public cooperation for the execution of development programmes, administered from above. There were several conditions which must be met, he thought, in order to establish functioning local government. Fundamentally, a radical social transformation at the grass roots level must be brought about. The Panchayati Raj institutions would not accomplish this, because, while concerned with development, they provided no mechanism by which village socialism might be established.

J.P. stressed that there must be education of the people and disinterested and non-partisan agencies. They must understand the necessity of a communitarian society where each person was a responsible participant with a concern for the welfare of the whole community. Secondly, political parties must refrain from interfering in these institutions, as factionalism would destroy the public spirit. Third, J.P. wanted to see real devolution of power. The people, he said, must be trusted. Fourth, local authorities should be provided with resources with which to get a development programme underway. And the local bodies should enable local people to participate in decision making through frequent meetings of the gram sabha, which consisted of the adult population of the village.[82]

While J.P. saw the local *panchayats* as the basic units of decision making in *Sarvodaya*, it is clear that he saw a role for the State until a degree of socio-economic change had been carried out. He wrote:

> The real remedy for the economic and social divisions in the village is (a) to hurry up with the needed economic and social legislation (b) to enforce strictly the existing laws in these regards (c) to intensify the vital neglected work of adult mass education...[83]

The single economic reform most needed, he thought, was "to vest ownership and management of all village lands in the gram sabha—so that each person becomes an equal shareholder." It is clear that J.P. wanted the government to accelerate the implementation of land reform legislation enacted by state legislatures. He believed the *Bhoodan* Movement had helped prepare the way for this "radical agrarian legislation" and now it must be implemented. It would be a step in the right direction but ultimately ownership of land must be vested in the entire village. He also suggested that the *gramdan* system could be extended to metropolitan areas by setting up local self-governments according to the administrative unit or *mohalla*.[84]

In "Swaraj for the People," J.P. took an optimistic view of the *Panchayati Raj* institutions, writing in 1961. He urged the *Sarvodaya* workers to support Panchayati Raj, pursuing efforts to improve the capacity of the villagers to effectively understand and use the institutions in accord with the spirit of *Sarvodaya*. The workers should engage, he said, in *lok-siksan* social education and training), and *lok-sakti* (creation of the necessary competence among the people). This would push the system in the direction of further devolution of power, decentralization and toward full fledged *Sarvodaya*. At this time, the central defect which J.P. saw in the *Panchayati Raj* system was that it didn't go far enough toward dissolving the State.[85]

There was much pessimism and many critics of the system at this time. But J.P. took the position that the new institutions should be given a chance to improve themselves. The critics charged that the pepple were not ready to govern themselves and that traditionally privileged classes would use the institutions to perpetuate their dominance of the poor and powerless. J.P. recognized the relevance of both charges. He knew that the people needed education and encouragement to break out of their isolation and develop a civic orientation. He also realized the potential danger that the institutions could be used by rural elites to shore up their socio-economic dominance. But he pointed out that the British had used the same argument, that is that the people were too backward, ignorant and ill informed to govern themselves to deny India independence. The Nationalists had replied that "Good goverrment can never be a substitute for self government," and the same rule must apply with regard to gram panchayats. Villagers must be educated and enlightened and given the opportunity to acquire experience in self rule, he argued.[86]

In answering the charge that the *Panchayati Raj* institutions would be captured and used by rural elites for their own purposes, J.P. realized that this would indeed happen in some cases. But he pointed out that the remedy for this was social education. Vinoba Bhave's position had been that *gramdan* should first be carried out in the villages before setting up gram panchayats. This would prevent the capture of the institutions by dominant castes and communities.[87]

In 1961, J.P. argued that the *panchayati raj* institutions could help to decentralize the economy and to make India more autonomous in the international arena. India, he thought, would be less dependent upon foreign aid and better able to utilize its own resources.[88]

But later in Communitarian Society and *Panchayati Raj*, J.P. looked at the institutions more critically. He wrote:

> It is time the protagonists of *Panchayati Raj* looked beyond the hackneyed phrases of political and economic decentralisation, fondly hoping that parliamentary democracy plus a large measure of local self-government would perform the trick and usher in the people's democracy of their dreams.[89]

J.P. also realized that many involved in the *Panchayati Raj* movement lacked faith in the concept of local self-government, and that in reality, there had been little real decentralization of power. Further he realized that the political parties had made use of the institutions to build up their power in rural areas, further reinforcing and politicizing the divisions of class, caste, and religious community. J.P. was aware that "far from flowering into a unique kind of people's democracy, *Panchayati Raj* may be developing into a convenient administrative arrangement under which the traditional local bosses, the dominant castes and factions, and the new economic dominants in the villages can maintain and extend their rule."[90]

From early on, in fact, J.P. had seen the basic contradiction in setting up the system of *Panchayati Raj* within the parliamentary system. In *Swaraj* for the People', he called the system a very unhappy mixture of two principles and processes of democracy that like water and oil, will not mix."[91] The parliamentary system would tend to concentrate power at the top, while the aim of the *Panchayati Raj* system was to disperse power.

But while he recognized this contradiction, it can be argued that a similiar contradiction existed in J.P.'s political actions, and in his thinking. On the one hand, he believed and argued that the social revolution and transformation could take place only from below, through a mass movement led by *Sarvodaya* workers, or a peaceful army of volunteers. On the other hand, he was impatient with the State because land reform legislation was not being implemented. After denouncing the role of the State in social reform and sharply criticizing the fundamental tenets of democratic socialism, he suggested that the democratic socialist state might be instrumental in achieving *Sarvodaya*. Immediately after Nehru's death in 1964, he spoke of the *Sarvodaya* movement as "complementary to that of the State whenever the objectives happen to be common," whereas, "in other spheres it functions independently." J.P. also attempted to identify the democratic socialism of Nehru with *Sarvodaya* at this time. Shortly before Nehru died, he had accused Nehru of being the chief road-block to the establishment of socialism in India. He said:

> There may be some people in this country who might think that democratic socialism and Sarvodaya are not only two different kinds of ideologies and ways of life but also two contradictory things. But having been a socialist ... I can say that democratic socialism as understood not only in this country but also in the East cannot be achieved in a day like this without the support of Sarvodaya.[92]

But if democratic socialism and the State are elitist, in the sense described by J.P., one must wonder how *Sarvodaya* could co-exist with it and contribute to its achievement. In the late 1960's the Naxalite Movement spread across India. This movement which originated in the Naxalbari District of West Bengal was led by a group of urban activists who urged small peasants and landless labourers to engage in terroristic activities against big landlords. Naxalites organized small groups to seize land and grain from the landlords, and in some cases to burn their homes and murder the landowners and their families.

J.P. was engaged in *Sarvodaya* work in Bihar during the peak of Naxalite activity. In 1969, when the Naxalites threatened the *Sarvodaya* workers in Muzaffarpur in Bihar, J.P. came to the district to work in the villages. He decided to come to this area, he said, because:

> The mind indicated that the Naxalite threat was an urgent call to demonstrate through positive action how the challenge of violence could be used to speed up the process of non-violent social change and reconstruction that Vinobaji [Bhave] had initiated through his *Gramdan Gram Swaraj* movement.[93]

A large proportion of the population of this area consisted of landless labourers who lived in extreme poverty under the dominance of landowning families. Amid this inequality, the poor lived in "utter poverty, misery, exploitation, backwardnes stagnation, frustration and loss of hope."[94]

While J.P. did not support the outbreak of violence, he could not unreservedly support the government authorities in the suppression of the outbreaks. He explained the violence was due mainly to the intolerable socio-economic conditions of the labourers. He criticized the government for neglecting their impossible condition and failing to implement social legislation which the state legislature had enacted. Laws in existence provided for home-steads, better share-cropping terms, ceilings on land holdings, minimum wages and regulation of money lending.

But, in fact, the workers often remained bonded labourers, under the semi-feudal relations of production. Concerning the violence, J.P. said:

> [I]t never would have taken root had not the ground been prepared for it by the persistence of poverty, unemployment, and a myriad of socio- economic injustices ... It is not the so-called Naxalites who have fathered this violence, but those who have persistently defied and debated the reform laws for the past so many years ... The big farmers who cheated the ceiling law, .. the gentlemen, ... who grabbed government lands and village commons; the land owners who persistently denied the legal rights of their sharecroppers and evicted them from their holdings or those who under-paid their labourers and threw them out from their homestead; the men who by fraud or force took the lands away from the weaker sections; the so-called

> upper caste men who looked down upon their *harijan* brethren and ill treated and socially discriminated against them; the money lenders who charged usurious interest rates and seized the lands of the poor and the weak; the politicians, the administrators and all the others who aided and abeted these wrongs—it is they who are responsible for the accumulated sense of in justice, grievance and hurt among the poor and downtrodden that is now seeking its outlet in violence. . .
> When the institutions and processes of democracy are found to be so woefully lacking, is there any wonder that discontentment, frustration, anger, and want should turn the minds of some towards violence as the only possible savior?[95]

But while the violence was understandable and could largely be explained by socio-economic conditions, J.P. maintained that history had shown that violence could never be the "savior it is promised to be." First, it is evident that political violence can be both revolutionary and reactionary. A violent revolutionary movement might lead to a social revolution, but on the other hand, it might produce a reaction and lead to a fascist dictatorship. Secondly, on a Marxian note, he suggested that social and historical conditions must be ripe for revolution to succeed. This might take a century or so, he believed. Moreover, even when a revolution does succeed, "it means no more than the old social order has been torn up and destroyed." A power struggle inevitably ensues and a new social order is established, but not the one "dreamed of by the revolutionaries. Fourth, although revolutions promise to give power to the people, "power is invariably usurped by a handful of the most ruthless among the ... revolutionaries. Nor can it be otherwise when power comes out of the barrel of a gun and the gun is not in the hands of the common people but in the hands of the organized instruments of violence that a successful revolution always throws up ... A violent revolution has always brought forth a dictatorship of some kind.[96]

In contrast to this sequence of events, J.P. said, Gandhi wanted to give the people power alongside the power of the State. "His means were ... service, constructive work and conversion by gentle persuasion, and when the situation required, non-violent non-cooperation or resistance."[97] J.P. conceptualized *Gramdan* in this instance, as an instrument by which the "balance of power" in the community, now in the hands of the propertied elite, would through communitarian ownership be held by all the community.[98]

In changing the attitudes and values of the people, Gramdan would prepare the way for *Sarvodaya*. But while J.P. rejected violence as a viable solution for social inequality, he did suggest that violent action for the purpose of social change, to help relieve the condition of the exploited was preferable to inaction. In "Revolution on The Agenda," he wrote:

> I have every sympathy with the Naxalbari people. They are violent people. But I have every sympathy with them because they are doing something for the poor. There is the limit to the patience of the people.[99]

This position reminds one of Gandhi's conviction that it is better to defend oneself through violence than to be a coward.

In 1970, J.P. criticized those who supported the landlords who adamantly continued to impede the implementation of land reform legislation and who illegally occupied government expropriated land.

It appears to me that what the Communists and the Socialists are doing ... is an attempt to rectify a great wrong by people's action which too, as long as it is open and peaceful and conducted in the right manner, is a part of the democratic way of life. Thus looked at, the parties' land movement may be also considered to be so much assistance rendered to the government retrieving property and dispersing justice to those who have been wronged ... The Government must back the squatters, put pressure on the landlords and persuade them to relinquish what does not rightfully belong to them ...[100]

J.P. thought that such takeover of land, rightfully belonging to the peasants and landless labourers, might mushroom into the mass movement needed to ensure social justice. Land seized peacefully, he suggested, could be distributed by the gram sabha, to the landless. He asked party leaders to reason with the landlords and persuade them to give up their claim to the lands. If this attempt at persuasion failed, then Satyagraha could be launched.[101] There was a sense of urgency and impatience in J.P.'s appeal.

> I say with a due sense of responsibility that if convinced that there is no deliverence for the people through non-violence, Jayaprakash Narayan will also take to violence. If the problems of the people cannot be solved democratically, I will also take to violence.[102]

But J.P. remained convinced that violence was "only half of the revolution," at best. He saw the participatory democracy of the gram sabha, in which communities would be rebuilt as self-governing, mutually cooperative, self-reliant bodies as the only real solution for genuine and lasting social reform in rural India.[103] And only in this way, he felt, could the community be brought together in unity, rather than being torn apart by factionalism.

Nevertheless, by 1970 many workers in the *Sarvodaya* movement, including J.P., felt that the opportunity for peaceful social change, in India was slipping away. Even in 1965, a majority of leaders in the *Sarvodaya* movement were dissatisfied with the strategy of the movement and desired more militancy.[104] They were also acutely aware of the fact that most of the Gramdan declarations remained on paper only. They were impatient to see the movement proceed into the second stage of pushti and begin the actual distribution of land to the landless.[105]

There were other factors which contributed to demoralization in the Sarvodaya movement. After the food crisis in the mid 1960's, the Indian Government greatly increased outlays in planning budgets for agricultural development. But the vision of a "socialist" pattern of development was largely abandoned. Emphasis was put upon the capitalization of agriculture through private rather than cooperative enterprise. Although agricultural cooperatives were established through which to channel inputs, production was to remain as private enterprise.

With increased inputs from the Government for capitalization of agricultural production, the *panchayati* institutions were increasingly dominated by new rural elites. In this way, these elites were able to work through these institutions to funnel government inputs into their own hands. Further, the *Panchayati raj* institutions became politicized, and were utilized by rural elites to gain political influence at the state and national levels. Ministers often began their political careers in these institutions.

Such a pattern of development was the very antithesis of that envisioned by Gandhi, J.P. and the other *Sarvodaya* workers. While development did occur in Green Revolution areas, the poor and landless labourers benefited much less than the landed elites. Further, politicization of the rural elites made control of food prices difficult for the Government. In the early 1970's increasing food prices led to widespread unrest in the urban areas of North India. With increasing unrest, the Central Government became more authoritarian. The protest movements in Gujarat and Bihar in 1974 and 1975, led J.P. to launch his campaign for Total Revolution.

Total Revolution

In 1974, J.P. called for a Total Revolution in India. Joining student activists in Gujarat, he challenged the policies of the Central Government, calling for an end to corruption and favoritism. This phase of his activity was, in some respects, a departure from his *Sarvodaya* activity of the past twenty years. The movement in which he participated was instrumental in uniting the forces which challenged the Ruling Congress Party in 1977 in the form of the Janata Party.

J.P. who had devoted the last two decades to constructive work in the villages of Bihar, now joined urban student activists in Ahmedabad. The movement drew upon the tradition of student activism in the subcontinent, dating to pre-independence days. Starting as a relatively minor protest on college campuses, the movement became widespread throughout urban areas of the state as government corruption and inflated food prices were targets for protest. J.P. supported the students and the urban poor, and used the movement to launch a national campaign for the reform of politics.

It is clear that by the 1970's, J.P. had come to the conclusion that the Gram Swaraj movement had largely failed. The enthusiasm of earlier years had dissipated and the imagination of the people, he felt, must be captured by a new dynamic concept. Thus, his vision for total revolution evolved. The programme of action which he conceived in 1974 was less visionary than Gandhi's vision of *Ram Raj* had been. He moved back toward organizational politics urging the people to establish a viable opposition party to balance the power of the Ruling Congress Party. J.P. and others involved in the movement sensed the mood of frustration in the country. They believed the time was ripe for action. They saw the politicians as corrupt and out of touch with the people. J.P. hoped to compel the Government to reform itself through launching mass Satyagraha. At the same time, he believed the people could help themselves by constructive programmes and through people's committees for direct action. The urban intellectuals and youthful students were given a central role in the movement to utilize their organisational skills. The work, as envisioned, would include four aspects: struggle, construction, propaganda and organisation.

J.P. had no ready explanation as to why the Gram Swaraj movement had failed in India. He wrote in 1975 that he remained convinced that *Gram Swaraj* was a "viable political organisation" but that it "was not capable of bringing about a systemic political revolution," although "theoretically, there is no reason why it has not ..." He once said, however, that the programme for *Sarvodaya* had been "narrow and doctrinaire." After more than twenty years of work, the movement remained "ineffectual."[106]

He explained that:

> During the *Bhoodan* movement, when hundreds of thousands of landlords donated their land, it might be claimed that a really

> widespread moral force ... was created. Perhaps it was so. But it was short lived and later uncounted doners took back ... what they had given. That moral force was soon dissipated ... and when gramdan came along there was little of that force remaining. Some of the ideas about land and property remained, but not as accepted ideas. Had the latter been the case, those ideas could have become a tremendous force for social change.[107]

By 1975, J.P. felt that the conditions had not been ripe for struggle when the *Bhoodan* workers moved into the villages and came to believe that dissatisfaction with the existing state of affairs must be widespread extending to the urban intelligentsia in order for the social movement to succeed. "It is only when the people generally, including the young and the students and the intelligentsia ... are in a state of disaffection, frustration, disillusionment and are alienated from authority..." he wrote, "that the conditions for a struggle are ripe."[108]

The goals for the "Total Revolution" included the Gandhian concept of inner moral change.

> This is a revolutionary movement. Let there be no mistake about it. Those who think it is not because it is peaceful, show a singular lack of intelligence. Do not think for a moment that the aims of eradicating corruption and unemployment, of bringing down prices and radical changes in the system of education can be achieved without a social, economic, political, moral and cultural revolution.[109]

J.P. pointed out that the social change brought about since independence had failed to adequately deal with the fundamental ills of Indian society. The worst of these, poverty, lack of opportunity, inequality, the dowry system, caste distinction, untouchability, communalism, and lack of social and cultural integration remained.[110] In Bihar, J.P. joined the students in their movement to demand morality in the public sphere. He said, "I saw the students in Gujarat bring about a big political change ... and I knew that this was the way out."[111] He called for the closure of colleges and universities for one year, and asked the students to participate in constructive work for the people. Education officials, he said, should use the year to reform the educational system to make it more relevant to the needs of the country.

Total Revolution was conceived as a "permanent revolution" that would continue to change both "our personal and social lives."[112] The larger question was "how to bring about revolution in every sphere and aspect of society," in a democratic manner and involving people's direct action. Constructive work was necessary, but also he called for widespread "civil disobedience, peaceful resistance, and non-cooperation in a general *Satyagraha*." It is clear that J.P. saw the breakdown of the Congress ministries in Gujarat and Bihar as an historic opportunity to revive the Gandhian methods of struggle while utilizing the energy, idealism and enthusiasm of the restless youth on college campuses. He believed that the change would not occur suddenly, but might be brought about in a decade or two. "The basic systemic changes would happen first and the individual and group adaptions, mostly psychological, later, he said.[113]

In rural areas, emphasis was to be put upon irrigation, medical care, rural education as well as agricultural production and family planning. People's lives should be enriched by the movement and they should become politically conscious. Agro-industrial communities were still seen as the ideal pattern of society. People's committees would be organized which would perform the tasks which the gram sabhas were supposed to perform. These Gram Jana-Sangharsha Samities (Village Committees for People's Struggle) would become *Janata Sarkars* (People's Governments). Led by radical youths, these institutions would bypass the panchayat institutions, and lay the groundwork for *Sarvodaya,* which the panchayats had failed to do. Urban intellectuals involved with the movement would be sent to the country-side to explain the principles of Gandhian socialism to the people. In 1975, J.P. reported considerable success in the workings of these committees. They sought to reach out and involve the most marginalized elements of the population, including the tribals and the agricultural labourers, living in grinding poverty.[114]

He invited political parties to join and to participate in the movement, and the Janata Party, which took office in 1977, evolved out of the movement. Yet, J.P. did not abandon his goal of a partyless society. But he felt that India was not yet ready for partyless democracy, and that at this point people could still work through the party. He maintained that both the Party and the State must be abolished in the future. My objective has not changed. It remains the same as that of socialism or communism—a Stateless society ... Marx envisioned a society in which the State would wither away. Political parties are instruments for the exercise of power. These can be no parties in a Stateless society.[115]

References

1. Jayaprakash Narayan, "A Long Battle," in *A Revolutionary's Quest*, ed. Bimal Prasad (Delhi: Oxford Univ. Press, 1980), p. 372.

2. Jayaprakash Narayan, *Towards Total Revolution* (Bombay: Popular Prakashan, 1978), pp. 273-279.
3. E. F. Schumacher, *Small Is Beautiful* (New York : Harper & Row, 1973), p. 6.
4. *Ibid.*, p. 4.
5. *Ibid.*, p. 9.
6. *Ibid.*, p. 210.
7. Jayaprakash Narayan, "From Socialism to Sarvodaya," in *Revolutionary's Quest*, p. 190.
8. Jayaprakash Narayan, *Socialism, Sarvodaya and Democracy* (New York: Asia Publishing House, 1964), pp. 190-191.
9. Jayaprakash Narayan, "A Plea for Reconstruction of the Indian Polity," in *Revolutionary's Quest*, p. 218.
10. *Ibid.*
11. Jayaprakash Narayan, "My Picture of Socialism," in *Revolutionary's Quest*, p. 19.
12. Jayaprakash Narayan, "The Objectives of the Congress Socialist Party," in *Revolutionary's Quest*, p. 19.
13. Jayaprakash Narayan, Towards A New Society (New Delhi: Congress For Cultural Freedom, 1981, p. 90.
14. *Ibid.*, p. 87.
15. Narayim, "From Socialism to Sarvodaya," in *Revolutionary's Quest*, p. 197.
16. Narayan, *Towards New Society*, pp. 90-91.
17. Narayan, *Socialism, Sarvodaya and Democracy*, p. 184.
18. Narayan, "A Plea for Reconstruction of the Indian Polity," in *Revolutionary's Quest*, p. 215.
19. Narayan, *Socialism, Sarvodaya and Democracy*' p. 185.
20. *Ibid.*
21. Narayan, *Towards a New Society*, pp. 87-88.
22. Jayaprakash Narayan, *Communitarian Society and Panchayati Raj* (Varanasi: Navachetna Prakashan, 1970), p. 122.
23. *Ibid.*, pp. 122-123
24. Narayan, "A Plea for Reconstruction of the Indian Polity," in *Revolutionary's Quest*, pp. 218-219.
25. *Ibid.*, p. 227.
26. *Ibid.*, p. 211.
27. Narayan, "From Socialism to Sarvodaya", in *Revolutionary's Quest*, p. 197.
28. Narayan, "A Plea for Reconstruction of the Indian Polity," in *Revolutionary's Quest*, p. 226.

29. *Ibid.*, pp. 223-225.
30. Narayan, *Communitarian Society*, p. 125.
31. Narayan, *Towards Total Revolution*, pp. 289-290.
32. *Ibid.*, p. 285.
33. Narayan, "From Socialism to Sarvodaya," in *Revolutionary's Quest*, pp. 198-199.
34. Narayan, "A Plea for Reconstruction of the Indian Polity," *in Revolutionary's Quest*, p. 209.
35. *Ibid.*, p. 215.
36. *Ibid.*, p. 216.
37. *Ibid.*
38. Narayan, *Socialism, Sarvodaya and Democracy*, p. 184.
39. *Ibid.*, pp. 185-186.
40. *Ibid.*
41. Raghavan Iyer, 'The Moral and Political Thought of Mahatma Gandhi' (New York Oxford Univ. Press, 1973), p. 252.
42. Narayan, *Towards A New Society*, pp. 163-164.
43. *Ibid.*, pp. 164-167.
44. *Ibid.*, p.168.
45. Narayan, "A Plea for Reconstruction of the Indian Polity," in *Revolutionary's Quest*, p. 212.
46. Narayan, "From Socialism to Sarvodaya," in *Revolutionary's Quest*, p. 991
47. Iyer, p. 47.
48. *Ibid.*
49. *Ibid.*
50. *Ibid.*, p. 71.
51. *Ibid.*, pp. 80, 115-116.
52. *Ibid.*, pp. 162-178.
53. Jayaprakash Narayan, Three Basic Problems of Free India (New York: Asia Publishing House, 1964), pp. 23-24
54. Iyer, p. 225 and Narayan, Three Basic Problems, p. 33.
55. Alan and Wendy Scarfe, *J.P. His Biography* (New Delhi: Orient Longman, 1975), p. 277.
56. *Ibid.*, p. 278.
57. P.D. Tandon, *Vinoba Bhave* (Bombay: Vora and Co. N.D.), pp. 68-69. Also see Scarfe, p. 278.
58. Scarfe, pp. 292-294.
59. Narayan, "From Socialism to Sarvodaya," in *Revolutionary's Quest*, p. 204.

60. *Ibid.*, p. 205.
61. *Ibid.*, pp. 205-206.
62. Jayaprakash Narayan, "Revolution: For Power or for People," in *Revolutionary's Quest*, p. 276.
63. Narayan, *Towards a New Society*, pp . 98--99.
64. Narayan, "A Plea for Reconstruction of the Indian Polity," in *Revolutionary' s Quest*, p . 219.
65. Narayan, "From Socialism to Sarvodaya," in *Revolutionary's Quest*, pp. 200-210.
66. *Ibid.*, p. 201.
67. *Ibid.*
68. *Ibid.*, p . 200.
69. Narayan, "A Plea for Reconstruction of the Indian Polity," in *Revolutionary's Quest*, pp. 220-221.
70. Narayan, "From Socialism to Sarvodaya," in *Revolutionary's Quest*, pp. 202-203.
71. Narayan, "A Plea for Reconstruction of the "Indian Polity," in *Revolutionary's Quest*, p. 223.
72. Jaraprakash Narayan, "Face to Face," in *Revolutionary's Quest*, p. 314.
73. *Ibid.*, p. 315.
74. Geoffrey Ostergaard and Melville Currell, *The Gentle Anarchists* (London: Clarendon Press Oxford, 1971), p. 57.
75. Narayan, "A Plea for Reconstruction of the Indian Polity," in *Revolutionary's Quest*, p. 231.
76. *Ibid.*, pp. 236-237.
77. *Ibid.*, p. 241.
78. *Ibid.*, p. 24.
79. *Ibid.*, p. 211.
80. *Ibid.*, p. 212.
81. *Ibid.*
82. Jayaprakash Narayan, "Swaraj for the People," *Revolutionary's Quest*, pp. 249-250.
83. *Ibid.*, pp. 254-256.
84. *Ibid.*
85. *Ibid.*, p. 288.
86. *Ibid.*
87. 0stergaard and Currell, p. 248.
88. Narayan, "Swaraj for the People," in *Revolutionary's Quest*, p. 123.
89. Narayan, *Communitarian Society and Panchayati Raj*, p. 123.
90. Ostergaard and Currell, p. 247.

91. Narayan, "Swaraj for the People," in *Revolutionary's Quest*, p. 263.
92. Narayan, *Towards Total Revolution*, pp. 285-86.
93. Narayan, "Face to Face," in *Revolutionary's* p. 203.
94. *Ibid.*, p. 307.
95. *Ibid.*, pp. 310-311.
96. *Ibid.*
97. *Ibid.*, p. 313.
98. *Ibid.*, p. 307.
99. Jayaprakash Narayan, "Revolution on the Agenda," in *Revolutionary's Quest*, p. 284.
100. Jayaprakash Narayan, "The Land Grabbers," in *Revolutionary's Quest*, pp. 298-299.
101. *Ibid.*, p. 300.
102. Narayan, "Revolutionary on the Agenda," in *Revolutionary's Quest*, p. 285.
103. Narayan, "The Land Grabbers," in *Revolutionary's Quest*, p. 301.
104. Ostergaard and Currell, p. 271.
105. *Ibid.*, p. 262.
106. Jayaprakash Narayan, "Total Revolution: Why and How?" in *Revolutionary's Quest*, p. 362.
107. *Ibid.*, p. 363.
108. *Ibid.*
109. Jayaprakash Narayan, "A Revolutionary Movement," in *Revolutionary's Quest*, p. 338.
110. Narayan, "Total Revolution: Why and How?," in *Revolutionary's Quest*, p. 369
111. Narayan, "A Revolutionary Movement," in *Revolutionary's Quest*, p. 340.
112. Jayaprakash Narayan, "A Long Battle," in *Revolutionary's Quest*, p. 369.
113. Narayan, "Total Revolution: Why and How?," in *Revolutionary's Quest*, p. 362.
114. Narayan, "A Long Battle," in *Revolutionary Quest*, p. 373.
115. Narayan, "A Revolutionary Movement," in *Revolutionary's Quest*, p. 340.

6

J.B. Kripalani on Democratic Socialism

As one of the most prominent leaders of the Indian Nationalist movement, J.B. Kripalani contributed immensely to the development of Indian Socialist thought. As both theorist and activist, Kripalani laboured to guide Indian polity towards the Gandhian pattern of a decentralized and democratic socialist structure. As an independent thinker, he maintained a critical distance from the conventional wisdom that 'development must proceed through large-scale industrialization and centralized planning'. He sharply criticized the pattern of development in both the West and in the USSR and other socialist countries. His embrace of the Gandhian conception of decentralized development and non-violent social change came about only after Kripalani became thoroughly convinced that such a path was the only one that could lead to complete freedom for India—to the pattern of society envisioned by many Indian Nationalists which included spiritual and moral, as well as political and economic freedom. He wrote :

> I am accused in some quarters of being a blind follower of the Mahatma. I wish to assure you that I have tried my best to resist him but found him irresistible. I have questioned him on many occasions, argued with him several times, differed with him most violently, but I must confess that he has always proved right and I wrong.[1]

Similar to M.N. Roy and J.P. Narayan, Kripalani travelled the arduous path from acceptance of a philosophy of political emancipation through terrorism to the embrace of Gandhi's philosophy of non-violence, although the period of his, prodigality was greatly attenuated in relation to the other two theorists. Unlike M.N. Roy and J.P. Narayan, Kripalani's moral and political thought remained firmly grounded in indigenous Indian soil throughout, as he never embraced an alien Western ideology as did the other two theorists. His imagination captured early in life by the compelling ideas of the nationalists, Kripalani felt a sense of revulsion from foreign rule and he became a rebel flirting with the philosophy of terrorism. But beginning in 1917, his work with Mahatma Gandhi, in Champaran in Bihar, in opposition to the injustices of the indigo planters to the peasants, initiated a slow reform in Kripalani's mind. His practice of non-violence, under the leadership of Gandhi, led to his conversion. Consequently, in contrast to M.N. Roy and J.P. Narayan, he arrived at the philosophy of non-violence relatively early in life, while maintaining a critical stance toward each of Gandhi's individual actions and positions on critical issues.

Jiwatram Bhagwandas Kripalani was born in 1888 in Hyderabad in Sind in a middle class family of Hindu *Kshattryas*, a community known locally as the Amils. The Amils or Dewans of Hyderabad were relatively well educated and members of the community enjoyed a virtual monopoly of administrative employment both under the Muslim rulers and also under the British until the early part of the twentieth century. The typical member of the community has been described as "bourgeios, with all the virtues and vices of this class addicted to a petty bureaucratic tradition."[2]

J.B. was the sixth of seven brothers, two of whom embraced Islam. His father was reputed to have been a man of "stern discipline whose irascible temper was dreaded by not only his own children but all children in the neighbourhood."[3] The young Kripalani is said to have had a passion for gambling, which he later said that "he never outgrew, but as he grew older, he discarded the dice and gambled with his life.[4] It is also said that Kripalani disliked book learning, preferring to learn through experience.[5] He was expelled from college twice for his radical views, first from Wilson College in Bombay and later from D.J. Sind College in Karachi.

After earning an M.A. degree, Kripalani worked as a school teacher, but was soon forced to leave by the headmaster of the school because the students became excited by Kripalani's political ideas which were considered dangerous. He then became professor of History at Muzaffarpur College in Bihar. At this point, his political and social thinking had largely been shaped by the political ideology of Tilak and Aurobindo. Several of Kripalani's students later became associated with the terrorist movement in Bengal.[6]

It was during this period that Kripalani first met Gandhi at Santiniketan in 1915, at the Phoenix boys school founded by the social reformer after his return from South Africa. " ... 1 was almost the first ... person, interested in the political life of the country and its freedom, to meet Gandhiji when in the beginning of 1915 he finally came to India,"[7] Kripalani wrote.

> My desire to meet him was due to the knowledge of what he had done for the Indian residents in South Africa by his novel movement of Satyagraha. It was due also to the fact that at that time India was bereft of all dynamic leadership. Political life was at a low ebb. The Congress had ... failed to inspire, enthuse or educate the people. It had become a body without a soul.[8]

During his short stay, Kripalani was profoundly influenced by Gandhi, more by his character than his political ideas, which he initially failed to comprehend. He could not, at this time, appreciate the enormous significance of Gandhi's ideas for the Nationalist Movement. Kripalani later described his experience at Santiniketan:

> I met him everyday for about a week, till he left for Calcutta. But what a week! If it had been merely a week of political talks, it might not have meant much to me. But in this week I was privileged to see his reforming zeal and organizing capacity for work ... What struck me most was the intensity of his character. He appeared to be a man who could, if need be, stand alone, provided he was convinced that the course of action he was following was the right one. He would not be deterred by the favours of friends or the frowns of opponents ...
>
> As for his political views, they appeared to me to be all wrong. He was, as I have said, under the spell of the moderates, as the Indian Liberals were called by their opponents in those days. He had been greatly impressed by the personality of Gokhale ... In spite of Gandhiji's new technique of political action against injustice, his attitude in those days towards the British Government in India was essentially the same as that of the moderates. He did not go so far as some of them and think that British rule in India was a divine dispensation; but he was convinced ... that the sum total of British activities in India was for its benefit and he wanted the Indians to act as good citizens of the empire, whatever their handicaps. This view appeared to me to be justified neither by history nor by contemporary facts. But I was not bothered about Gandhiji's views. What I was concerned about was the man's character. I clearly perceived that he was a man who was serious about his business. He

would see to it that his personal conduct was in keeping with what he kept before others. This had not been so with political leaders in India ... Therefore, in spite of what I thought of his political views and his estimate of public men, I had no hesitation in telling him ... that if he ... thought my services could be of any use, he could count on me ...[9]

The distance between the political thinking of Kripalani and Gandhi in 1915 is again seen in Kripalani's account of his first reading of Gandhi's prospectus for his *Satyagraha Ashram* at Sabarmati in Ahmedabad, a few months later. Kripalani recalled:

The Ashram prospectus made me revise my estimate of Gandhiji. I thought that like the religious reformers of old, he was concerned with saving the souls of a few exceptional individuals rather than reforming the lives of average men and women living in India. His kingdom, like that of the old prophets, was not of this world but of the other. I read this prospectus carefully but could see no light. For instance, it said that if a man used super fluous buttons on his shirt or coat he would be 'stealing.' In married life the couple must live as brother and sister. Though I was not married then, I used more buttons on my shirt and coat than were absolutely necessary. I threw the book in irritation on my table. I thought that if a person was so hopelessly unrealistic, it was no use making any suggestions to him ... Thus I dismissed proved that Gandhiji from my thoughts. But subsequent events proved that he was not one to be so easily dismissed.[10]

When Gandhi began his work among the peasants of Champaran in Bihar in 1917, Kripalani for the first time became involved in working with Gandhi to improve social conditions. Kripalani jeopardized his position at Muzaffarpur College by arranging for Gandhi to stay with a friend in the college compound. Kripalani, who was a warden at the college hostel claimed Gandhi as his guest. The European principal objected to Gandhi's presence and asked Kripalani to make other arrangements for him. It is said that Kripalani later lost his professorship because of his association with Gandhi.[11]

The result of Kripalani's work in the Champaran Campaign was to bring him into direct contact with the villagers and convince him of the worth of Gandhi's approach to social reform. Kripalani noted that the educated had little contact with the masses and knew little about what was happening in the villages.

We, the educated, lived more or less an isolated life. Our world was confined to the cities and to our fraternity of the educated. Our contact with the masses was confined to our servants and

> yet we talked of the poverty of the masses and were anxious to free the country from foreign yoke![12]

While Gandhi and his team of lawyers inquired into the peasant's complaints in Champaran, Kripalani went to work in the nearby villages, being concerned mainly with the education of the villagers and the improvement of hygiene. Kripalani recalled that while Gandhi was aware that he was a follower of Tilak, he never asked him whether he believed in terrorist methods, but took it for granted that he would do nothing to jeopardize the mission to Champaran, "One could not even think of deceiving a leader who had such abundant faith in the goodness of human nature, Kripalani wrote.[13]

During 1917, Kripalani's discussions with Gandhi on the history of India shook his faith in his own competence as a historian and he began to doubt whether his previous interpretation of Indian history was correct. There discussions centered upon the role of violence in history. Kripalani's reconsideration of history, under Gandhi's influence, led him to formulate the concept of a natural and logical historical progression toward greater cooperation and less violence in human society, free, however, of historical necessity, which Kripalani rejected.

In 1917, Kripalani told Gandhi that he believed that independence from British rule could not be attained through non-violence and pointed out that history showed that no people had ever achieved freedom without the use of force. Kripalani found it difficult to appreciate Gandhi's faith in the "goodness of the British." Kripalani recalled that:

> He had also another argument to advance in favour of his theory which he thought was historical. He said India was the most non-violent country in the world. This amused me. The whole of Indian history is a series of wars ... How could I believe that India was more non-violent than other countries? It was in after years when again I thought over what Gandhiji had said that I could understand his point of view. I saw that a superficial view of Indian history would show that India was as much involved in wars as any other country from the times of the *Ramayana* and the *Mahabharata*. But a penetrating study of Indian history, especially of the people, would show that the Indians were less prone to violence than people elsewhere.[14]

Upon leaving Muzaffarpur, Kripalani secured employment as a lecturer at Benaras Hindu University. But in 1920, he left the school, along with a number of his students and founded the Gandhi Ashram for *Khadi* and Village work at Benaras. This Ashram was later moved to Meerut. Kripalani organized workers to carry out Gandhi's constructive programme in the villages, believing that such grass roots efforts were the basic preparation needed for a non-violent struggle for political and economic freedom.[15]

In 1923, Gandhi called upon Kripalani to become the *Acharya* (principal) of the Gujarat Vidyapith, the national college which Gandhi founded at Ahmedabad. He held this post for five years, returning to constructive work in the villages in 1928, with the emphasis upon establishing centers for the production of Khadi or homespun cloth. Kripalani was also involved in the non-cooperation movement in 1930. He wrote:

> I happened to be the director of one of the largest *khadi* and village industries organizations—Gandhi Ashram. As soon as a call for *Satyagraha* was given, we marched off to jail, not caring what happened to our *khadi* and other works. All our production and sale centers were confiscated, along with the goods and funds.[16]

In 1934, Kripalani became Secretary of the Indian National Congress, a position which he held for twelve years.[17] Kripalani was largely responsible for building up the Congress organization during this period of his leadership.

Also in 1934, Kripalani was asked to join the Indian Socialist Party, led by its President, Acharya Narendra Dev and its Secretary, J.P. Narayan, but he stated that he "did not regard himself as an alternative to Gandhi and suggested that the Socialist Party was likely to do more harm than good in India. He remained skeptical of the Socialists' agenda, which he feared would divide the people politically along the lines of class, when unity was of paramount importance, given existing caste and communal divisions. G. Ramachandran commented that Kripalani is at heart a socialist. Nevertheless he dislikes most of the socialists and most of the socialists dislike him. His socialism might be described as *Satyagraha* Socialism. It aims not at controlling capitalism but at destroying it, root and branch, by breaking it up into pieces through ruthless decentralization."[18]

On October 22, 1946, Kripalani was elected President of the Indian National Congress, just after the Interim Government was formed.[19] After independence, Kripalani continued to participate actively in Indian national politics, serving as a member of the Constituent Assembly from 1946 to 1951. In 1951, he left the Congress Party and organized the Krishak Mazdoor Praja Party which merged with the Socialist Party in October 1951 to form the Praja Socialist Party. Kripalani served as the secretary of the PSP until December 1954, resigning his membership in 1960. He was elected to the Lok Sabha or lower house of Parliament, serving from 1957 to 1962 and again from 1963 to 1970. Kripalani died on March 19, 1982 in Ahmedabad. His body was cremated on the banks of the Sabarmati near the Harijan Ashram which he helped found.

Kripalani's independent and sharply critical mind, his skepticism regarding apocalyptic totalistic solutions, his pragmatic approach which recognized the potential in humanity for both, great good and great evil and his mistrust of a foreign model or solution as the basis for future Indian society enabled him to develop an extensive critique of Western Parliamentary Democracy, Socialism and Communism and the orthodox pattern of centralized development inherent in each of these ideologies. Kripalani rejected the fundamental tenets of Marxism, questioning their validity both, from a universalistic perspective and in terms of existing social and economic conditions in India.

As a political thinker, Kripalani was more systematic and less eratic than either M.N. Roy or J.P. Narayan, and he placed greater emphasis upon pragmatic and gradual social reform, rather than upon apocalyptic solutions. Refusing to be swept off his feet by any foreign doctrines, his initial rejection of totalistic formulations resulted from an instinctive skepticism rather than a systematic analysis of the fundamental tenets of Marxism and Communism which was to come later. There was in Kripalani a certain Burkean mistrust of sweeping social movements which threatened to destroy at its roots the social fabric of society. All genuine revolution, he argued," was an evolutionary rather than an apocalyptic process. The quantum leap made by societies in a revolution, he believed, was simply the end result of a long period of preparation, during which change accurred subtly beneath the surface. The utmost a violent revolution, in itself, might accomplish, he argued, was to remove the hindrances to the evolutionary processes of history created by the reactionary holders of power.[20]

Consequently, Kripalani argued that the most radical and effective social change was that which was pragmatic and reformist. Revolution, rather than sweeping away ancient moral and ethical principles, was that which rediscovered such truths beneath the decrepit institutions of society, and restored them to their proper place as the basis of social polity. Social action embodying the least amount of violence resulted in the greatest change in the shortest time.

It is clear that Kripalani's conviction that genuine revolution came about non-violently was derived from his actual experiences. In 1969 he wrote:

> It has been my experience, living and working with Gandhiji, that what he achieved by his satyagraha appearead at the time to be small but the rest was subsequently accompliseed through the combination of various circumstances. These generally favoured greater justice between man and man and group and group. It is true that if the first small step had not been taken by Gandhiji, the other forces that brought about the final result might have remained dormant for a long time.[21]

Although Kripalani, like Gandhi, saw non-violent social change as the ideal, he was not given to despair when the actual practice fell short of this goal. He laboured to build the organisations for the political mobilization of the Indian people, while acutely aware of the dangers and pitfalls of the institutionalization of ideas. He was aware of degrees of truth and perceived that actual practice would always involve a degree of violence. But violence, he thought, must be minimized because the result of violence in society would be an accumulation of the *karma* of violence, which must inevitably harm society in the future.

Kripalani's moderate approach to social reform enabled him to acknowledge the State and the Party as imperfect institutions, but he was unwilling to renounce them as did M.N. Roy and J.P. Narayan. Consequently, he was less critical of the State and the Party in general and of the liberal democratic regime in particular.

The remainder of this chapter will explore Kripalani's philosophy of Socialism and the State, his philosophy of history and his critique of the Marxist concept of "class struggle." Kripalani believed that the natural and logical progression of a democratic pattern of society was toward democratic socialism.[22] The real meaning of democracy," Kripalani wrote, "is that people can bring about a revolution as often as 'they desire, without creating confusion or civil strife."[23] A just society must be built upon an ethical foundation and the fundamental principle was the practice of non-violence. This necessarily entailed a decentralized pattern of institutions and of production. Kripalani rejected historical materialism, arguing that it was impossible to formulate scientific laws which would describe historical movement and believing that the driving force of history was never class struggle, arising from objective economic conditions, but rather psychological and ideological factors.[24] He noted that history is sometimes profoundly changed because of the life of a lone visionary who rediscovers ancient ideas and is totally dedicated to the reform of society. Leadership may play an important role. "In history," he once wrote, "all reforms have been made possible through the efforts of gifted individuals and advanced minorities."[25] It is not the masses which rediscover these ideas and often the reformer must resist the passions and prejudices of the majority. He must walk alone. History, although a progression, is at best a "zig-zag" or ascending spiral. Kripalani denied the existence of class struggle in history, but argued that if such a phenomenon ever existed the result would be historical regress, rather than progress, as Marx supposed, because the concept necessarily embodies the practice of violence. In such a society humanity would remain alienated from its ultimate goal of true freedom, which, rather like M.N. Roy and J.P. Narayan, Kripalani defined in spiritual terms:

> Bread may be a substitute for liberty when people are starving, but the ultimate aspiration of humanity will always be for freedom and more freedom. That is also a man's spiritual requirement. That is what is prescribed as the individual's goal in Hindu Philosophy—*Moksha*—freedom from all limiting impediments and imperfections.[26]

Socialism and the State

The fundamental dilemma facing modern society, Kripalani believed, "was the concentration of power in the State apparatus. The State, for Kripalani, is not an abstraction. It is a concrete entity and as such is managed by individuals who exercise its power."[27] This collectivization of power is, in turn, bound up with the centralized economic structure of contemporary society and has critical implications for the cultural and moral values of the society. "Centralisation in economic life must of necessity bring about greater concentration of power in the State, to the detriment of democracy,"[28] he wrote. And, "any concentration of power in the State would not only adversely affect the fundamental rights of the individual but would also be inimical to cultural and moral values." Only "democracy puts the necessary controls on the power of those with whom lies the management of the State."[29]

This perspective regarding the State and society was the foundation for Kripalani's critique of Communism, Western Democratic Socialism, and Capitalism, each of which he found defective in terms of its capacity for achieving not only material equality but also the moral autonomy of the individual. In order for democracy to function and moral values to remain strong, there must be a "devolution of political power." This can best be accomplished, according to Kripalani, not by, "dispensing with the central authority of the State" but rather by establishing a "balance between decentralization and centralization" in both politics and economics so that "the strength of the center" is "built on the strength of its local units and not at their expense."[30] Such a balance must be maintained if local units are to retain their autonomy and take the initiative for self-government. Likewise, industry must not be fully centralized but also dispersed and under the control of local authorities.[31]

Each of the presently existing politico-economic systems, Kripalani thought, shared characteristics inimical to the political, economic and spiritual freedom of the individual, although his critique of existing Communism was the most severe. First, each of these systems displayed overcentralization, both politically and economically. Such a structural arrangement made machines the masters of men and was impotent in solving the basic problems of unemployment and distribution of material needs to the masses. Secondly, each of these systems appeared as an institutional and material device for achieving economic equality, as they had all transformed the moral and spiritual principles underlying them into such an apparatus, while, in practice, undermining moral and spiritual freedom. Thirdly, they gave rise to a "theory of justification by success."

Communism creates "a crushing centralisation" from which "there can be no escape for the mere individual."[32] The individual is a mere "ensemble of social relations." Springing from violent revolution, such a system is built on a "psychology of fear." Rapid industrialization and mechanization typically leads to great suffering of the people, exploitation, poverty and misery of the masses for a number of generations. Western Democratic Socialism is superior to Communism in advocating a greater decentralization of political power, but typically, theorists fail to realize the necessity of parallel decentralization in economic life.[33] Western Liberal Democracy, Kripalani thought, had, as its logical and natural end, a superior form of democratic socialism, based on the central principle of individual moral and spiritual freedom. But historically, this evolutionary process was derailed by capitalism and imperialism, which destroyed political equality before it was fully realized, by creating great economic inequality.[34]

The notion of "democratic centralism" in Communism, Kripalani observed, is a myth. "... [M]ore of centralism means less of democracy. Centralisation and democracy are realy contradictions in terms.[35] And in the absence of democracy based upon the moral integrity of the individual, the power of the State increases :

> Marxism assured us that the State would automatically fade away ... The idea of the State fading away is simply the extension of the individualist and liberal theory that the State is best which rules the least. The fading away of the State can be accomplished only in favour of the culturally and morally self-regulated

> individual. For Communism which does not believe in the individual but the group, such a consumation can be neither desirable nor possible. The State instead of fading away will become increasingly powerful and all pervasive.[36]

For Kripalani, Communism was clearly regressive in terms of historical progress.[37] Whilst the eighteenth and nineteenth centuries led to the "emancipation of the individual" from the joint family, the caste and the guild, Communism appeared "to reintroduce in a new and more rigid form the old handicaps." The "State assumes the duties of the parent, the family, and the social, industrial, political, cultural and spiritual group."[38] Structurally, society is so bureaucratically complex that the ordinary citizen must leave things to the "experts," the bureaucrats and the politicians, while "individual genius" is discouraged.

Communism, Kripalani charged, struck at the very root the basic principle of democracy.

> Theoretically, democracy is based upon the recognition of the individual as a free, moral and spiritual entity. Communistic philosophy, however, does not believe in the free moral individual. According to it, the individual is only 'an ensemble of social relations ... Such a view deprives man of his moral dignity as an individual. To compensate him for this loss, he is guaranteed economic competence ... He is as much of a cell in the State as under fascism and nazism. Such a position, assigned to the individual, cuts at the very root of democracy. Practically, the individual slaughtered at the alter of Communism can never be resurrected.[39]

Another crucial objection to Communism is bound up with Kripalani's philosophy of history, which will be discussed in more detail in the next section of this chapter. This involves the concept of historical *karma*. Kripalani believed that the authoritarian nature of existing Communist .. societies was an inevitable consequence of the very nature of the revolution which produced them. Since these revolutions were based on violence, the *karma* resulting from this violence must adversely affect the future evolution of society. Those in power are gripped by a "psychology of fear." Since they came to power through terrorist methods, they fear that they will be overthrown by terrorist methods. So they must scramble to make their regime powerful, while continuing to rely upon terrorist methods of suppression through a secret police apparatus. The military arm of the state apparatus must be strengthened, which in turn requires the development and centralization of heavy industry. Consumer industries, in relation to heavy industries, are largely neglected. In a backward country, such rapid centralization can only be accomplished under a political dictatorship. Consequently, political and economic centralization and suspicion and repression of the individual are the end result of a chain reaction stemming from the use of violence. The principles of the revolution are inverted and the precious goal of a free society crumbles under a new reign of tyranny.[40]

Kripalani's critique of large scale and centralized industrialization applies to both "private capitalism and state capitalism." He wrote:

> No student of modern history can deny the fact that both these types of industrialization ... have resulted in the exploitation, poverty and misery of the masses, not for one or two generations but for several generations ... ln the wake of capitalist industry, [there was] poverty and exploitation of the masses in the home country and slavery in colonial lands ... The rivalries of capitalist countries in search of colonies, to get raw materials and dump their finished products, led to imperialism. The rivalries of the imperialist nations of the West ultimately led to the last two global wars. [41]

Kripalani listed four general characteristics of large industries: a large investment per unit of production, ever diminishing human labour, purchasing power of the producers lagging behind production and the rapid utilization of natural resources. The capitalization of heavy and centralized industry, it was pointed out, requires enormous sacrifices by the masses, regardless of the form which capitalism assumes. Centralized industrialization cannot occur under conditions of equitable social welfare.

> If the labourers get fair wages and other social benefits they are entitled to and if the agriculturalists get a fair price for their produce, there will be little left for capital formation to serve the needs of rapid industrialization ... The real sacrifices, to build up capitalist industry and increase production in the future, were made by the toiling millions in the field and factory in many lands and not by the so-called captains of industry.[42]

Kripalani agreed with Keynes that in the West the "immense accumulations of capital built up in the half century prior to WWI" could not have accurred in a society were wealth was equally distributed.[43]

The improved condition of the masses in capitalist countries was brought about by exploitation of colonial areas, a long struggle waged by the trade union movement which again involved sacrifices and suffering, and the increased political influence of labour in the West, Kripalani said.

In the Communist countries, particularly the USSR, Kripalani pointed out that industrialization was achieved in record time only by establishing a political dictatorship.[44] He saw Communists as cynical, for the most part, in their attitude toward the masses. Although the Soviets fully realized that the masses must suffer to build the "classless society" built upon heavy industry, and were prepared to liquidate large numbers of resisting peasants, they justify their actions in terms of their final goal. Meanwhile, they "deceive the people into thinking that they can both enjoy increased consumption while building up large industries."[45]

Kripalani concluded that:

> Communism ... whatever its economic merits is distinctly a political, cultural and spiritual regress for humanity. It solves the economic problem by extracting a heavy price ... Economic equality must not be purchased at the price of political and spiritual slavery. There must be an amount of free activity in every sphere of life. This can best be guaranteed under an economic system of decentralised industry which affords free play to the choice and initiative of individuals and groups under the minimum necessary controls.[46]

Another fundamental defect underlying Socialism and Communism, in practice, according to Kripalani, is that followers have "turned the moral and spiritual principle underlying socialism into an institutional and material device for achieving economic equality."[47] This development was seen by Kripalani as the result of the theory of dialectical materialism, which views correct action in history as "scientific" rather than that which is grounded in moral will and values. A new "morality" arises. "Whatever means changing times and circumstances dictate are moral means. Morality, therefore is an ever changing device for the achievement of success."[48]

For Kripalani, justification by success is insufficient. unless action in history is based upon moral principles, the result of human action may miscarry, regardless of intent.

> If results are to be the measure of human conduct, and if theory is to be adjusted to convenient practice and the latter is to justify the former, it would require divine power and perfection to act correctly and justly ... The fact is that human reason is neither perfect nor omniscient. Nor again is human power the deciding factor in world affairs. Human beings can but see a section of the truth at a particular time. Their light must be illumined by some higher values and principles ... The theory of justification

> by success takes for granted that the results are in human hands and that particular results flow from particular causes without fail. Both propositions are not quite true Human beings can at most initiate action.[49]

In contrast to Communist and newly developing countries, the process of industrialization in the West was "unconscious," Kripalani explained.[50] The principles of liberal democracy arising from the eighteenth and nineteenth centuries provided for the preservation of the moral autonomy of the individual. The germ of this idea could be traced to the stoics who "held that there were certain moral principles inherent in human nature," which "should be followed by all human beings."[51] Capitalism, however, "failed to recognize that concentration of power in the State would adversely affect the rights of the individual in society."[52] The logical end toward which liberal democracy was moving, Kripalani thought, was democratic socialism, but capitalism, a necessarily centralized system and its extension, imperialism, cut short this development. The "plenty" of capitalism is "illusive" because wealth is ill distributed, there is much waste, foodstuffs must be destroyed to manipulate prices, vast populations remain unemployed and the purchasing power of the producers does not keep pace with the production of goods.[53]

In the Western world, then:

> The democratic vote had no value in an economically maladjusted society. Capitalist production divided society between the few haves and have nots. The equality that was scarcely achieved in politics was soon lost by the back door of economic inequality. Capitalism also created the modern empire. Thus the democratic idea instead of expanding itself in the economic and the international fields, was narrowed even in the internal political field ... Capitalism and capitalist imperialism have therefore almost completely destroyed political democracy in the Western countries.[54]

The fundamental task, according to Kripalani, was to "rescue the principle of democracy from capitalism and imperialism. It must be combined with social and economic democracy. This is possible only by the establishment of economic socialism. In the international sphere empires must be liquidated if democracy is to prevail all round."[55] The wrong direction taken by social reformers in democratic countries was due to a misguided belief that political democracy gave rise to capitalism.

> If humanity has to advance, the moral principle underlying political democracy must be safe-guarded. Its real enemies are

> within the so-called democratic countries ... Scientific Socialism ... instead of realising that political democracy was being smothered by capitalism and the modern empire, made the former (political democracy) responsible for the latter. In earlier days of Communist propaganda political democracy, which was wrongly confused with chaotic individualism of the capitalist order, was as vehemently and bitterly attacked as capitalism and imperialism.[56]

The perception of democracy as an "external and organizational device" abscured the "fundamental values of oneness, tolerance and love on which it was based," Kripalani said. This allowed capitalism and imperialism to arise undetected. Only when the threat of totalitarian states arises do those, who value democracy, regain sight of the moral principles of democracy. A few, he noted, have realized that this moral principle is inconsistent with economic capitalism and politico-economic imperialism. The logic of such a position is so apparent that the British politicians deny the very, existence of the Empire, without in the least, relinquishing their hold on it."[57]

The fundamental question, then, is how to establish a pattern of industry in society which would avoid the misery, suffering and waste of capitalism while preserving political and individual liberty; a pattern that will provide immediate employment and equitable distribution of material goods while preserving democratic liberties and social values.[58] The answer, for Kripalani, was to be found in Gandhi's conception of cottage industry. He argued that the establishment of cottage industry, embodying both economic socialism and political democracy would go far toward eliminating the causes of imperialism and war. Kripalani agreed with the Marxists that modern empires had been made possible by centralized industry, although there were causes other than economic, he thought. Cottage industry, on the other hand, would need no foreign markets and production would be "automatically adjusted to internal consumption and if need be to mutually beneficial trade."[59]

Kripalani also argued that cottage industry would go far toward preventing dictatorial rule and militarism with its inordinate waste of national wealth.

> After all, the boss in the factory is the prototype of the dictator in the State. Those who have been habituated ... to work under a petty dictator in the industrial field are not the likely ones to protest against dictatorship in the State. What is dictatorship but overcentralisation in government? The proletariat used to socialised and centralised industry, even when it creates a

> revolution, can think only in terms of Communism and not of democracy.[60]

Consequently, the proletariat stripped of individuality and accustomed to regimentation will yield to a dictatorship. On the other hand, with the existence of an independent class in industry and agriculture, political democracy would be combined with economic socialism.[61]

Kripalani also explored the nexus between centralized industry and armaments. Modern industry, he observed, made possible both, the necessary organization and the weapons for modern warfare, whereas cottage industry would "check the manufacture of deadly weapons and machines."[62] While war might not end, its "destructiveness and cruelty" would diminish and as a result also "ill will and hate" would also decrease.[63] Kripalani also argued against the buildup of arms in India in a strongly pragmatic vein. Since India could not succeed in competing with big industrial nations, such a policy would be wasteful, inflicting enormous suffering on the people. A stronger defense, he believed, could be built on the "unity of purpose" of the people and their willingness to sacrifice, to eliminate poverty, and improve the overall quality of life. He also argued that a nation that achieved independence non-violently should not have to rely upon arms to retain national independence. He supported Vinoba Bhave's suggestion that India disband one-half of its armed forces.[64] Finally,

> The soundness of non-violent methods as more economic is ... self-evident. All the wealth that is blown away in war, if utilised for increased production and more equitable distribution, would banish poverty from the world.[65]

Cottage industry, Kripalani believed, provided the soundest basis for democratic socialism in India. First, the principles of cooperation and non-violence would finally extend democracy to the economic realm. "The purpose fulfilled by socialism in the economic field is the same as that of democracy in the political field," he said.[66] Secondly, it would embody spiritual and cultural values. Thirdly, it would eliminate the extraction of surplus value from the worker, a major vehicle for the exploitation of the masses. Fourthly, rather that eliminate mechanization, which Gandhi considered amoral, it would eliminate the underlying evil, the accumulation of capital through centralized private and state owned industries. Fifthly, it would represent the proper use of science and technology, in harmony with moral values, and as such be revolutionary. Sixthly, it could eliminate the worst physical and psychological ills associated with the tedious division of labour in large industries. Consequently, work could once again become pleasurable, embodying art and creativity, closer to the utopian and Marxian ideal of work as a free creative activity. Seventhly, it would inculcate into the worker the independence and self reliance required for a functioning democracy, rather than breeding habits of mass psychology and the herd instinct. Eighthly, it would embody the principle of voluntary limitation of wants, integral to self-discipline, creativity and mastery of the self. Finally, from the economic perspective, it would diminish unemployment, increase the national production, increase the purchasing power of the poor and boost the collective wealth of the nation.[67]

At the root of Socialism, for Kripalani, lay the principle of economic equality. This assertion of equality in the economic field is also an assertion of the "dignity of man," and "the externalization of the principle of human oneness and solidarity."[68] The spirit of non-violence and cooperation, he believed, would greatly increase human solidarity. "Narrowness and fanaticism," he wrote, "are not caused so much by the lack of communications and contact as by the lack of ... cooperation ... The barriers separating man from man and nation from nation are more psychic and moral than physical. So far as they are based upon greed, exploitation and material inequalities they will be greatly diminished with decentralised industry."[69]

Considering that the essence of Socialism consists in the theory of surplus value, which takes the form of profit, rent and interest, khadi industries, Kripalani pointed out, must be considered socialistic. (Kripalani, however did not fully agree with the Marxian formulation of the theory of surplus value.) The instruments of production (the spinning wheel and loom) are directly owned by the producers.[70] The producer also owns the product of his labour and thus avoids the exploitation inherent in both private and state capitalism.[71] Since village industry leaves no surplus for an employer of labour, it embodies the essence of Socialism.[72]

Kripalani was anxious to dispel the misconception held by some that cottage industry could not make use of improved technology to ease the toil of production. The underlying evil in large scale mechanization, he argued, following Gandhi, is the accumulation of capital, owned by a small class, rather than mechanization itself. While cumbersome steam power was unsuited to small scale production, electrification would provide mechanical power in small units for efficient village production. With small units, man would remain the master, rather than becoming' enslaved by machinery. In practice, however, Kripalani realized that some centralization was unavoidable.[73]

He disagreed with the Marxists and other critics who argued that cottage industry was "reactionary." Rather, he said, it was revolutionary because it brought "consciousness, purpose and direction" to decentralized industry. It was not based on circumstances of helplessness but on the higher objective of freedom. Through such self-help the real revolution could proceed even before political independence was gained formally.[74]

Another revolutioanry aspect of cottage industry was that it encouraged a proper use of science and technology. Technology, Kripalani pointed out, could be used for both, good and evil. His fundamental concern was that science and technology must be subject to moral restraint.[75] He said that "the best or principle use of science was not to increase material goods and power or for exploitation ..."[76].

> Science, for Kripalani, was primarily a search for Truth.
> Basically science is a ... rational method of searching for truth in all departments of knowledge and life ... All tested and verified knowledge, whether it deals with material nature or the more complex inner nature of man is science. It has a triple aspect. It is first and foremost a method of investigation by observation, experiment, experience and verification. Science also means the basic laws of material and human nature discovered through ... investigation. The last use of science is to obtain power in the external and internal fields by the application of the laws discovered through scientific investigation.[77]

The contemporary confusion, he thought, resulted from the fact that science had become confounded with material results and the acquisition of power. But "one may accept the scientific method of investigation as also the general laws based upon it, without caring for the resultant material advantages if they happen to be inimical to higher life and human happiness."[78] Some of the practical results of science would have to remain unexploited if certain higher moral values were to be preserved. This requirement would not involve a renunciation of material progress, but only the insistence upon the principle that "material advances must subserve higher ends."[79] He suggested, for example, that before atomic energy could be used for constructive purpose's, "war, by common consent, must be outlawed."[80]

In a decentralized society, a blind faith in technology would be checked and the dangerously accelerating appetite for more and more material goods restrained. This would result in the use of science and technology for social and moral purposes :

> Let us not think that science and technology in the absence of social and moral restraints are the *summum bonum* of life ... There can be no moral or spiritual progress without some restraint in the use of material goods, services and comforts ... If for moral and social purposes there is some restraint put upon the expanding use of technology ... humanity need not be the loser in terms of the good life ... If science and technology are reallyto be used to enhance virtue and happiness they, like other instruments of power, will have to be put under proper restraints. This, we believe, can be done by harnessing them to social ends ... through decentralisation of ... industry.[81]

Kripalani's vision of decentralised socialism separated him from Marxist and Socialist theoreticians by a wide gulf. In the mid 1930's he defended Gandhi's ideas concerning *Sarvodaya*, or the social uplift of all, against the Socialist and Marxist camps which at that time included J.P. Narayan and M.N. Roy. He recalled that "I had ... to defend his ideas against the so-called 'scientific' socialists, who held that freedom and socialism could be achieved in India simultaneously! I had to explain to the sceptics the value of the constructive programme and the scientific nature of Gandhiji's new scheme of basic education."[82]

For Kripalani, there was no conflict between Gandhi's aims and those of the Western socialists, and he found the Marxist assault on Gandhi's thought "unjustified." Moreover, he believed that their programme was counterproductive in terms of both national political independence and the broader goal of Swaraj, which included moral and spiritual freedom.[83] Kripalani's critique of the Marxian analysis of Indian society, particularly in relation to the concept of class struggle, will be examined more fully below.

As a belief in spiritual and moral values was an integral part of Kripalani's concept of socialism, he took issue with the Marxists who insisted that one must believe in philosophical materialism to be a "scientific socialist." Kripalani viewed "materialism" as merely a hypothesis which arose in earlier ages to assist physical scientists in the laboratory. As such, it was not "confused ...with the moral teachings of their religion, or their faith in spiritual experience."[84] But Marxists made it a pillar of their "scientific" analysis of society. If one rejected the materialist dogma, "he could only be a "utopian' socialist which, with Marxists, meant that he did not understand the working of society and the way of changing it through revolution..."[85] For Kripalani, such a view demonstrated a misunderstanding of the essence of democratic socialism.

Kripalani again viewed the Socialist and Marxist doctrines as flawed in their approach to industrialization. There was a contradiction, he pointed out, between the socialist attack on modern governments that are run "directly or indirectly by big business in the interests of capital" and the prevailing concept of "socialist" development in unindustrialized countries. In fact, 'Kripalani wrote, "There is no other way known to history, apart from oligarchical concentration of power, for the industrialization of an agricultural country."[86] The obvious alternative for Kripalani was a pattern of development through *swadeshi* or cottage and village industries. But for the Marxists, such a programme was "reactionary."

> The Marxists believed in big, centralised and mechanised industry. They believed in it both for economic reasons and for the political reason of capture of power in the State. They held that the industrial proletariat was the vanguard of the revolution and that the agricultural proletariat was reactionary or at best stood for the status quo. The only way to create a revolution on the Western pattern was through the establishment of centralised and mechanised big industry which could create an industrial proletariat.[87]

Kripalani believed that the Marxist programme for revolution had little relevance to Indian society and existing economic conditions. The establishment of cottage industry, on the other hand, could make use of available resources to relieve poverty immediately. Moreover, the masses understood the ideas and the language of the constructive programme better than the "alien Communist jargon." Social uplift must be pragmatic and proceed one step at a time, insuring that means are in harmony with the ends.

After independence, Kripalani warned Indian planners that unless a decentralized pattern of democratic socialism was achieved, India would accumulate the same problems of institutionalized violence seen both in the capitalist West and in the Communist and Socialist sphere.

> "... [I]t is thus that we can escape the dichotomy of capitalism and State capitalism ... lf we follow ... nationalising and bureaucratising industry we shall only be producing State capitalism which would pave the way to a totalitarian State and dictatorship," he wrote.[88]

Philosophy of History

J.B. Kripalani's philosophy of history was based both on empirical observation and theoretical considerations. His close contact with

Mahatma Gandhi, beginning in 1915, led him to reconsider his view of history, particularly the role of violence in history. While in his youth he had viewed violence as a vehicle for progressive change in history, his reevaluation of history led him to view the role of violence in history as regressive. Secondly, his leadership role in the Indian Nationalist movement required that he defend Gandhi's philosophy of non-violence against the view of history put forward by the Socialists and Marxists in the movement. Consequently, Kripalani developed a critique of the Marxist view of history . . Thirdly, Kripalani formulated his own independent view of history which, for the most part was based upon Gandhian principles, but also upon his own independent observation and thought.

This section will explore Kripalani's view of history, first considering his approach to the methodological problems of social science. Secondly, Kripalani's view of the Marxist approach to history and his criticisms of this school of thought will be delineated. Finally, Kripalani's own view of history will be explained.

From a methodological perspective, Kripalani observed, there are certain essential differences between physical science and the social sciences:

> The difference lies in the fact that while physical sciences deal with material objects, social sciences deal with the conduct of men and women and their groupings. While the former (material objects) are more or less static and non-self-regulative, the latter are dynamic and self-regulative. They have consciousness, feelings, intelligence and will; material objects have none of these. The difference between human individuals and their various aggregates, is not merely quantitative, capable of exact measurement as in the physical sciences, but also qualitative, and not subject to exact measurement. Moreover, human conduct is guided and influenced by certain standards and values. These are not subject to measurement. One value cannot be translated in quantitative terms of another value. What quantity of material goods or objects will produce the true and the beautiful cannot be scientifically calculated.[89]

Another serious methodological problem arises from the fact that social phenomena are always in a flux. Consequently, the possibility of repeating an experiment is severely limited. Moreover, it is more difficult for the investigator of social phenomena to be as neutral as the physical scientist.[90]

The methodological problems of the social scientist are further compounded by the confounding of a host of inseperable variables, many of which are elusive in terms of measurement. But the temptation to simplify the problem by undue reduction would, at the same time, defeat his purpose.

> [D]ifferent social activities, such as economic, social, political, ethical, aesthetical and even religious ... are all organically interconnected. They act and react upon each other affecting and modifying and even cancelling the effects of each other ... Social sciences have often to deal with men's immemorial beliefs, customs, conventions, manners and even their superstitions and, illusions. All these defy scientific weighing and measurement; nor would it be possible to obliterate all differences and distinctions between various aspects of human life and reduce them to a unitary cause, whether physical, biological, economic, political, moral or religious, which would explain in its terms all change and evolution. That would be a kind of material mysticism, seeking for a formal cause which would explain everything.[91]

As a result of these insurmountable methodological difficulties, it must be acknowledged by social scientists, Kripalani argued, that "fixed and inexhorable laws" which "must work themselves out by logical and historical necessity," can never be established in the social sciences.[92] The best that social science investigation can establish is "certain tendencies." These tendencies "can be modified and even annuled ... for long stretches of time, by other tendencies working in the same field or in ... interrelated fields of human activity. They may be altered by human ingenuity, wisdom and will.."[93] Consequently, it would constitute a fatal flaw in the social scientist to be "positively certain, dogmatic or fanatical" in seeking to establish fixed laws concerning the movement of history and social change.

In his, critique of the Marxist view of history, Kripalani exposed its inadequacy to explain historical movements and social change, both in universalistic terms and in terms of conditions in the Indian subcontinent. Class struggle, a central concept of Marxism, he believed, was valid neither in terms of universal application nor to conditions in India. Kripalani's critique of the concept of class struggle as it relates to universal history, will be discussed in this section.

A frequent error of the Marxist analyst, Kripalani pointed out, was the application of basic assumptions of Marxism without adequate knowledg e of local conditions to determine if they actually apply.[94] In the same way, concepts of Marxism such as "class struggle" were seen to be universally applicable to revolutionary social change in history.

Kripalani listed nine basic assumptions in Marxist thought from which arose the theory of class struggle. First, it was assumed that "sociology and even history are exact sciences, with their Laws as inexorable as those of the physical sciences. Secondly, it was assumed that "the primary moving force in history and society was economic." Thirdly, it was claimed that "human history so far has been the play of the tragic conflict between two classes, the masters and the slaves, the exploiter and the exploited ... In the present stage of human history these two classes are the capitalists and the workers." Fourthly, "in some industrial countries in the West the polarisation of these two classes has been achieved." Fifthly, polarization of classes "would mean progressive deterioration of the condition of the mass of workers leading to class war." Sixthly, "in the ensuing struggle the organised strength of the proletariat will be pitched against the wealth of the capitalists. The victory ... will be with the proletariat." Seventhly, to create a new 'social order of a classless society, it will be necessary to establish the dictatorship of the proletariat. Eighthly, "with the establishment and consolidation of a classless society not only the dictatorship but along with it the State will fade away." Finally, "in whatever country the proletarian revolution takes place it will have to be international in its scope. This [is] because the interests of world capital are identical and so are those of the world proletariat."[95]

Kripalani argued that actual history did not support these central assumptions of Marxism. First, "the view that the primary moving force in history and society is economic ... is not historically correct."[96] Further, he said, class struggle rather than being the driving force of history has never existed, "in the Marxian sense if at all," as claimed by the Marxists.[97] In fact, he argued, history and social change was often "governed by custom, convention, fixed belief and superstition." For example, in medieval times, the primary moving force was "either religious or military or a combination of the two. Economics played a subordinate role and that was often modified by religious, political and military considerations." He also pointed out that in medieval India, although "the priestly class did not have economic or political power, it enjoyed great social prestige." In ancient Greece and Rome, on the other hand, the military, political and intellectual classes had a "dominant influence."[98]

Kripalani believed that Marx overgeneralized from one phase of history in one part of the world to a universal view of history. Kripalani acknowledged that with the rise of capitalism in Europe the "economic power of the new industrial and economic classes was the dominant factor in society," coloring also moral and religious practice. Due to this, "Marx concluded that economic power was at the root of all social arrangements..."[99] In fact, Kripalani charged, Marxian historiography was "a successful effort at rationalising a preconceived theory."[100]

To support his thesis that revolts in history were never attributable to economic disparities and class struggle, Kripalani examined several revolutionary movements. He argued that past revolutions were more the result of a conscious tyranny and perceived injustice, and departures from convention rather than class struggle or awareness of economic exploitation.[101] The wealth of classes was not a cause of revolts. Many rebellions occurred because of the corruption of individual rulers or of a ruling class.[102]

> The will of these classes was the law in their respective spheres of activity or jurisdiction. It was this royal, aristocratic, administrative and priestly tyranny and lawlessness that on rare occasions drove the common people into riot, revolt or insurrection. In such riots the property of the privileged classes was often looted and destroyed. But the revolt was against injustice and tyranny of the privileged classes, and not against their economic power.[103]

Kripalani believed that the poor ordinarily blamed their "fate" rather than the rich for their poverty. While the idea of exploitation was "not altogether absent," exploitation was, seen in "moral terms of injustice and cruelty." The poor did not hold the rich responsible for inequalities, Kripalani said, but rather considered such injustice in "the nature of things." Moreover,

> Every artisan was in a sense a capitalist, the owner of the tools and machines, the instruments of production that he used ... As for property rights, ... they were considered sacred by the rich and the poor alike. Society was not based upon contract or cash nexus but on custom and status.[104]

More often, according to Kripalani, what provoked the resentment of the people was "discriminatory laws that assigned indefined privileges to the nobility."[105]

Looking at particular revolts in history, Kripalani argued that in ancient Rome, the plebians revolted against the patricians because they wanted to enjoy the rights of citizenship, not because of the wealth of the patrician class. He said their goal was to secure political power, not a classless society.[106] The revolution in seventeenth century England was fought to "assert the supremacy of Parliament as against that of the King in the matter of taxation," he argued.[107] The Levellers, on the other hand, drew inspiration from the teachings of Christ and not from economic and material forces, in setting out to establish an equalitarian order.[108] In the French Revoution, and the Puritan Revolution in England, "economics played a subordinate part." In the French Revolution the idea of equality was derived from reason. The American Revolution, Kripalani believed, was based on the principles of "Liberty, equality and fraternity."[109] "The English, American and the French Revolutions were basically political, their aim being the establishment of the reign of law, individual liberty and political democracv ... "[110]

Kripalani also denied that the Russian Revolution was brought about by class struggle. He noted that it was directed against the Czar and the war, rather than against the capitalist class. The landlords were forcibly deprived of their lands by the people, but he did not see this as class struggle in the Marxian sense. The Revolution threw up a liberal government under Kerensky, which was overthrown by the Bolshevik "military coup" before things could settle down.[111] "The Government was displaced by a political and military coup and not by any democratic process or due to war between economic classes." Kripalani believed that the "military coup" which overthrew Kerensky could hardly be called "class struggle" and that the political reforms under the Bolsheviks were carried out in the early years through the "personality, determination and will of Lenin."[112]

Kripalani found it significant that none of these revolutions followed a course consistent with Marx's vision of revolution. In Russia, the revolution did not involve a challenge to the capitalist class by a proletariat but rather the polarization of society between the landlords and the tenants. Both the French and Russian Revolutions were rebellions against the aristocracy and both began when "an exasperated mob sprang to action," rather than through "deepening class struggle."[113]

Such considerations led Kripalani to dismiss the Marxian theory of revolution as well as any theory of history which tried to establish social change as a predictable or pre-determined process, as unscientific.

"A revolution arises from so many causes interacting upon each other that to say that it will come necessarily through class war or class conflict is to be unhistorical."[114]

The entire Marxian approach, for Kripalani, is not only wrong but harmful in that one must conclude that it is built on the notion that the end justifies the means. For Marx it is a historical necessity that the proletariat establish its dictatorship. The theory of such a world engulfing revolution is "derived from the labour theory of value, with its two corollaries of surplus value and ever increasing misery of the masses.[115]

According to this formula, then, a revolutionary should logically work to worsen the condition of the proletariat in order to "sharpen the edge of their discontent ... Any action, however adverse to the interests of the masses, would be justified in the interests of the coming revolution ... This would be to carry to its logical and diabolical conclusion the doctrine that the end justifies the means."[116]

Kripalani acknowledged that all movements in history do require sacrifices to bring about the desired end. "Some life will have to be sacrificed so that larger life today or in the future may be conserved ..." But when such sacrifice is raised to a general principle, people come to be seen as "pawns in history" and the "reign of terror" is established.[117]

Finally, Kripalani thought there was no set of circumstances under which a revolution would be an inevitable event. There was, he thought, no such historical necessity. "If there are ... any conditions precedent," he said, "they are psychological and ideological rather than economic."[118] Thus did Kripalani dispense with the Marxian theory of revolution.

Kripalani's own philosophy of history was of far greater complexity than that of Marx. He believed that social change only appeared to be a revolutionary process, but in fact was evolutionary. "Real political, social and economic advance of the masses " he wrote , "has always been brought about by an evolutionary process. An upheaval or revolution can at best take away the hindrances created by reactionary holders of power and allow the evolutionary process to resume its course."[119] He claimed that historical analysis showed that what is known as revolution is "only the last step in an evolutionary process." Further, revolution, he said, "is the law of life in all stages of nature, geological, biological, and socio-political ... Revolutions in all spheres, in all stages of the revolutionary process, beginning from the inorganic, developing into the vegetable, animal and human kingdoms, are always due to a long and laborious evolutionary process which often goes on unobserved."[120]

Kripalani argued that generally historical evolution was in a progressive direction toward democratic socialism. "In all spheres of human life and activity the direction of progressive civilisation has been toward greater honesty, fairness, cooperation and non-violence."[121] The practice of non-violence represented the highest stage of social evolution. Nevertheless, all change is not progressive. Violent action in history can produce periods of stagnation and even retrogression. The path of human history is at best a "zigzag."[122] And sometimes regress may be necessary for progress, he said. For example, an apparently failed movement may establish powerful ideas.[123]

The concept of human progress, for Kripalani, involved both "internal and institutional reform," and for true reform he said both of these must be in balance.

> Human progress throughout history is marked both by internal, and institutional reform. If the inner being is reformed but the appropriate external and organisational machinery through which the spirit is to manifest itself is lacking, there will be loss of balance and consequent reaction. On the other hand if human nature is sought to be reformed merely through external and organisational devices, unregenerative human nature will soon assert itself and upset the balance.[124]

It should be noted that there is a marked similiarity between the concept of human nature as explained by Kripalani in this paragraph and that of J.P. Narayan.

This concept of human progress meant, for Kripalani, that those who organized external social relations must be "informed and guided by moral principles." This was why Plato believed that "kings must become philosophers and philosophers kings."[125]

The institutionalization of truth in history, although seen as necessary, is problematical for Kripalani. This is because to embody truth, institutions must remain flexible since "truth keeps changing in its facets" throughout history. He believed, with Plato, that there is one eternal and absolute truth, the Idea of Truth, but that "the actual form that Truth takes under a particular set of circumstances varies." Further, while a particular set of customs and institutions may embody truth at a particular time in history, they may later "come to lose the original impulse and meaning, and become only empty forms and devoid of the spirit of truth ..." In such a case, an institution can become the "vehicle of evil" rather than the "expression of the good." This is why throughout history progressive change must mean reverting back to the "fountain-head" of truth, and devising new institutions to embody it more perfectly. The problem in modern times, Kripalani believed, had been the tendency to abolish all moral values, rather than those customs and institutions which prevented the proper application of established moral values. And while men have largely succeeded in controlling natural forces, they have become enslaved by "the group forces of caste, class, race and nation" thereby losing will and direction.[126]

The driving forces in history for Kripalani, then are psychological rather than material. "The essence of a revolution", he said, "is the idea behind it."[127] Kripalani's theory of revolution recognizes an array of forces which may contribute to revolution and to human progress. These include human ingenuity, will, personality, charisma, spiritual fervor, moral values, ideas, slogans and the irrational element in man. Revolution may come about because of an idea, for example, the rediscovery of Truth, in a new conception applicable to contemporary conditions. An able leader with a clear vision, will and perhaps a charismatic personality may capture the imagination of the people. Social change may originate with "persons who are not contented with the status quo and want change in some field of life's activity, spiritual, social, political, economic, intellectual, scientific or artistic."[128] "Equality," for example, is only a "mechanical principle," but "its driving force must ... come from a moral and spiritual principle."[129]

Another element of the psychological condition may be a mental restlessness, a widespread feeling that a change for the better is insight. It may be that people become unwilling to bear certain conditions because "their moral values and intellectual outlook have undergone a revolutionary change."[130] There is also an element of irrationality in revolution. "Man has yet to become rational...," Kripalani wrote.[131] In revolution "an enthusiasm or fervor may take possession of humanity." This could be triggered by a dynamic personality or by a slogan such as the "natural rights of man," "liberty, equality and fraternity," and "workers of the world unite." Such mantramic phrases may often be based on half-truths, but nevertheless are powerful catalysts for social change.[132]

Kripalani placed primary importance on the exceptional individual as the moving force behind historical change.

> The new hope and the new gospel are incarnated in a personality ... The idea alone counts. The man with an idea is a desperate person. He therefore becomes contageous ... Reason or logic do not count for the time being ... He produces ... a kind of fever which spreads ... Such are the personalities by whom revolutions are usually brought about.[133]

He also said that "in history, all reforms have been made possible through the efforts of gifted individuals or advanced minorities ... The reformer and the revolutionary have very often to plough their lonely forrows. They have always to resist the passions and prejudices of the majority. They walk alone."[134] Again he pointed out that since the true social reformer seeks to remove "superstitions, bad customs and conventions" which have crept into ideologies and to return to the Truth of the original teachings, he may "appear to be a traditionalist, revivalist or a reactionary ..." such reformers, he said were Buddha, Christ, Mohammad, Nanak, Kabir, Dayanand, Vivekananda and Gandhi.[135] A requirement for success is that the social reformer must live in conformity with the reforms which he proposes. A movement, Kripalani said, needs an "able leader with clear vision and an iron will who is capable of organising." If the ideas are not organized, they will die with the reformer.[136]

Kripalani also saw a "large element of chance" in history.[137] That the "physical and economic fields" are merely the "necessary background to the psychological and ideological fields" was seen in the role of poverty in revolutions. He denied that revolutions ever result from poverty alone.[138] "Many times poverty and degredation rendered the masses lifeless when it seemed conditions were ripe for revolution," he wrote.[139]

> " ... [The] poor never revolt. It is when the condition of the poor begins to improve that they find that there is a wide gap between what exists and what they expect."[140] Also "ideas of what is just and equitable make better materials for a revolution than poverty," he said.[141]

Perhaps the greatest danger for the revolutionary, Kripalani thought, was the doctrine that the end justifies the means. He held that man must have a "measure for his conduct" because without it, "humanity is driven to the brutal doctrine that might alone is right and that success justifies everything."[142] He recalled that in history, thousands of saints and scientists were martyred for the medieval doctrine of a single exclusive religious loyalty. The eighteenth and nineteenth century enlightenment was a protest against such brutality, but modern revolutions have often shown tendencies similiar to religious movements. "Heterodoxy and non-conformity are deadly sins against the revolution! They are just like apostasy in religion, worthy of the cross, the gallows and the stake ..."[143] Revolutions, moreover, according to Kripalani, are "unpredictable" and may turn on their makers. Also, "the result of human actions are not altogether in human hands, they depend upon a combination of circumstances not always known, and when known, not always under human control."[144] Social change, then, should always be guided by moral values.

The fundamental revolution, for Kripalani, is the change toward a non-violent society. He believed that Gandhi had a "historic mission." Gandhi, he wrote, "combines in himself not only the necessary moral and ideological basis of the new reform but also the capacity to organise it in appropriate external institutions."[145] Using Gandhi's methods, he thought, social change could come about with little violence. This would then be a real revolution. The Indian Revolution, conceived by Gandhi, Kripalani said, was a "synthetic revolution." It was not concerned only with the transfer of political power, as many revolutions are, but also with the transformation of both the individual and society. It contained the moral principles of Truth and non-violence.[146] Kripalani believed that non-violent methods would prove to be the shortest route to achieving the good society.[147] Further, he thought the genuine revolution launched by Gandhi had universal application.

Finally, Kripalani believed in historical *karma*. Violent actions would result in evil *karma* for society, he thought, while non-violent action would "create a stock of *karma* for peace and good will."[148] He believed that such a view was supported by history. He said that the history of such nations as Italy, Germany, America, France, England and Russia were examples where "nationalism triumphant has generally turned jingoist and imperialist." There is a national *karma* and when "freedom from from foreign yoke has been achieved by war, violence and crooked diplomacy, of these create their own momentum and produce their own national *karma*. This momentum, this *karma*, has to be worked out. It works itself out in foreign expansion."[149] Kripalani said that class struggle, if such could be induced, would be harmful because "once mass passions are excited even for a good cause they are likely to leave behind the residue of evil *karma*."[150] On the other hand, Kripalani believed, during the nationalist struggle, that if India could achieve independence and the social transformation of society non-violently, it could act as a powerful force in the world, not for imperialism, but for disarmament, international cooperation and world peace.[151]

At the root of positive social change in history, then, for Kripalani, was the "law of non-violence." While man once lived in a so-called state of nature, he learned to cooperate only by applying the law of non-violence to his affairs. " ... Human nature was once as red in tooth and 'claw as animal nature ... [Humanity] survived because it discovered and evolved something other than the law of war and violence."[152] To the extent that human institutions such as the family, religion, commerce, industry, politics, government and law had embodied the law of non-violence, it had marked progress for mankind.

Ultimately, Kripalani came to see the goal of humanity in history in much the same way as M.N. Roy and J.P. Narayan. The "ultimate aspiration" of humanity, he said, is freedom and this is defined spiritually as "*Moksha*—freedom from all limiting impediments and imperfections."[153]

Class Struggle

Kripalani's critique of the concept of class struggle, as it applies to the Marxian philosophy of history has been explained above. In this section, additional criticism of the concept of class struggle will be discussed as well as the ways in which Marxist theorists themselves have modified and revised the concept.

In addition to failing to account for the driving force behind history, Kripalani also argued that the concept of class struggle failed to acknowledge that in all societies, cooperation is of far greater importance than class divisions and antagonisms. In fact, he argued that the concept of "class struggle" could not really describe how societies function. This is because societies are not ordinarily polarized into opposing and antagonistic classes. Further, with regard to production, he argued that not only does the production of the national wealth involve the cooperation of all classes, but the benefits do not accrue to only one class, for example, the capitalist class as for Marx. Secondly, through an analysis of actually existing conditions in India, Kripalani explained why the concept of class struggle lacked explanatory power when applied to the subcontinent. In the first place, he saw the concept as harmful to the nationalist struggle. Secondly, one could find no single exploiting class in India. Thirdly, caste was more divisive and pervaded the consciousness of Indians much more than did class. Fourthly, a scientific analysis of social conditions, he argued, would show that generally the interests of urban dwellers, including industrial labourers, were in opposition to the rural masses, who lived in relative poverty. This situation was foreign to the Marxian notion of class conflict. Fifthly, granting the theoretical possibility of a Marxian class struggle in India, it would be limited to a few large urban areas. Finally, Kripalani believed that the decentralization of industry in India would make the concept of class struggle obsolete.

Kripalani argued that although conflict exists in every sphere of activity in all societies, the absolute division of society into opposing classes engaged in struggle has never existed and that mutual cooperation is more important to the functioning of society than such class antagonism. In all societies, he pointed out, cooperation and trust are necessary and integral. In the trade union movement, for instance, mutual trust between parties is essential.

> There is conflict between labour and management, management and capital, between the members of the learned professions and the mass of workers. There is conflict between the urban and rural interests ... Conflict of various interests can never be altogether eliminated. There is conflict within every state, every

city, every village and family. Above all, there is conflict between nation and nation.[154]

But if all conflicts were to be solved through violence, he said, it would mean perpetual strife. A great many disputes are solved non-violently in society through mutual cooperation.

Further, all wealth is a social creation requiring the cooperation of more than one class in society. Kripalani did acknowledge the problem of unearned income, but, he pointed out that "surplus value and, unearned income are not the creation of labour alone but of many classes ..." He said that it is the State itself that makes production and exchange in modern civilization possible.[155] Thefundamental question for modern society is how to equitably distribute wealth. The concept that "capital and labour live in separate worlds of their own ... with no connecting bridge of ideas, forms of thought and action" is also criticized.[156] He stressed that capitalism in practice has shown that it is flexible enough to distribute economic benefits to the working class as well as to those who own capital. Historically, in capitalist countries, the standard of living of the worker has increased due to trade unions and greater political influence of the workers, he stated.[157]

In terms of India specifically, Kripalani urged Socialists and Communists to abandon the concept of class struggle. In regard to the Congress Resolution of 1933 condemning the Socialists for engaging in "loose talk about class war," he said that while the Congress recognized existing class antagonisims, it did not encourage it.[158] At this time Acharya Narendra Deva was the leader of the Congress Socialist Party and J.P. Narayan was the General Secretary. Kripalani recalled:

> The main point of difference between the so-called old leadership and the Socialists was whether the country could afford to divide different sections of India's population to wage a class war when they were all united on the question of eliminating foreign rule from India and achieving independence .. At that time there was no powerful capitalist class in the country. Almost the whole of the business class was with the Congress. Even many *zamindars* [landlords] favored the Congress demand for *swaraj*. This they did even though Gandhiji had made it clear ... that the Congress stood for the poor ... Any doctrinaire socialist approach would have divided the forces working together for Independence.[159]

As for the Socialists' concept of "non-violent class struggle," Kripalani said such a phenomenon was impossible as "the very idea of class struggle" was "surcharged with hate and violence."[160]

Moreover, there was no single exploiting class in India, Kripalani argued. The essential polarization in India in terms of exploitation was between the masses in the villages with uneconomic land holdings along with the landless labourers and the rest of the population. The workers in the villages, he said, "are exploited even in the interest of organised industrial labour."[161] Further, he stressed that the lower caste labourers resented the upper caste Brahmins more than they did the capitalists. This showed that caste consciousness was more powerful than class consciousness in India.[162]

As the industrial proletariat was a small minority in India, Kripalani felt it was illusory to look to it for revolutionary impetus. The center of Indian life was in the thousands of villages and it was here, where the masses must be organized for the non-violent revolution he envisioned.[163] The attempt to organize along class lines in India, Kripalani thought, would risk communal conflict and play into the hands of the imperialists. This would clearly be counterproductive.

Essentially what was required, Kripalani concluded, was the modification of capitalism in India through decentralization of industry. The struggle would be waged through cooperation, democracy, *Satyagraha* and trade unionism.[164] Finally, he stated, the idea of class conflict was outmoded. It was not the "way of wisdom" to face the workers with what could not be translated into action. The concept confused the workers as well as the rest of the public. The concept was superfluous in India and should be dropped.[165] Rather than a belief in the concept of class struggle, "The way of wisdom is to believe in the sociobility, goodness and unity of human beings, and to devise means which instead of increasing and accentuating, would ease tensions and reduce conflicts..."[166]

It is important to note that Kripalani's critique of class conflict is supported by the ways in which Marxists themselves have modified the concept of class struggle. In the *Communist Manifesto*, Marx and Engels wrote that "The history of all hitherto existing society is the history of class struggles."[167] In 1888, Engels modified the statement to refer to *written* history in order to account for earlier communal societies where class divisions were absent. In 1927, Karl Kautsky wrote that some of the "class struggles" referred to in the *Communist Manifesto* were actually "conflicts between status groups." While Marxists came to agree that class conflict was most acute in capitalist society, the crucial issue became whether there had been an intensification of class conflict. Eduard Bernstein argued in 1899 that due to the growth of the middle class, the growing complexity of class structure, and rising levels of living, that an intensification of class conflict was not occurring.[168]

In *Class Struggle and The Industrial Revolution*, John Foster found a decline in revolutionary class consciousness in English towns in the second quarter of the nineteenth century as a result of extension of suffrage, growth of mass parties and legal recognition of trade unions. Also, C. Wright Mills dismissed the concept of a fundamental class conflict in American society. Herbert Marcuse argued that in advanced capitalist society, the working class had largely been incorporated. Nicos Poulantzas in *Classes in Contemporary Capitalism*, reexamined class conflict in the twentieth century "in terms of alliances between various social groups which on one side dominate and direct economic and social life and on the other side are subordinated and directed."[169]

This chapter has explored the political philosophy of J.B. Kripalani, in terms of his views on democratic socialism, history and the Marxist concept of class struggle. Kripalani envisioned a non-violent society, based on moral values to provide for individual moral autonomy and a decentralized institutional structure. He rejected historical materialism and the concept of class struggle as he believed that such an approach necessarily led to the doctrine that the end justifies the means. His philosophy of history placed the individual moral reformer at the center, emphasizing the importance of psychological; factors, particularly the will, over material factors. He also believed in a historical *karma*. Only non-violent historical change, he believed, would result in genuine revolution. In his interpretation of the Gandhian philosophy of non-violence, which will be delineated in Chapter Seven, he contributed immensely to twentieth century Indian political thought.

References

1. P.D. Tandon, "A Rare Intellectual," in *Acharya J.B. Kripalani*, ed. P.D. Tandon (Bombay: Hind Kitabs Ltd., 1948), pp. 129-130.
2. Krishna Kripalani, "The Rashtrapati," in *Acharya J.B. Kripalani,* pp. 34-35.
3. *Ibid.*, p. 36.
4. *Ibid.*, p. 35.
5. *Ibid.*, p. 36.
6. Mohan Lal Saxena, "President Kripalani," in *Acharya J.B. Kripalani*, pp. 46-47.

7. J.B. Kripalani, *Gandhji His Life and Thought* (New Delhi: Publications Division, Ministry of Information and Broadcasting, Government of India, 1970), p. viii.
8. *Ibid*, p. 52.
9. *Ibid.*, pp. 54-55.
10. *Ibid.*, p. 56.
11. *Ibid.*, pp. 59-61.
12. Kripalani, *Gandhi: His Life and Thought*, p. 61.
13. *Ibid.*, p. 71.
14. *Ibid.*, pp.73-74.
15. Kripalani, "The Rashtrapati," in *Acharya J.B. Kripalani*, p. 38.
16. Kripalani, *Gandhi: His Life and Thought*, p. 109.
17. K.K. Bhattacharya, "Our Rashtrapati," in *Acharya Kripalani*, p. 17.
18. G Ramachandran, "A Devoted Gandhi-ite," in *Acharya B. Kripalani*, p. 87. Kripalani, *Gandhi: His Life and Thought*, p. 171.
19. *Kripalani, Gandhi: His Life and Thought*, pp. 250- 251.
20. J.B. Kripalani, Class Stuggle (Rajghat, Kashi: Akhil Bharat Sarva Seva Sangh Prakashan, 1958), p. 64.
21. Kripalani, *Gandhi: His Life and Thought*, p. 69.
22. *Kripalani Class Struggle*, pp. 30-31.
23. *Ibid.*, p. 70.
24. J.B. Kripalani, *Gandhian Thought* (Rajghat, New Delhi: Gandhi Smarak Nidhi, 1961), p. 23.
25. J.B. Kripalani, *Someray Thoughts* (Ahmedabad: Navajivan Publishing House, 1979), p. 56.
26. Kripalani, *Class Struggle*, p. 73.
27. J.B. Kripalani, Planning (New Delhi: Praja Socialist Party, 1957), p. 25.
28. *Ibid.*, p. 26.
29. *Ibid.*, p. 25.
30. *Ibid.*, p. 26.
31. *Ibid.*, p. 25.
32. J. B. Kripalani, *Politics of Charkha* (Bombay: Vora & Co., Pub., Ltd., 1946), p. 56.
33. Kripalani, *Planning*, p. 26.
34. Kripalani, *Politics of Charkha*, pp. 52-53.
35. Kripalani, *Planning*, p. 26.
36. Kripalani, *Politics of Charkha*, p. 56.
37. *Ibid.*, p. 58.
38. *Ibid.*, p. 55.

39. *Ibid.*, pp. 54-55.
40. Kripalani, *Planning*, pp. 46-47.
41. *Ibid.*, p. 10.
42. *Ibid.*, p. 12.
43. *Ibid.*
44. *Ibid.*, p. 45.
45. *Ibid.*, p. 13.
46. Kripalani, *Politics of Charkha*, p. 58.
47. *Ibid.*, p. 38.
48. *Ibid.*
49. *Ibid.*, p. 43.
50. Kripalani, *Planning*, p. 45.
51. Kripalani, *Some Stray Thoughts*, p. 57.
52. Kripalani, *Planning*, p. 25.
53. Kripalani, *Politics of Charkha*, p. 69.
54. *Ibid.*, pp. 52-53.
55. *Ibid.*, p. 53.
56. *Ibid.*, pp. 53-54.
57. *Ibid.*, p. 53.
58. Kripalani, *Planning*, pp. 20-21.
59. Kripalani, *Politics of Charkha*, pp. 61-62.
60. *Ibid.*, p. 60.
61. *Ibid.*, pp. 60-61.
62. *Ibid.*, p. 64.
63. *Ibid.*
64. Kripalani, *Planning*, pp. 47-49.
65. Kripalani, *Gandhian Thought*, p. 75.
66. Kripalani, *Politics of Charkha*, p. 51.
67. Kripalani, *Gandhian Thought*, p. 11.
68. Kripalani, *Politics of Charkha*, p. 51.
69. *Ibid.*, p. 63.
70. Kripalani, *Thoughts*, p. 67
71. Kripalani, *Politics of Charkha*, p. 70.
72. *Ibid.*, p. 29.
73. *Ibid.*, pp.10-12.
74. *Ibid.*, p. 33.
75. Kripalani, *Planning*, p. 43.
76. *Ibid.*, p. 4.
77. *Ibid.*, p. 5.
78. *Ibid.*

79. *Ibid.*, p. 6.
80. *Ibid.*, p. 43.
81. *Ibid.*, pp. 43-44.
82. Kripalani, *Gandhi: His Life and Thought*, p. vii.
83. Kripalani, *Thought*, p. xi.
84. *Ibid.*, p. ix.
85. *Ibid.*
86. *Ibid.*, p. 1.
87. *Ibid.*, p. vi.
88. Kripalani, *Planning*, p. 51.
89. Kripalani, *Class Struggle*, p. 3.
90. *Ibid.*, p. 4.
91. *Ibid.*, pp. 4-5.
92. *Ibid.*, pp. 5-6, 23-24.
93. *Ibid.*, pp. 5-6.
94. *Ibid.*
95. *Ibid.*, pp.1-2.
96. *Ibid.*, p. 6.
97. *Ibid.*, p. 45.
98. *Ibid.*, pp. 6-7.
99. *Ibid.*, p. 7.
100. *Ibid.*, pp. 7-49.
101. *Ibid.*, pp. 45, 65.
102. Kripalani, *Some Stray Thoughts*, p. 256.
103. Kripalani, *Class Struggle*, p. 48.
104. *Ibid.*
105. *Ibid.*
106. *Ibid.*, p. 49.
107. *Ibid.*, p. 50.
108. *Ibid.*
109. *Ibid.*, p. 51.
110. *Ibid.*, p. 52.
111. *Ibid.*, pp. 53-54.
112. *Ibid.*, pp. 54-55.
113. *Ibid.*, p. 58.
114. *Ibid.*, p. 63.
115. *Ibid.*, pp. 19-20.
116. Kripalani, *Gandhian Thought*, p. 28.
117. *Ibid.*
118. *Ibid.*, p. 23.

119. Kripalani, *Class Struggle*, p. 64.
120. Kripalani, *Politics of Charkha*, p. 31.
121. Kripalani, *Gandhian Thought*, pp. 52-54.
122. Kripalani, *Some Stray Thoughts*, p. 8.
123. Kripalani, *Politics of Charkha*, pp. 35-36.
124. *Ibid.*, pp. 36-37.
125. *Ibid.*, p. 38
126. *Ibid.*, pp. 46-47.
127. *Ibid.*, pp. 33-34.
128. Kripalani, *Some Stray Thoughts*, p. 8.
129. Kripalani, *Politics of Charkha*, p. 35.
130. Kripalani, *Gandhian Thought*, p. 23.
131. Kripalani, *Some Stray Thoughts*, p. 6.
132. Kripalani, *Gandhian Thought*, 24
133. *Ibid.*, pp. 25-26.
134. Kripalani, *Some Stray Thoughts*, p. 56.
135. *Ibid.*, p. 10.
136. *Ibid.*, pp. 10-13.
137. Kripalani, *Gandhain Thought*, p. 21.
138. Kripalani, *Gandhian Thought*, pp. 19-20 and *Some Stray Thoughts*, p. 31.
139. Kripalani, *Gandhian Thought*, p. 20.
140. Kripalani, *Some Stray Thoughts*, p. 31.
141. Kripalani, Politics of Charkha, p. 32 and *Some Stray Thoughts*, p. 250.
142. Kripalani, *Politics of Charkha*, p. 43.
143. Kripalani, *Gandhian Thought*, p. 26.
144. Kripalani, *Politics of Charkha*, p. 48.
145. Kripalani, *Gandhian Thought*, p. 54.
146. Kripalani, *Some Stray Thoughts*, p. 239.
147. *Ibid.*, p. 141.
148. J.B. Kripalani, *The Indian National Congress* (Bombay: Vora & Co. 1946), p. 15.
149. *Ibid.*, pp. 13-14.
150. Kripalani, *Class Struggle*, p. 71.
151. Kripalani, *The Indian National Congress*, p. 15.
152. Kripalani, *Gandhian Thought*, p. 46.
153. Kripalani, *Class Struggle*, p. 73.
154. *Ibid.*, p. 42.
155. *Ibid.*, p. 20.

156. *Ibid.*, p. 35.
157. *Ibid.*, p. 31.
158. *Ibid.*, pp. 76-77.
159. Kripalani, *Gandhi: His Life and Thought*, p. 171.
160. Kripalani, *Class Struggle*, p. 68
161. *Ibid.*, p. 77.
162. *Ibid.*, p. 79.
163. Kripalani, *Politics of Charkha*, p. 92.
164. Kripalani, *Class Struggle*, pp. 43-44.
165. *Ibid.*, p. 93.
166. *Ibid.*, pp. 43-44.
167. Karl Marx and Friedrich Engels, *The Communist Manifesto*, ed. Samuel H. Beer (New York: Appleton-Century-Crofts, Inc., 1955), p. 9.
168. *A Dictionary of Marxist Thought*, 1983 ed., s.v. "class conflict," by Tom Bottomore, p. 78.
169. *Ibid.*, pp. 78-79.

7

J.B. Kripalani on Gandhian Democracy

J.B. Kripalani was one of the first thinkers to attempt a systematic interpretation of the complex moral and political thought of Mahatma Gandhi. He was also one of the first to recognize that Gandhian thought represented a significant contribution to political philosophy. Kripalani began his commentaries on Gandhi's thought in the 1930s and continued to interpret and systematize his organic philosophy as it evolved. Kripalani's contribution to understanding the moral and political thought of Gandhi is made more significant by the widespread neglect of his thought, especially in India, until recently.[1]

Although Kripalani wrote widely on Indian politics, his basic works are, in large part, broad interpretations of Gandhi's thought. These writings were approached from a consistent standpoint of duty and service to the nation. While Gandhi was often too busy to explain systematically and elaborately defend his ideas against his critics in India, Kripalani took the burden upon himself to do so. Moreover, it was not Gandhi's practice to engage in extensive polemics. The spirit of Kripalani's endeavor was not so much that of a follower as that of a fellow traveller and social worker convinced of the moral value and practical utility of his schemes. He realized that most intellectuals in India would fail to understand the significance of Gandhi's thought unless it was presented in a rational and systematic way. This chapter will examine Kripalani's intepretation of the Gandhian conception of democracy including non-violent revolution and social change, economic principles, the institutional decentralization of society and Basic Education. Together these comprise, in Kripalani's words, an organic or integral philosophy, which could serve as the foundation of a fundamental revolution.

For Kripalani, Gandhi was a fearless revolutionary, a *karma-yogi* or man of action, a dynamic and ever-growing personality, a leader and organizer, an innovator in his attempt to spiritualize politics, a creative genius and a practical reformer. Kripalani accorded Gandhi a giant status as an original political thinker and revolutionary. He suggested that the period since the French Revolution had produced only two great revolutionaries, Gandhi and Marx.[2] And whilst both Gandhi and Marx set out to end exploitation of all sorts, a humanitarian goal, Kripalani drew the sharpest distinction between the two thinkers. Whereas the ends were similiar in some respects for both thinkers, the actual means to those ends were in dialectical opposition. For Marx, violence could be used to attain a humane end. For Gandhi, on the other hand, the means must be consistent with the end, and means are indistinguishable from ends. This made Gandhi more revolutionary than Marx, in Kripalan's view, because his method of reaching the end was in itself revolutionary. Marx's method followed the conventional mode of social change, through violence. Gandhi's method of non-violent social change, on the other hand, represented a new and fundamentally different approach to the renovation of society and politics.[3] For Gandhi, Kripalani pointed out, the means must never deviate from the principles of truth and non- violence. Kripalani viewed Marxism and Gandhism as "two distinct ideologies ... separated by an unbridgeable gulf." "They are based," he said, "upon diametrically opposite immoralities and philosophies of life."[4]

The basic principles laid down by Gandhi led Kripalani to value the system of functioning liberal democracy, as he believed it partly embodied the Gandhian principles of truth and non-violence. Thus while the Gandhian critique of the modern State led Jayaprakash Narayan and M.N. Roy increasingly in the direction of anarchy, that is, toward a conception of a partyless and stateless society, it led Kripalani toward a greater appreciation of the functioning parliamentary system as an embodiment of and a practical approach to the institutionalization of the principles of non-violence. Kripalani continued to believe that it was possible to construct political institutions through which the Gandhian principles of truth and non-violence could function more freely. Jayaprakash Narayan and M.N. Roy, on the other hand, became increasingly skeptical of this enterprise.

Not only did Kripalani believe that workable institutions could be constructed through which the principles of Truth and non-violence would be preserved, but he also held that Gandhi had a special ability and mission to accomplish this. In fact, organization, Kripalani argued, was essential for the success of non-violence. Gandhi's great capacity for organizational work," he felt, had largely been overlooked.[5] He wrote:

> To Gandhi belongs the credit of demonstrating on a large scale that the standards of moral and gentlemanly conduct that are good in individual and social realtions are also good and efficient in political and intergroup relations and conflicts; and, also, that truth and non-violence can be organized into external effective action."[6]

Whilst both Marx and Gandhi wanted to establish "equality, freedom, brotherhood and democracy," Gandhi held that the State could disappear only when "each person was a law unto themselves."[7] For Kripalani, democracy was a step in the right direction toward establishing such a society as it provided greater moral autonomy for the individual. Further, he argued that much of the institutionalized violence of politics, in an earlier age, had been eliminated under liberal democracy. But it was retrogressive, he thought, that violence in the form of a system of exploitative capitalism had been introduced through the back door.

The basic problem, in Kripalani's view, was that progress in group and inter-group morality, particularly on the level of the State in international relations, had not kept pace with the improvement in inter-personal relations. While the institutionalization of democracy in the liberal state represented remarkable progress in reducing the level of violence between individuals in society, intergroup and inter-state violence remained and was widely accepted, as a result of the dual morality which posited the moral individual in an immoral society. Kripalani saw in *Satyagraha* and institutional decentralization the guidelines, through which the practical reform of the group could finally be carried out. Basic Education could instill the necessary moral values and discipline in the individual for the pursuit of this goal.

The Non-violent Revolution

Kripalani compared Gandhi to the prophets of the great religions. He had established the moral guidelines for the non-violent society, but no systematic body of philosophy. *Satyagraha,* encompassing all aspects of social behavior, provided a method of renovating politics and society. It was the challenge facing mankind, Kripalani believed, to follow Gandhi's example in experimenting with Truth to establish institutions through which Truth and non-violence might emerge. The Marxist methodology of social change had, in his view failed. Surely the hope of twentieth century mankind lay in the organic moral and political thought of Gandhi.

Liberal democracy, for Kripalani, represented man's best effort to attain the non-violent revolution in the present historical era.

> Democracy asserts the moral value of the individual in society and stresses his dignity and worth. It also puts an end to or at least reduces to some extent, the political exploitation of the individual. Democracy ends violence inside a group ... Democracy represents moral and spiritual principles operating in the political sphere.[8]

But democracy alone could not usher in the non-violent revolution. Capitalism "abolished the free and responsible individual" and Socialism, while embodying moral and spiritual principles, was seen by its adherents in materialist terms. The individual, Kripalani said, could not be resurrected through material forces. The "chaotic individualism" of the modern democracy, in which the "individual was divested of moral responsibility" could not lead to altruism and humanism through the pursuit of self-interest, as some theorists had suggested. The integral philosophy, on the other hand, might lead to such a society, Kripalani believed.

> His practical programme based on truth and non-violence is aimed at providing the moral man with a moral society. Gandhian philosophy of life for the individual and society, gathers up in one sweeping whole the moral, material and organisational gains of political democracy and economic socialism. It thus sums up the different trends of modern history. It works for a non-violent revolution and a new social order free from political, economic and social injustice and exploitation.[9]

Kripalani stressed that the non-violent revolution pursued by Gandhi must revolve around the principle that there can be no dual morality in society. "Moral man and immoral society cannot pull together for long," he wrote.[10] This condition was pinpointed by Kripalani as the essential difference between Gandhism and Socialism. The difference is that "Gandhi holds that one's means should be as pure as one's ends are high; that high ends cannot be served by low and crooked means."[11] At another time he stated:

> There are not to be two sets of morality, one in the social and the other in the political sphere ... Means can never be justified by ends. Means are as important as the ends. Sometimes they become even more important ... Such a conception of society progressively rules out the use of hate and violence in political relations.[12]

This dual set of moral standards explained why there had been so little progress in improving inter-group and international relations, Kripalani believed.

> While the individual and the social field has improved considerably, ... group life today recognises no law except that of the jungle ... Untruth and downright dishonesty mark the mutual intercourse of nations ... Men are used as cannon fodder for ends that are not quite clear even to the politicians who use them.[13]

Kripalani also developed the abstraction of the "group mind." The group mind, he said is "morally less advanced and more mechanical than the individual's mind. It is less amenable to reason and moral influence."[14] But with *Satyagraha*, he said, the urge for the dominant group to use violence greatly reduced. This is because they "exhaust themselves in ineffective action" and are "denied the good will and sympathy of neutrals." The *Satyagraha* group itself, on the other hand, "cannot be as non-violent, dispassionate, truthful and pure as an individual *Satyagrahi*."[15]

An essential pillar of the non-violent revolution, for Kripalani, was the use of *Satyagraha*. He explained his understanding of the concept in relation to the actions of Socrates in *Crito*. The term *Satyagraha*, he pointed out, is made up of the root meaning *sat* or truth and *agraha*, to hold fast. "Gandhiji used this term as it applied to the removal of political, economic, social and moral wrongs."[16]

The following related Kripalani's understanding of the concept of *Satyagraha* in relation to Socrates' actions in *Crito*. It is useful to follow Kripalani's interpretation of Socrates' argument in *Crito* in order to appreciate his understanding of the concept of *Satyagraha*.

Socrates, Kripalani recalled, refused to go along with his friends and escape from the Athenian prison to save his life. In *Crito*, Socrates related his hypothetical conversation with the laws of the state. The laws pointed out to him that the city could not continue to exist if the legal judgements were destroyed by private persons. Further, they pointed out that Socrates had agreed to abide by the outcome of the trial. The laws also reminded Socrates that they had given him life, and provided for the institutions of marriage and education. The laws asked Socrates if he had forgotten that his country is "far more precious, more venerable, and more sacred" ... than his mother and father and other ancestors.[17] They also told Socrates that "if you cannot persuade your country, you must do whatever it orders and patiently submit to any punishment which it imposes ... You must do whatever your city and your country commands or else persuade it in accordance with universal justice; but violence is a sin even against your parents, and it is a far greater sin against your country."[18] The laws also pointed out that to evade the law would confirm the opinion of the jurors that Socrates had a destructive influence on the youth. If Socrates died by the jurors' decision, on the other hand, he would have been a victim of the wrong decision of his countrymen rather than a victim of the laws.

Kripalani believed that this episode brought out the philosophy underlying *Satyagraha*. This is "that *Satyagraha* is not the destroyer either of the State or of the laws." He said that Socrates did not identify the judges with the laws of the State. But if he broke the order that condemned him to death, he would be doing an injury to the laws of the State.[19]

There is an apparent contradiction, Kripalani said, in that while Socrates refused to obey the order of the court to stop guiding the youth, he would not disobey the order that he be put to death. But for Socrates, there was no contradiction here.

For Kripalani, law is "a commandment to do or refrain from doing a certain act." But he goes on to say that no authority can oblige a free individual to do anything against his will. "And because the human will is held to be free, a person is considered responsible for his positive and negative actions ... Only in freedom can there be responsibility."[20] Kripalani contended that the State, realizing the limits of its power," gives the citizens the choice of either not to break the law or to undergo the 'punishment for the disobedience of the laws." He wrote:

> If a person accepts any of the two alternatives, provided by the law, he is not violating the law but fulfilling its obligation in the alternative provided by the law itself ... A person accepting willingly the alternative of punishment or any equivalent thereof, provided by the law, is in reality not disobeying the law but is fulfilling its requirements in the alternative, provided by the law itself. His disobedience is only in the language used.

But one who tried to escape the Law would be "refusing to accept any of the alternatives."[21]

Kripalani further pointed out that there is another aspect of *Satyagraha* brought out by Socrates and by Gandhi at Champaran. This involves the "contradiction between the individual citizen and the State as represented by the authorities in power for the time being ..."

> It is the conflict ... between the awakened conscience of a free citizen and the state authorities. The *satyagrahi* resolves this contradiction by willingly undergoing the penalty awarded by the court. The authorities cannot permit the violation of their orders, otherwise there will be confusion as Socrates points out. On the other hand if the citizen suppresses his awakened conscience, he ceases to be a free man. The *satyagrahi* by willingly accepting the punsihment, awarded to him by the authorities, does no injury to the state and the laws and also proclaims himself to be a free man. After all, the progress of man in the world had been made possible by individuals who were or considered themselves to be free and were willing to bear the hard and the harsh consequences of exercising their freedom. The history of human progress is the print of the martyrdom of man.[22]

Kripalani stated that this attitude toward the law was also brought out by Gandhi's statement to the court at Champaran:

> As a law-abiding citizen, my first instinct would be to obey the order served on me. But I could not do so without violence to my sense of duty to those for whom I have come. I feel that I could just now serve them only by remaining in their midst (i.e. in disobeying the order) ... It is my firm belief that in the complex constitution under which we are living, the only safe and honorable course for a self-respecting man is, in the circumstances ... to submit without protest to the penalty of disobedience .... I have disregarded the order served upon me not for want of respect for lawful authority, but in obedience to the highest law of our being, the voice of conscience.[23]

Kripalani argued that Gandhi's trial at Sabarmati jail in 1922 showed that Gandhi did not disobey the law. "He pleaded guilty and wanted the judge to award him the highest penallty under the law. Gandhiji thus accepted one of the two alternatives that the law provides."[24] It is emphasized that the real disobedience is in avoiding the punishment provided by the law. Kripalani held that "When one obeys a higher law, he fulfils the requirements of the lower law and does not destroy it." Gandhi, he said, "was not trying to destroy the institutions but to reform them." For this purpose, *Satyagraha* could be offered in the family, in the village and in the country. *Satyagraha* has a "positive content," holding fast to truth, and "it reconciles the two seemingly contradictory terms. obedience and non-violence."[25]

> *Satyagraha* therefore cannot be conceived of as an anti-social activity. It recognises the social utility and necessity of the State and the laws and yet allows the individual to enjoy his liberty as a human being. The *Satyagrahi* even in chains is a free man.[26]

The application of truth and non-violence to politics through *Satyagraha* was a new idea which originated with Gandhi, Kripalani argued. "It must be considered as Gandhiji's original contribution to sociology," he wrote.[27] Gandhi's ideas about Truth and non-violence, according to Kripalani, came from his Vaishnavite faith and the *Upanishads* and the *Gita*, rather than from the *New Testament*. Kripalani emphasized the difference in Gandhi's approach, grounded in his background, and that of the Christians.

Whereas the Jains and Hindus had considered *ahimsa* the highest virtue, Christianity has never considered non-violence as superior to all other virtues.[28] And whilst the New Testament's mission is spiritual, Gandhi did not separate the spiritual and the material realms. According to Kripalani,

> Christ said that his kingdom was not of this earth but of heaven. When shown a coin bearing the effigy of Caesar and asked to whom it belonged, he said 'Give unto God the things that belong to God.' Gandhiji, on such an occasion, would not have given the same reply. He would have said that Caesar was the trustee of the people and he was only entitled to his wages as such, and that all worth belonged to the people who were instrumental in its creation.[29]

Christ and Tolstoy, Kripalani contended, thought in terms of changing the individual, whereas Gandhi wanted to change both the individual and society.[30]

> In *Satyagraha*, ... there is no quarrel with individuals. It is with systems, which have degenerated through ... the perverted actions of generations of men and women. These have created unjust vested interests ... *Satyagraha* ... seeks to bring about a moral transformation and not the liquidation of individuals."[31]

Also, in *Satyagraha*, it is thought that when the individual works to change the system, the individual is, himself, transformed.[32]

Kripalani interpreted Gandhi's approach to the philosophy of non-violence as setting up "graded" levels of morality in a hierarchy. "The lowest in the scale was the man who was full of fear and was cowardly...and who did not resist tyranny. Such a one encouraged tyranny to function. Higher than this came the violent resister. The third was the physically non-violent resister. He resisted non-violently out of necessity because he could not organise violent resistance." This type of resistance would be typical of most industrial strikes. "The highest form of non-violence is the non-violence of the strong, of one who has made it the law of his life. He is non-violent in thought, word and deed. Such a one has shed all fear. His is the purest form of non-violence."[33]

The *Satyagrahi* must follow these principles of truth and non-violence, Kripalani said. The emergence of the non-violent society was tied up with the moral renovation of all spheres of life, social, political, economic and spiritual.[34]

Kripalani pointed out that the Western concept of pacifism or opposition to war could not contain the full blooded concept of *Satyagraha* which embodied the aim to end exploitation in all spheres of life. Gandhi's concept is closer to the Buddhist concept of the path which included a concern for morality in all activity. All actions, thoughts and works must avoid evil. One's desires must be contained. There must be a two-fold renovation of the society involving reform of the social, economic and political structure of society as well as the reform of the individual.[35] "Both individual and society act and react upon each other. Both have, therefore, to be treated simultaneously," he said.[36]

In Chapter Six it was stressed that the concept of class struggle in society as a driving force for positive social change was foreign to Kripalani's world view. For the *Satyagrahi*, this view must also be firmly rejected. "The *Satyagrahi* hates no human being. For him humanity is not divided in two opposing classes, one having all the virtues and the other having all the vices, the eternally saved and the eternally damned. It therefore cannot think in terms of class war, class struggle or coercion."[37]

Kripalani saw in non-violent non-cooperation a revolutionary method of bringing about the moral reform of society. For him it went far beyond the moral approach offered by the old reformers, Buddha, Mahavira and Christ. Kripalani believed that their

> resistance to evil was psychological and not external or organisational. Moreover, their mission was to guide individuals in their pursuit of the supreme good, their salvation ...they did not directly concern themselves with politics or international problems ... Gandhi's *Satyagraha* attempts to do both, i. e. to guide the individual towards the goal of higher life and also to solve political and .. international problems. This is his special contribution as a reformer.[38]

Further, he pointed out that "*Satyagraha* ... is both an individual obligation and a social and political duty ... *Satyagraha* provides also for corporate and group action." It aims to take collective action and "if need be, to bring about the end of a bad social, economic or political system, by making its working impossible ... The *Satyagrahi* raises the fight to a higher moral level, and at that level conflict can only be temporary ..."[39]

Kripalani pointed out that the non-cooperation of the *Satyagrahi* is for the sake of free and full cooperation. Group conflicts and rivalries are minimized and points of common interest emphasized.[40]

Kripalani also suggested that *Satyagraha* was particularly appropriate due to the complex nature of modern society.

> What was perhaps not possible in former ages is possible now. The world today is so organised that the functioning of its complex machinery can be effectively stopped by *Satyagraha*, by downing tools and withdrawing co-operation. It has also become increasingly sensitive to public opinion, with the modern annihilation of distance and the advance of political democracy, with its freedom of conscience and speech, and of the press and association ... Machines of war and destruction would lie idle without the co-operation of labour of various kinds.[41]

This means that "to keep tyranny going," the "active co-operation of the oppressed is necessary ... The chains that bind the poor and oppressed are to a great extent of their own forging. Once they refuse their help or co-operation, the whole fabric of industrial, commercial and governmental injustice, exploitation and oppression would collapse."[42]

For this to happen, however, the ideology of non-violence must be institutionalized, according to Kripalani. Gandhi was successful, he said, in part because he had "organised truth and non-violence in civil resistance distinguished from armed resistance."[43]

> The *satyagrahi* bears no ill-will. Yet he does not solely rely upon his inner individual soul force, he canalises it, he organises it and makes it work through institutions. He works not only through purely moral and psychological but also through external means. As every spiritual force loses some of its purity when it is translated into external activity, so does *Satyagraha* get partially diluted by the very organisation it creates and the material it employs...[44]

There will always be some violence and some gulf between the ideal and the actual, between theory and practice, Kripalani said. "But in *Satyagraha* the gulf is the narrowist."[45]

The institutionalization of the "law of love and non- violence" and its application to group relations qualitatively distinguishes Gandhi's approach to its application historically. In the past, the law of love was applied primarily to individual relations, while evil was organized to "monopolise all the good things of the earth." Whereas the old law of love was "the law of non-resistance," from *Satyagraha* emerged the "strategy" and "machinery" to resist evil.[46] Gandhi, Kripalani said, "does not want submission to evil. He wants it to be resisted. He does not advise us to turn the other cheek; he wants the cheek to be made so tough that the striker may find it inconvenient to strike."[47]

Kripalani cited the efficacy of the modern weapon of the strike as an example of the importance of non-violent resistance in modern society, while sharply distinguishing between the strike and *Satyagraha*. The fundamental difference was that a strike was the "non-violence of the weak." The labourers during a strike do not cease hating their oppressors.[48] Strikers recognize a conflict of interest based upon "class antagonism."[49] "*Satyagraha*, "on the other hand, he said, "is a strike plus something more ... A *Satyagrahi* is a better non-cooperator or striker. His judgement is not clouded by passion, anger and hatred."[50] The non-violence of the striker is only "external" but that of the *Satyagrahi* must be "non-violent in thought, word and deed."[51] "While the *Satyagrahi* cheerfully bears the penalty attached to his disobedience to law and does not want to inflict any injury on those who enforce it, the striker in the industrial field would, if he could, avoid the penalty attached to his disobedience, and if possible try to injure his opponents."[52] This is why the *Satyagrahi* "must possess a higher morale born of their belief in ethical principles and truth and non-violence." The *Satyagrahi* is non-violent out of "free-choice" and not from weakness.[53] Finally,

> *Satyagraha* properly organised will have all the virtues claimed by war without the destructive qualities, material and moral. In addition to bravery and courage, *Satyagraha* claims for itself the great virtue of fearlessness ...[54]

Kripalani saw in the philosophy of non-violence radical implications in the field of international relations. He said that disarmament is non-violence in the international field. He believed that the only way to escape from hate, violence and war was through the application of the principles of Truth and non-violence to international relations. He felt that history had shown that external organization was insufficient. There must also exist the internal will to attain peace.

> War is not an isolated phenomenon. It is intimately connected with our individual and social life. We cannot stop its recurrance if we leave its psychological and sociological causes untouched.

> Peace in the world can only be the ripe fruit of our ideas, beliefs and modes of thought and action. If there is no proper integration and harmony in our lives, external institutions ... like the United Nations Organisation alone cannot bring about peace. If the right understanding and the right will are not there or if the social organisation is not built upon equality and justice, the mere external organisation for peace can achieve only what is called a balance of power. A balance of power produces an unstable and temporary equilibrium liable to be upset at any time by a shift in the circumstances. External machinery for peace can succeed only when it is organised in response to a psychological and social will to peace.[55]

With regard to war itself, Kripalani, like Gandhi, was not a pacifist. It is clear that he did not take the point of view that war had always been without virtue. But he did believe that with new and more destructive technology, war is "only a bad historical habit, bereft of all virtue."[56] Whereas in the past the virtues of "bravery, sacrifice, patriotism and discipline" had been associated with war, with new technology, this was no longer true. He saw *Satyagraha* as a "moral substitute for war."[57]

Yet in specific instances Kripalani realized that practice would fall short of the ideal. He applied Gandhi's graded levels of non-violence to the international sphere. By this principle, it would be more virtuous to go into battle for the defense of a good cause than to submit passively to evil without waging war.

Kripalani's application of this principle is seen in his analysis of India's options in the conflict between East and West Pakistan in 1971. He responded to a question as to what Gandhi would have done if faced by the policy of Yahya Khan, President of Pakistan, against East Pakistan. Kripalani calculated that Gandhi would have first exhausted all avenues in seeking a peaceful solution. Yahya Khan would have been asked to stop the military operation in the East and to confer with Sheikh Mujiber Rahman, the leader of the Awami League.[58]

But Kripalani believed that Gandhi-would have advised the government that if no peaceful solution could be found, they must help their neighbours in a fair and just cause. In defense of this position he cited the case in 1947 in which Gandhi advised Nehru to send the army to Kashmir to defend against invading tribes.[59]

> I am sure ... if all the peaceful solutions had failed ... Gandhiji would have advised our government to recognise the *de jure* Government of Bangladesh elected by the people. If recognition

had led to war with Pakistan, Gandhiji would have advised India to march its armies to help Bangladesh ... It must be remembered that Gandhiji was not a pacifist like the Western Quakers. If people did not believe in non-violence he wanted them to use the weapons in which they believed, be it that of violence, provided the cause was just. Gandhiji was against all fearful and cowardly submission to unjust, brutal and soul-killing violence of the tyrant and the oppressor ... He held that non-violence is the better and the most effective weapon. But failing that, violence could be used in a just cause. This is what I know of Gandhiji. Others may be knowing more and better.[60]

Gandhian Economic Principles, Decentralization and Sarvodaya

Kripalani's analysis of the relationship between political centralization and economic centralization have been explored in Chapter six. In this section, Kripalani's insight into Gandhi's conception of economics as an alternative conceptual framework will be discussed.

Kripalani saw that Gandhi's economics challenged the assumptions of classical economics as well as those of the Marxists and Socialists. Gandhi's approach challenged the building of economic systems upon abstract economic formulations or laws. "Economics," Kripalani said, "deals with living human beings who have intelligence and will of their own and are subject to passion." The abstract laws of economics cannot deal with the fact that the economic needs of different peoples and nations differ.[61] It was also true, he said, that "life does not move in consonance with the rules of formal logic. It is dynamic and is always transcending these rules."[62] Gandhian economics transcended the traditional approaches to economic thought. This was because it placed people and their material, moral and spiritual needs at the center. It was built upon the concrete rather than the abstract and it embodied human values in accord with a rich and open view of human nature.

Kripalani realized that Gandhi's approach was highly original and represented a paradigm shift with respect to traditional economic theoretical frameworks. That Gandhi's thought represented a radical departure is implicit in his writings, but Gandhi himself never systematized his insights. Kripalani attempted to show how the assumptions of Gandhi's economic thought differed from those of the existing science of economics. He stressed that one must put the assumptions of traditional economics out of one's mind. To understand Gandhi's ideas, "one must rid oneself of ... ideas derived from the economic thought of the West."

He said, "Gandhi's economics must be studied from the viewpoint of his own moral and spiritual principles and ideals as also from the conditions that existed and still exist in India."[63]

Gandhian economic thought placed the individual and his manifold needs at the center. In India this principle required that economics also place the village as the basic unit at the center. Kripalani considered it tragic that so many Western educated intellectuals and policy makers in India were unable to make the paradigm shift and see the need for an economics suited to Indian conditions and Gandhian moral and spiritual principles.[64]

Kripalani realized that economic thought, whether of the capitalists or of the Socialists or Communists was basically within the same conceptual framework. Both systems were built upon the principle of accumulation. If accumulation was "Moses and the Prophets" for the capitalists, it was equally true for the Socialists and the Communists. Centralization was a logical end in both systems and was seen as desirable. Similiarly, violence and exploitation were integral to both systems.

Both capitalism and Communism also built upon the concept of a theoretical or hypothetical "economic man." In the West, Kripalani said, the economic man "always sought his advantage to the exclusion of every other consideration—religious, moral, intellectual, national ..." There was a different concept of the economic man in Marxism. The Communists believed "that the conflict throughout history was not between individuals but between economic classes." Further, it "saw religion, morality, art, culture and nationalism as by products of the play of economic forces ..."[65]

But Kripalani stressed that Gandhi's conceptual framework lay between these two extremes. He believed that "man does not live by bread alone," but also that "man cannot live without bread ..." "He ... held that economic activity was but one, though a very important, part of social activity. It was connected with religion, ethics, politics etc."[66]

Other basic differences can be pointed out between the traditional approach and the Gandhian approach, and which emerge from Kripalani's analysis of Gandhian economics. For example, value is not seen in terms of abstract quantity which can be measured quantitatively and equated with other values. Marx, for example, in *Capital* equated an abstract value to the amount of labour contained in a thing. On this basis, the value of a commodity could be equated with other commodities. Whilst for Marx higher humanitarian values are to emerge from Communistic society, in practice, Communists lost sight of these humanitarian ends.

Gandhi, on the other hand, was not willing to wait for the emergence of a future superior morality in society to establish an alternate criterion for value. Gandhi, for example, would have been unwilling to measure the products of village industry, such as *khadi*, in abstract terms. This was because more than a commodity was being produced. Self-reliance and discipline were being taught whilst an organization was forged for the freedom struggle. Principles of truth and non-violence were being practised. So the production of value was seen in a broader sense. Kripalani said that *khadi* was conceived in terms of the nation, and the wealth of the nation, as used by Adam Smith .. "No society ... can dispense with moral and spiritual values in the arrangement of its economic life."[67]

Further, in Gandhian economics, technology could be seen as a means rather than an end in itself. And it must serve the welfare of all, not just one economic class. It must serve as a means to moral ends and be subject to them. Moral and ethical values must not be undermined by technology. In traditional economics, on the other hand, there was a built-in logic of ever increasing technological complexity, overlooking the immediate and future consequences,with regard to individuals.

Also in Gandhian economics, the material product of the productive process was treated in a pre-capitalist way. It was a means to an end rather than an end in itself, as in Aristotle's economy in the *Politics*. It was not a commodity for marketing, first and foremost, but something with a use value, and the object of an indivudual's creative initiative, which served to promote higher ends.

When man is no longer seen as "economic man," that is, as a Hobbesian automaton, but in accord with an open view of human nature, as a perfectable being, capable of altruism, economics becomes subservient to man. Economics serves humanity, rather than individuals serving the economic system. Therefore the development of the individual, seen comprehensively in terms of all round development, including spiritual self-realization, becomes the end. Individuals are no longer seen as means serving the system itself.

Kripalani also discussed the idea that with Gandhi, economics is no longer only a matter of relations between things. He wrote:

> The main basis of the *khadi* programme ... was its economic value, but an economic value which is not divorced from political, social, moral and even artistic value; in short from human values. Gandhiji's economics was not a matter of relations between things merely but of relations between things and human beings. Human relations have to be often deliberately designed. Material goods

> and services must not be allowed blindly to impose their will on men and their behaviour. Mutual relations of human beings imposed simply by material goods and processes often work for tyranny and injustice. If here is to be justice, fair play and a solicitude for human happiness, material goods, that is, their production, distribution etc., must be made to subserve human values.[68]

This addresses a central concern of Marx, although it could be argued that Marx did not go as far as Gandhi. Marx said that a characteristic feature of capitalism was that material objects in the market place come to control men. Material objects confront each other as subjects in the market place, whilst men, who by nature should be in control, confront each other in society as material objects. There is thus a perverse subject-object relationship. Men come to be ruled by external material forces over which they have no control.

Gandhian economics is not just economics in the narrow sense of the distribution of goods and services, or political economy in the broader sense as Adam Smith used it, i.e. the wealth of nations, but rather moral and political economy. Gandhian economics places the individual at the center, both in contemporary society and from a historical perspective. As Kripalani expressed it:

> For the materialist, the individual as such is no end in himself. He has in fact no existence beyond the temporary one in which he happens to find himself today ... There is no personal immortality. Society is continuous and it has a sort of immortality. This immortality consists in the ever increasing mastery over nature and the resultant refinement of culture and civilisation ... The individual disappears and dies. Society lives on, progresses and works out ever higher forms ... Individuals must therefore necessarily be means to its ends.[69]

In the Gandhian conception, on the other hand:

> The individual must work out his perfection in a spiritual society. Such a society must be based on principles that will lead the individual on to his divine destiny ... These principles are those of love, non-violence, truth and justice. A social order based upon these, excludes all exploitation, economic, social, political or even religious.[70]

Basic Education and Integral Philosophy

Gandhi believed that the proper education of the child must be an integral part of the revolutionary transformation of society. Kripalani took it upon himself to explain the central principles of Gandhi's programme of Basic Education more systematically than Gandhi, himself had done. In doing so he became one of the first to interpret Gandhi's ideas on education for the nation.

The aim of Gandhi's programme of basic education was to prepare the individual to live according to the principles of Truth and non-violence in every sphere of activity. Kripalani suggested that the heart of the problem was the "artificial division between the concept of the individual and society." In fact, he said, the individual and society cannot be separated in reality, and "the human individual attains his individuality only in a group, in some sort of society."[71] This meant that education must have a "social setting and a social aim," while also providing for the individual.

The inter-relation between the individual and society, Kripalani felt, was crucial. He expressed his view of the relationship in the following way.

> This inter-relation can only be ignored at the peril of the individual and society. Any over-emphasis of the one will be at the expense of the other. Such over-emphasis destroys the balance which a true and lasting civilisation needs. Most of the trouble of the world has been due to the loss of this balance. Sometimes the individual with his anarchic tendencies produces confusion in society. At other times society so crushes the individual that his initiative and personality are lost and he becomes a mere automaton. Humanity has been oscillating between the thesis of the individual and the antithesis of society. The proper synthesis, if it has been achieved has 'been short lived'.[72]

Kripalani cited three educational models which aimed at a synthesis of the individual and society. The first was from John Dewey who said that education was the process of remaking experience, giving it a more socialistic value through increased individual experience by giving the individual better control of his powers."[73]

The second and third models were found in ancient civilization. For Confucius, education promoted "duty" which "has both an individual and a social content." Under the Hindu system, "the four duties, *Arth, Kama, Dharma* and *Moksha* had to be performed through the four *varnas* and *Ashrams*." Kripalani observed that the fulfilment of these has reference to the individual and society."[74]

In Gandhi's programme of Basic Education, the molding of the individual would also "give direction to the society." And since for Gandhi, the individual is a spiritual being, the aim of society must also be spiritual. Only in such a society can the individual avoid being used as a means. The individual has a divine destiny but this must be worked out in society. Society must, therefore place the individual as a divine being at the center if he or she is to attain self-realization.

The goals of society, then, must be spiritual rather than material. For the materialist, the historical evolution of society is placed at the center and the individual, seen as temporal, is only a means to the perfection of society.[75]

The fundamental problem with education in India in the 1930s, Kripalani felt, was that it had no social purpose. In 1939, Kripalani pointed out that formal education in India was "cut off from all life and reality." It was "abstract," dealing with symbols rather than concrete objects. Emphasizing writing skills and memory, it had little to do with practical knowledge.[76]

Gandhi's Basic Education, on the other hand, was based on the principle that all education was to be woven around a craft and that the produce of the craft must be made economically remunerative so as to defray a part of the cost of education, namely, the teacher's salary.[77]

If the programme of cottage industry was to succeed in India, manual work must be seen as respectable. But this was not the main purpose of Basic Education. If all the faculties of the child were to be developed, including the will and the personality, education, it was argued, must provide healthy activity to the child.

According to Kripalani, the revolutionary aspect of the scheme was that it would "change the medium of instruction." With this change in methodology, "labour ... becomes a unifying and integrating factor. It helps to combine the intellectual, artistic, scientific and physical development of the pupil."[78] Kripalani argued that Gandhi's Basic Education "follows the natural evolution of the individual and the race, the evolution of all knowledge, art, science, philosophy and religion."[79]

Kripalani, taking a historical view of man's development, spoke of a natural process of education throughout history through which the individual came to dominate the forces of nature and know the world and himself. He said, "there has been a double process of education, by observation and experiment." Man "observed and then tried his hand on material nature." He came to "dominate natural forces." While working with his hands, he discovered general laws. These were further generalized to create philosophy. Kripalani said that man was the only animal that could fashion and invent. "He turned his gaze inward and discovered the laws that regulate the inner workings of his being thus creating psychology, the science of his soul and religion."[80] The need for cooperation among those working on the same field, Kripalani speculated, led to the creation of castes, classes and nations and introduced civic life and government. Man, he said, "creates his social and political rights, duties, obligations and loyalties, introducing in his personal life and in the life of society practical and theoretical ethics, law and politics."[81] He argued that if society was not to "succumb to decadance," this same process must be emulated in education.

Kripalani said that the child begins to function as a "wild primitive animal." He must "be raised and civilised by education." He expressed this idea as follows.

> It is ... certain that if the system of education follows the natural course of education of the individual and the race he will be educated better and quicker. All his capacities and not his brain alone, will be exercised and consequently strengthened and evolved. His eyes, hands and other senses will be trained. They will be alert. His imagination and his inventive capacity will flower forth in fruitful activity ... He will develop and become a unified and integrated personality.[82]

Through activity, work and play, the child is "directed to discover for himslef not only facts but the laws of investigation and thinking ... He automatically acquires the habit of scientific thinking."[83]

Kripalani held that even though education through craft work was an original idea for Gandhi, in the field of education it was "neither new nor revolutionary." First, it is a principle of psychology that up to the age of fifteen, the "child has a remarkable capacity for grasping the concrete." Education, then, should be connected with "objective facts," as education through abstractions is likely to "cripple" the child.[84]

Kripalani, believed that abstract education came about as a result of scholasticism. Primitive education was through observation and work. But when in medieval times education was taken over by the priestly class it became more abstract. Contemplation was considered the highest activity while the craftsman and labourer were looked down upon.[85] But with the Renaissance, there arose a protest against abstract learning, Kripalani said. Education eventually came to stress objective facts, experiment and investigation, i.e. induction, rather than deduction.[86]

Rousseau's *Emile* contained the basic ideas of the new method of education. Rousseau "wanted to follow nature and to treat the child as a child and not as a grown up."[87] Through activity, it was thought, the "child will learn simply and naturally" and "become a philosopher while he thinks he is only a workman."[88] Others advocating practical knowledge, Kripalani said, were Johann Heinrich Pestalozzi, Johann Friedrich Herbert, Friedrich Froebel, John Dewey and the Bolsheviks.

For Pestalozzi, "education is the organic development of the individual, mental, moral and physical, and is obtained through physical activities.[89] Froebel, according to Kripalani, also stressed the psychological need of the child for activity and education through constructive work. For John Dewey, three principles were stressed. First, "each individual should be capable of self-respecting, self-supporting, intelligent work". Secondly, "never before did the work of one individual affect the welfare of others on such a wide scale. Thirdly, "industrial methods and processes depend today upon knowledge of facts and laws of natural science in a much greater degree than before."[90]

Kripalani considered it significant that socialists had recognized labour and activity as a sound basis of education. For Marx, education meant intellectual development, physical development and polytechnical education. Kripalani argued that Marx would have no argument against education in the use of simple technology.[91] Another social thinker mentioned was Peter Kropotkin who said, "To the division of society into brain workers and manual workers we oppose the combination of both kinds of activity; and instead of technical education which ... [maintains the present dichotomy], we advocate the education integrale, or complete education which means the disappearence of that pernicious distinction."[92]

Kripalani also discussed the Soviet experiment in which education had been built around a practical curriculum. In this respect, he said, Gandhi's ideas were close to those of the Soviets. Lenin, he pointed out, wanted the "eradication of the whole division of labour, intellectual and manual."[93] Kripalani was concerned that the Indian Socialists realize this similiarity and lend support to Gandhi's programme of education.

In Kripalani's view, past experiments in practical education had failed for several reasons. First, the industrial revolution wiped out the craft industries and the new unskilled labourers could afford little education.[94] Secondly, the industrial revolution increased the gap between the city dwellers or middle class and the rest of the population, the urban and rural workers and peasants. He said that while in medieval times "education filtered down to the common people," the new education became confined to the upper classes. This produced an urban and rural proletariat. Kripalani believed that the reason craft education had not been introduced into the schools was that preparations for war took most of the national wealth.[95]

But Gandhi's Basic Education was designed to make craft education available to all under Indian conditions. It was thought that such education would provide a basis for modern scientific education and for earning a living under Indian economic conditions.[96]

Kripalani explained that Basic Education would be centered around training for a specific occupation but the curriculum would be broadbased. Inter-related subjects would be learned through studying the way they relate to the student's intended vocation. For example, someone studying agriculture would learn science but also something about both economics. and politics.[97]

Craft-centered education would also have the advantage of avoiding what Kripalani called the "tyranny of words." The avoidance of verbal and theoretical knowledge in favour of the concrete was sound, Kripalani felt, because of the misunderstanding caused in the world by the careless use of abstract terms, which, he said, resulted in the "tyranny of words."[98] An example was the use of the term "materialism."

> [M]aterialism is but a theory. It is not a scientifically verified fact. It is only a hypothesis in science...Yet many philosophers, economists and practical reformers and politicians would use this hypothesis as if it were a scientifically demonstrated fact, and base upon it their practical programmes. A generation ago it was mechanical materialism that was conclusive. Today it is dialectical materialism. Both are unproved hypotheses for facilitating the work of scientists, but they have been taken to be scientifically verified truths.[99]

Another problem was that general and abstract terms, such as "capitalism, fascism, communism, Gandhism, etc." excite passions and lead to theoretical quarrels without examining the content. This contributed to "wars, class hatred and class conflicts." Kripalani believed that a concrete education, on the other hand, would lead to a "rigorous discipline in the use of words."[100]

Kripalani argued that to prepare the individual to live morally and ethically in society, a "genuine organized society" must be set up in the school itself which would provide real problems for the student to solve. This was in keeping with the trend of education since the Renaissance when the emphasis had shifted from a focus on the afterlife to that of becoming a useful citizen. Kripalani cited Thomas Jefferson who said that in a democracy, the people must have a basic education. The student will learn "self-discipline" and "self-government" through "creative labour."[101]

Kripalani spoke of inculcating a "current morality," which must "periodically change with the advance of knowledge." He wrote :

> When such a morality is given an extended form and is institutionalised, the institutions created should be in accord with the results of science and the economic, social and political ideas and ideals prevalent in modern times ... The principles of cooperative labour cannot fail to evolve ideas of truth, love, justice, peace and discipline.[102]

To assure that education was grounded in "reality," Gandhi insisted that the student must produce enough value to pay his own way. As Kripalani explained:

> [I]f the work done has no economic value it is cut off from reality and the facts of life. Work done becomes only a means and as a means it is likely to fail. Gandhiji's scheme is one whole ... For Gandhiji, craft work is not merely a means of literary education; it is also an end in itself.[103]

The experimental nature of the programme of education was also emphasized by Kripalani. In enumerating the ten principles of Basic Education, Kripalani argued that the plan went further than previous educational reformers had gone. The ten principles of Basic Education were as follows.

1. Education up to a particular minimum standard should be universal for all citizens, male and female.
2. The course of this education is to run for seven years, beginning from the age of seven.
3. Basic National Education does not concern itself, for the present, with the pre-school stage or the post-basic stage.
4. Basic National Education must be imparted through the mother tongue.
5. In its method it must be woven round some art or handicraft. All intellectual instruction must be imparted through the instrumentality of the craft chosen.
6. The craft chosen must be learnt systematically and scientifically with a view to efficiency and practical results. It must not be learnt merely as a means either for intellectual work or for economic self-sufficiency. It must be both a means and an end.
7. The product of the craft must be economically paying.
8. Effort should be made to see that the money value of the work done covers the pay of the teacher.

9. The state should provide the rest of the expenses, of school buildings, furniture, books, maps, and the whole of the apparatus including tools etc. for the craft taught.
10. The state should undertake to utilise the produce of the craft by which it may meet its own requirements or those of the local bodies where the school is established. For any excess of goods produced, the state should provide marketing facilities.[104]

Kripalani called Gandhi's Basic Education the "coping stone of Gandhiji's socio-political edifice."[105]

Throughout his writings, Kripalani emphasized the integral or organic nature of Gandhi's thought. "The principles and programmes are organically connected. They form a whole."[106] 'Analysis of Gandhi's programmes revealed that they were based on a "complete philosophy."

> This unity in principle, and the unity that runs through his concrete schemes and plans, makes Gandhiji's programme a single whole. It makes of it a complete system of philosophy, with its distinct ideology.[107]

Accordingly, all aspects of human life should form a harmonious whole, as did the life of Gandhi.

> Gandhi believed in the unity of human life, which is a synthetic whole. It cannot be divided into separate watertight compartments—religious, moral, political, economic, social, individual and collective...
>
> Gandhiji's own life was lived in conformity with certain basic principles and was, therefore, integrated and coordinated. It made a harmonious whole ...There is basic unity of purpose and aim.[108]

Kripalani compared Gandhi's concept of the integration of spheres of life to Jayaprakash Narayan's concept of Total Revolution.[109]

Gandhi's synthetic approach, Kripalani observed, was consistent with the historical tendency of the Indian people to change through assimilation of the new. This largely explained Gandhi's appeal in India, he thought.

> In his synthetic attitude Gandhiji works in conformity with the genius of his people. The Indian tendency is not so much to analyse and separate as to co-ordinate the different trends and urges, to synthesize and to combine the new with the old ... The credal and the separatist movements have been few and have generally not taken root in the soil. The Indian effort has always been to resolve apparent contradictions through a dialectical process of its own. This does not require destructive revolutions

> to eliminate the thesis and the antithesis and establish on their destruction a temporary and unstable synthesis. Co-ordination is achieved through the force of thought and by virtue of certain basic ideas. The genius of the Indian people is constructive, catholic and assimilative. It is neither negative nor destructive.[110]

If Gandhi's thought often appeared inconsistent with the formal rules of logic, it was because synthetic thought, based on "creative, dynamic and revolutionary thought" refused to conform easily to a rigid system.[111]

Kripalani saw Gandhi's programme as revolutionary in all its aspects, and he argued convincingly that Gandhi must be seen as a revolutionary whether in terms of his skill as a political actor or in the more comprehensive sense of a moral and social reformer. But he argued that both aspects of Gandhi's life was vital to the success of his mission.

> His revolutionary application of moral and spiritual principles to group life would never have succeeded, if he had not been able to assess properly the political and economic situation in the country and take requisite action at appropriate and psychological moments.[112]

From the perspective of Gandhi as a successful political actor, Kripalani believed that Gandhi's "genius" lay in his "intuitive recognition of the situation as revolutionary." Kripalani explained that he understood that neither the path of terrorism as advocated by Tilak and the radicals, nor constitutional reform as advocated by Gokhale and the moderates could bring about a non-violent revolution. Rather, "direct action suited to a disarmed people" was required. Analytically, Kripalani argued, this aspect of Gandhi as a revolutionary could be separated from Gandhi as a moral reformer. "All this has nothing to do with the novel doctrines of truth, non-violence and the philosophy of means and ends, by which Gandhiji sought to moralise and spiritualise politics," he wrote.[113] His argument was that any competent political strategist, after a careful analysis of the Indian situation, would have advocated direct revolutionary action in the form of non-cooperation on a nation-wide scale, just as Gandhi had urged. Non-violence as a policy would have been "sufficient," from practical considerations, as a labour leader sees when preparing for a strike, he said. "...[T]he assessing of the situation as 'revolutionary, was then the triumph of Gandhiji as a politician and statesman of his time, judged by strictly orthodox standards."[114]

For Kripalani, Gandhi was more than a saint in politics. He saw that the second part of his agenda, "to spiritualise and moralise politics" depended upon his skill as a politician. He could have been a saint through his technique of Truth and non-violence, but this would not have succeeded without the political skills.[115]

Another crucial distinction for Kripalani was that Gandhi, unlike many in the past, wanted to reform politics by ethical reconstruction, rather than exploiting religion for political purposes.

> He did not want to make spirituality political, as priests of many religions through the ages have tried to do, to the injury of religion. They have employed the amoral or immoral methods of mundane activity to a superior and purer activity of the spirit.[116]

Kripalani viewed Gandhi as an economic reformer in an analogous manner. In economics, "Gandhi took an organic view and insisted upon the retention of moral and spiritual values."[117] But the moral reformation of economics, as in the political sphere, would have failed, Kripalani thought, had not Gandhi's ideas on economics been sound in their own right, apart from the moral and ethical aspects. "Gandhiji had the wisdom and the foresight of a true and scientific economist, one who does not merely calculate in terms of industrial goods and commodities but for whom human beings are more important."[118] The second half of the agenda, the most important for Gandhi—to make economics ethical—added to his stature as an economist. "In economics he was a great economist inasmuch as he correlated economics with sociology, and ethics, without which it has very little human value and is likely to produce more misery than happiness."[119]

Similarly, Kripalani saw Gandhi as a revolutionary in his own right, quite apart from the complementary aspect of insisting upon the non-violent character of revolution. Kripalani outlined four characteristics which all great revolutionaries, including Gandhi, shared. The first of these was the ability to recognize a revolutionary situation and take appropriate action. It means recognizing a situation where "the slow process of evolutionary reform and gradualness" will only increase tensions in society. For example, Kripalani argued that the French and the Russian revolutions had been particularly violent because reform had been repressed. Revolutionary action must be appropriate to accelerate change and relieve tensions in society. He argued that in the early Nationalist Movement in India, reform could be brought about neither by the terrorism of the radicals, as political repression would be greatly increased by the authorities, nor through Gokhale's agenda for constitutional reform, as the authorities were not convinced that they must institute such change. Only direct action through non-cooperation was appropriate and could be effective in bringing about lasting change in a non-violent manner, Kripalani argued. In this way, Gandhi avoided many of the "pitfalls" which accompany most violent revolutions.[120]

This analysis also reveals Kripalani's thinking concerning the dialectical relation between historical and material forces and human action or will. While recognizing the existence of historical and material forces, and their momentum, Kripalani believed that these can, to a large extent be overcome by actors who exercise the will to do so.

Kripalani said that the second quality of a revolutionary was that he understood that "genuine revolutions are a movement of the people—of the masses, although it may be initiated by an individual, a group or a class ... [I]t is they, the people, who lend to the struggle their will and their collective spiritual force."[121]

Kripalani believed that revolution could be compared to spiritual rebirth:

> Revolutions are no accidents. They are historical events with their roots in the past. They are the result of preceeding social and economic circumstances coming to a head at a particular historical time. A revolution is something like a spiritual rebirth of an organised portion of humanity. As an individual's spiritual rebirth is preceeded by a crisis which comes as a violent break with the past, changing his ideas, ideals and modes of thought, feeling and action, so is a revolution a spiritual crisis in a particular social order. It means a more or less radical break with past ideas, ideals, modes of thought, feeling and action. It is the rebirth of a people. Therefore the people must participate in it.[122]

The third characteristic of the revolutionary was that he leads a revolution under a "compelling sense of urgency." He feels that society will destroy itself without the cleansing force of the revolution. Again, the analogy is seen in relation to spiritual rebirth.

> ... [T]his sense of urgency may be a spiritual illusion but it is of the essence of spiritual rebirth ... It does not square with reason of logic. It has a logic of its own. It is regulated by the logic of revolution.[123]

But the sense of urgency must be accompanied by patience, during which "every act is a preparation for the appropriate opportunity." Kripalani said that as a revolutionary, Gandhi demonstrated such "impatient patience."[124]

The fourth characteristic of the revolutionary was that every action was seen in terms of the revolution, and how it contributed to its fulfilment. Kripalani believed that Gandhi viewed action in this way.[125]

Kripalani argued that each of these four characteristics of the revolutionary was possessed by Gandhi, but that he went further in requiring that the revolution proceed non-violently in accord with an integral or organic philosophy.

Finally, Kripalani pointed out that freedom was the goal of the individual in society. And only a moral and spiritual person is a free person. He stated that the "march of history" had ever been striving toward a social order which would provide for the emergence of such free individuals.[126]

> By moralising politics through the three principles of truth, non-violence and purity of means and fighting injustice and tyranny through *satyagraha* and by his constructive programme, Gandhiji sought to co-ordinate and synthesise social, political and economic life, establish effective democracy and lay the foundations of a new social order based on justice and equality and prove the way for world peace."[127]

This chapter has expounded J.B. Kripalani's interpretation of Gandhian Democracy, particularly in regard to the philosophy of *Satyagraha* or non-violent revolution, people-centered economics, the principles of Basic Education and the integral or organic nature of Gandhian thought. Kripalani, like M.N. Roy and Jayaprakash Narayan, believed that only in a truly democratic society could the individual attain the ultimate, goal of spiritual freedom. For Kripalani, Gandhi established the fundamental parameters of such a free society.

References

1. Raghavan Iyer, *The Moral and Political Thought of Mahatma Gandhi* (Oxford : Oxford Univ. Press, 1973), p. 11.
2. J.B. Kripalani, *Gandhi: His Life and Thought* (New Delhi: Ministry of Information and Broadcasting, Government of India," 1970), p. 306.
3. J.B. Kripalani, *The Latest Fad* (Allahabad: The Hindustani Talimi Sangh, 1939), pp. 98-100.
4. *Ibid.*
5. Kripalani, *Gandhi: His Life and Thought*, p. 306.
6. J.B. Kripalani, *Gandhian Thought* (Rajghat, New Gandhi Smarak Nidhi, 1961), p. 114.
7. Kripalani, *Gandhi: His Life and Thought*, pp. 415-416.
8. Kripalani, *Gandhian Thought*, pp. 134-135.

9. *Ibid.*, p. 140.
10. *Ibid.*, p. 44.
11. J.B. Kripalani, *Fateful Year* (Bombay: Vora and Co., 1948), p. 71.
12. Kripalani, *The Latest Fad*, p. 88.
13. Kriplani, *Gandhian Thought*, pp. 40-41.
14. *Ibid.*, p. 65.
15. *Ibid.*
16. J.B. Kripalani, *Freedom in Peril* (Madras: Gandhi Samaj, 1977), p. 44.
17. *Ibid.*
18. *Ibid.*, p. 45.
19. *Ibid.*, pp. 45-46.
20. *Ibid.*, p. 46.
21. *Ibid.*, pp. 46-47.
22. *Ibid.*, p. 47.
23. *Ibid.*, p. 48.
24. *Ibid.*
25. *Ibid.*, pp. 48-49.
26. *Ibid.*, p. 50.
27. J.B. Kripalani, *Some Stray Thoughts* (Ahmedabad: Navajivan Publishing House, 1979), p. 24.
28. *Ibid.*, p. 25.
29. *Ibid.*, p. 24.
30. Kripalani, Gandhi: *His Life and Thought*, pp. 356-358
31. Kripalani, *Gandhian Thought*, pp. 68-69.
32. J. B. Kripalani, Class Struggle (Rajghat, Kashi: Akhil Bharat Sarva Seva Sangh Prakasan, 1958), p. 38.
33. Kripalani, *Gandhian Thought*, p. 44.
34. Kripalani, *Gandhi: His Life and Thought*, p. 348.
35. Kripalani, *Gandhian Thought*, pp. 150-151.
36. Kripalani, *Class Struggle*, p. 37.
37. *Ibid.*, p. 40.
38. Kripalani, *Gandhi: His Life and Thought*, p. 351.
39. Kripalani, *Gandhian Thought*, pp. 64-65.
40. Kripalani, *Gandhian Thought*, p. 68, and *Class Struggle*, p. 41.
41. Kripalani, *Gandhian Thought*, p. 59.
42. Kripalani, *Gandhi: His Life and Thought*, pp. 352- 353.
43. Kripalani, *Gandhian Thought*, p. 56.
44. *Ibid.*, p. 56.
45. *Ibid.*

46. *Ibid.*, pp. 56-57.
47. Kripalani, *Gandhi: His Life and Thought*, p. 351.
48. *Ibid.*, p. 60.
49. Kripalani, *Gandhian Thought*, p. 60.
50. *Ibid.*, p. 116.
51. Kripalani, *Gandhi: His Life and Thought*, p. 353.
52. Ibid., pp. 353-354.
53. Kripalani, *Gandhian Thought*, p. 61.
54. Kripalani, *Gandhi: His Life and Thought*, p. 350.
55. Kripalani, *Gandhian Thought*, p. 151.
56. Kripalani, *Gandhi: His Life and Thought*, p. 347.
57. *Ibid.*
58. Kripalani, *Stray Thoughts*, p. 311.
59. *Ibid.*, pp. 312-313.
60. *Ibid.*, p. 313.
61. Kripalani, *Gandhi: His Life and Thought*, p. 371.
62. J.B. Kripalani, *Planning* (New Delhi: Praja Socialist Party, 1957), p. 4.
63. Kripalani, *Gandhi: His Life and Thought*, p. 306.
64. *Ibid.*, p. 375.
65 Kripalani, *Gandhian Thought*, pp. 194-195.
66. *Ibid.*, p. 195.
67. *Ibid.*, p. 235.
68. *Ibid.*, p. 234.
69. Kripalani, *Latest Fad*, pp. 80-81.
70. *Ibid.*, p. 81.
71. *Ibid.*, p. 76.
72. *Ibid.*
73. *Ibid.*, p. 73.
74. *Ibid.*, pp. 77-78. The four *varnas* designated the four great classes of Aryan society. The four classes were the priest (*brahmana*), warrior (*Ksatriya*), peasant (*vaisya*), and serf (*sudra*). Varna is a Sanskrit word meaning "color." The four *ashrams* designated the four stages of life. The first was *brahmacharya* or celibacy, a period of preparation in which an individual leads a disciplined and dedicated life in the pursuit of knowledge and in gaining self control. During the second stage or *grahasthashram*, the individual became a householder and enjoyed life. The third stage or *vanaprastha* required the individual to withdraw from active life. The last stage or *sanniyasin* was one in which the individual-had totally withdrawn

himself from life and welcomed death, which was perceived to be a merging with the infinite. See A.L. Basham, *The Wonder That Was India* (New York: Grove Press, 1954), p. 35. J.P. and Naik, "Development and Gandhian Tradition in India," *The Review of Politics* 45 (July 1983): 348.

75. *Ibid.*, p. 80.
76. *Ibid.*, p. 11.
77. *Ibid.*
78. *Ibid.*, p. 14.
79. *Ibid.*
80. *Ibid.*, pp. 15-16.
81. *Ibid.*, p. 16.
82. *Ibid*, pp. 16-17.
83. *Ibid.*, pp. 17-19.
84. *Ibid.*, p. 21.
85. *Ibid.*, pp. 22-23.
86. *Ibid.*, pp. 25-26.
87. *Ibid.*, p. 26.
88. *Ibid.*, p. 27.
89. *Ibid.*, p. 28.
90. *Ibid.*, pp. 33-34.
91. *Ibid.*, p. 34.
92. *Ibid.*, pp. 35-36.
93. *Ibid.*, pp. 38-40.
94. *Ibid.*, p. 43.
95. *Ibid.*, pp. 44-45.
96. *Ibid.*, pp. 47-48.
97. *Ibid*, p. 49.
98. *Ibid.*, pp. 51-52.
99. *Ibid.*, p. 52.
100. *Ibid.*, pp. 55-56.
101. *Ibid.*, pp. 57-60.
102. *Ibid.*, p. 61.
103. *Ibid.*, p. 65.
104. *Ibid.*, pp.74-75.
105. *Ibid.*, p. 102.
106. *Ibid.*, p. 102.
107. *Ibid.*, pp. 96-97.
108. Kripalani, *Gandhi: His Life and Thought*, pp. 305-306.
109. J.B. Kripalani, *The Nightmare and After* (Bombay: Popular Prakashan, 1980), pp. 12 -127.

110. Kripalani, *Gandhi: His Life and Thought*, p. 317.
111. *Ibid.*, pp. 317-318.
112. J.B. Kripalani, *Gandhi The Statesman* (Delhi: Ranjit Printers and Publishers, 1951), p. 1.
113. *Ibid.*, pp. 18-19.
114. *Ibid.*, p. 20.
115. *Ibid.*, pp. 20-21.
116. *Ibid.*, p. 21.
117. Kripalani, *Gandhi: His Life and Thought*, p. 306.
118. Kripalani, *Gandhi The Statesman*, p. 24.
119. *Ibid.*, p. 31.
120. *Ibid.*, pp. 63-67.
121. *Ibid.*, p. 69.
122. *Ibid.*, pp. 69-70.
123. *Ibid.*, pp. 87-88.
124. *Ibid.*, p. 91.
125. *Ibid.*, pp. 93-94.
126. Kripalani, *Gandhian Thought*, pp. 132-133.
127. Kripalani, *Gandhi: His Life and Thought*, p. 356.

8

Democracy, Decentralization and Total Revolution

It has been argued in this work that there is a distinctive approach to democracy in modern Indian political thought, which is grounded both in ancient Indian thought and also follows the line of critique of parliamentary government running through Vivekananda and Aurobindo to Mahatma Gandhi and on to Jayaprakash Narayan and J.B. Kripalani.[1] Chapters Two through Seven have expounded the political thinking of M.N. Roy, Jayaprakash Narayan and J.B. Kripalani. This chapter will summarize their approach to democracy, especially with regard to the key concept of organizational decentralization, which they see as making possible the multifacted renovation of society including individual moral and ethical transformation. This is seen as a comprehensive or "total revolution." Chapter Nine will summarize the Indian vision of socialism or *Sarvodaya*, the real challenge of the revolution.

A central concept of the Indian approach to democracy is organizational decentralization, both politically and economically. This line of thinking parallels in significant ways the major themes in Western socialist thought. Each of the three thinkers discussed in this work contributed enormously to twentieth century Indian political thought in developing an extensive critique of contemporary society and its economic and political institutions. This broad critique includes a critical appraisal of both Western parliamentary government and the capitalistic pattern of society as well as existing Socialist and Communist societies. The main thrust of the argument involves the contention that the Renaissance vision of the individual as the central concern of society must be restored. It sees modern ideologies and the economic and political systems built upon them as shot through and through with contradictions and unable to advance human freedom in accordance with the Renaissance vision. The critique developed by these thinkers offers a challenge to contemporary society and goes to the heart of the contemporary global economic and political crisis. The critique also coincides with particular theses recently articulated by perceptive theorists such as Rudolph Bahro and Jurgen Habermas.

The theses embodied in the social critique of the three theorists discussed in this work, challenging the central concepts of Liberalism and Marxism which have emerged since the eighteenth century, deserve serious consideration by today's leaders and policy makers. If policies based upon these principles could take root widely, they could surely alleviate considerably the current economic and political crisis, as well as diminish human alienation, restore creative initiative and human solidarity and go far toward building a truly human global community.

Democracy

Today the dominant dogmas about modern society and the State must be thoroughly reexamined and carefully probed. The relationship between political and economic organisation, technology and violence, needs to be better understood if humankind is to survive and human society is to advance. As Robert C. North pointed out, " ... from today's perspective ... the overall trend through human pre-history and history may have been toward greater domestic and external violence rather than less.[2] This is contrary to the expectations of Thomas Hobbes who saw in modern political organisation the basis for greater rationality and securtiy. Similarly, modern Liberalism has failed in important ways to create a society of free and ethical individuals. The modern dependendence upon the State, based upon a predominantly utilitarian ethic, has proved only partially successful in providing greater material equality whilst failing to enable individuals to fulfil their most basic moral and spiritual needs in a humane and just society.

The arduous path travelled by M.N. Roy, Jayaprakash Narayan, and J.B. Kripalani led them to a perspective upon society radically different from that widely accepted today which places the State and the Party at the center. Beginning from diverse standpoints ideologically, they came to see economic and political decentralization as essential for the establishment of a democratic society which could ensure individual moral autonomy. They urged the renovation of society and politics through the application of moral values to the public sphere. They believed that the will is capable of triumphing over historical and material factors, thus rejecting economic determinism. Drawing from the Indian cultural tradition, they viewed freedom in terms of spiritual self-realization as the highest goal of the ethical individual in a free society.

M.N. Roy was a brilliant but in some respects an unsystematic political thinker. The great latitude of his thinking which moved terrorist and later Marxist to a view of freedom in spiritual terms, while insisting upon a thoroughly materialist ontology, resulted in serious contradictions in his thought as a whole. Nevertheless, one can profit enormously from his rich insights into the basic nature and internal contradictions of parliamentary democracy, dogmatic or reductionist Marxism and contemporary Socialism and Communism. Roy's Radical Humanism offered a vision of what a total ethical and institutional renovation of society would require, which in some respects conformed to that of Mahatma Gandhi. His perspective upon the Party and the State somewhat influenced Jayaprakash Narayan and his idea of a "Total Revolution."

As a revolutionary in Bengal, M.N. Roy was influenced by the Indian spiritual tradition through his study of religious literature. He again turned to this tradition late in life after he had given up his orthodox Marxist perspective, although he rejected the non-materialist or what he considered the metaphysical doctrines of Indian philosophical writings. Times of adversity, particularly the years of his imprisonment, set Roy thinking deeply about the essential nature of man and induced him to see freedom in spiritual terms.

Roy's first systematic analysis of society was attempted only after his study of and embrace of Marxism in the United States and Mexico. He fully accepted the fundamental tenets of historical materialism and economic determinism while he participated actively in the Communist International. Yet he was never completely comfortable with the iron discipline required of members of the organisation. He began to question and doubt that the Marxist analysis of history and society was infallible only after his official expulsion from the Communist Party and the International. With his disillusionment about developments in the Soviet Union in the 1930s and his close observation of political developments and society in India, his ideological blinders began to fall away and his extensive critique of orthodox Marxism was developed.

Roy viewed Marxism as a system of thought which, freed from its most serious contradictions, could become a basis for a radical humanist philosophy of the future. But he also argued that its historical evolution had introduced elements which led to man's slavery under contemporary Socialism and Communism. Roy believed that Marxism had two sides, materialist and teleological, and that the major contradictions were introduced by those whose approach was teleological. This teleological conception, he said, made men puppets. Marxist scholastics had made social forces and the means of production into modern gods. Roy urged man to develop instead the humanist side of Marxism. Man would again be seen as the creator of the world and the root of historical change. This was the direction in which Marx began before he moved to a strictly economic interpretation of history.

Roy ultimately rejected the Marxist and Hegelian view of freedom because according to this view man must recognize necessity before he is free. He observed that historical necessity in Marx is incompatible with the idea of man as a free human being who makes revolutions and all of history. Marxist historiography, it was argued, contradicts itself in trying to combine historical determinism with freedom of will. This cannot succeed because there is a teleological view in Marxism. He believed that his system of Radical Humanism, on the other hand, could combine historical determinism with human free will because it was free from the teleological view.

As a steadfast materialist, Roy rejected the Marxist theory of economic determinism but not historical determinism because in his view historical materialism does not exclude freedom of the will. His reason for rejecting economic determinism were firstly, that economic determinism is dualistic, philosophically, whereas a strict materialism is monistic. Secondly, it leads to the contradiction seen in the conclusion that the classless society will lack class struggle and thus be devoid of progress. Thirdly, Marx's ideas about the future of the State proved to be empirically false as it did not wither away. Fourthly, economic determinism does not recognize the autonomy of the mental world.

The economic interpretation of history, it was argued, is deduced from a wrong interpretation of materialism which involves a dualism in which one thing, i.e. the economic base, acts upon another, i.e. the ideological superstructure. Roy considered such thinking dangerous because it leads to empiricism, leaving out the factor of human will. Causality, he contended, is a logical rather that an empirical concept. History is a determined process, in his view, but it includes will as well as economic factors. The Marxist direction of causation between historical events and ideas, he said, must be rejected.

Philosophical materialism for Roy is a principle which cannot be compromised. He accused all systems of philosophy other than Materialism of being "dishonest religion."[3] In his view, mankind had made real progress toward freedom and human liberation only when a scientific and materialistic view of the world was emerging. He noted three such periods in history: classical Greece and ancient India, the European Renaissance and the period beginning with Ludwig Feuerbach's materialist criticism of religion. For Roy, "Materialism is the philosophy of revolution. Revolutions are inherent in the process of human development. Therefore, materialist philosophy is a necessity in all ages."[4] Roy effectively narrowed his view of true philosophy, stating that materialism is the only philosophy. He believed that the rejection of materialism by modern man had left only two alternatives: the protection of the totalitarian State or religious revivalism which constituted spiritual slavery. Roy's dogmatism concerning philosophical materialism led him to neglect the concentration in traditional Indian philosophy upon the spiritual which historically played the major role.

Marxism, Roy believed, was based on a wrong interpretation of materialism. The vulgarization of Marxism, including its theory of economic determinism, could, he thought, be traced to a major mistake made by Marx. Marx, as a humanist, wanted to correct Feuerbach's conception of man as an abstraction. But seeking a scientific explanation of human activity, Marx saw man's struggle as "economic." Roy, on the other hand, argued that it was not "economic" but rather a "biological" struggle for existence. But Marx's mistaken view led to the conception of man as an economic automaton. It should be noted, however, that such a view is not characteristic of the young Marx.

Roy concluded that Marx did not give adequate credit to the utopian socialists and agreed with Martin Buber that Marx's ideas were apocalyptic, and consequently eschatological and utopian. He pointed out that many of Marx's ideas were not original, the contributers including Vico, Edward Gibbon, Georg Hegel, Francois Guizot, Augustin Thierry, Louis Saint-Simon, Francois Mignet and Jules Michelet. Also contributing to his socialist views were Philippe Bounorotti, Louis Blanc and Jerome Blanqui. Roy considered it unfortunate that Marx rejected the humanist traditions of the utopians and eighteenth century materialism, seeing it as mechanical. He believed that Marxism, departing from its philosophical tradition, came to embrace a vulgar form of materialism.

There were other damaging contradictions in Marxism, according to Roy. If the "bourgeios ideologies" developed by British political economists could become the ideology of the proletariat, as Marx believed, then how could ideology be the product of economic necessity? He concluded that the concept of ideas associated with class structure in history must be rejected. Rather, ideas grow out of the material world and are a part of it. Ideas have a history of their own, he said, and develop progressively rather than dialectically. Roy believed that while no science of history could predict the future, his historical materialism showed that one could reconstruct history from the history of human thought.

Roy saw the violence associated with Marx's theory of social change as the "romantic extravagance" of revolution and antithetical to rationalism. He charged that Marxism was cynical because it held that human beings are never motivated by moral impulses. But believing that revolutionary action is the decisive force of history leads to the idea of the dictatorship of the proletariat and a political dictatorship.

On the positive side, Roy believed that Marxism contributed to philosophy, offering a solution to Cartesian dualism, a sharp separation between mind and matter. Marx formulated, he said, the fundamental principles of material monism. Marx was at heart a revolutionary and an idealist, but allowed philosophical dualism and a teleological outlook into his system, imposing shackles on man's freedom. Ultimately, the individual was replaced by the collective ego of society.

Roy also criticized modern Liberalism. The most damaging aspect, he believed, was the tremendous gap between its doctrine and its application in practice. Liberalism based on the scientific naturalism of Hobbes and the psychology of sensation put forward by John Locke gave man a new faith in himself. Roy believed Liberalism began the struggle for emancipation from religion and spiritual serfdom. The secular thinking of Hobbes with its scientific, materialistic and mechanistic cosmology, laid the foundation for Liberalism. In this scheme, man was a part of Nature and Nature was a rational process. The Hobbesian system was a sound foundation for democracy, Roy said, because the purpose of social organisation was to promote the individuality of its members. Borrowing from the Enlightment and Stoic and Christian ideas about the nature of man, Liberalism put faith in the individual as a moral entity.

But Liberalism, according to Roy, fell short of true democracy. Its two main concepts, parliamentary rule in the political field and *laissez faire* in economics, were defective. The parliamentary system was in effect a dictatorship of the Party, Roy argued. The individual sought shelter in the collective—the Party and the State. A utilitarian ethics underpinned and justified the system. With social atomization, the individual was rendered powerless. Elections were largely appeals to emotions, resulting in mass hysteria. There was a universal desire to capture power among the contending parties. The delegation of power through representation resulted in surrender of power. Under parliamentary "democracy" the executive could not be controlled by the people. In the collective sphere, confused, powerless and helpless citizens could not be individuals. As such the system was politically bankrupt, in Roy's view. Liberalism was further mistaken in the view that a good society could be ensured by good laws. Only good individuals could produce a good society.

The theory of *laissez faire* also impeded individual freedom, as it appeared to justify exploitation. It negated many gains made in the political realm.

Consistent with his materialist view, Roy thought the root of the problem was that Liberalism was not secular enough. It inclined toward natural religion, reason coming to be viewed as metaphysical, as something transcendental. God came to be seen as "immanent in nature" and reason came to be seen as conscience. This rebirth of pantheism created a secular religion, again rendering individual freedom impossible. Roy also argued that Liberalism was morally ambiguous. De-secularization and Comptean positivism were damaging trends. Utilitarianism led to moral relativism and spiritual slavery.

Roy's New Humanism or Radical Humanism viewed man as a free creative being. Building on positive elements from the Renaissance, Marxism and Liberalism, Roy sought to construct a philosophy which would transcend contemporary political thinking which tended toward a concept of the individual ego merged into the collective ego of society. Roy began with the notion that the individual needed democracy as a result of the individual urge for freedom which was inherent in human nature. Roy defined freedom as "the progressive elimination of all the factors, physical, social and psychological which obstruct the unfolding of man's rational, moral and creative potentialities."[5] He said that freedom is real only as individual freedom. Rejecting the concept of group morality, Roy posited the goal of a government of spiritually free individuals accountable to their consciences. In this respect his view of human freedom as spiritual liberation or *Moksha*, was similiar to that of Aurobindo, Vivekananda and Mahatma Gandhi. This view sees the fundamental urge in man as toward spiritual freedom, and the development of this creative urge as a prerequisite for social and political freedom.

Human nature for Roy is sufficient cause for the endless progress of mankind. It is not an immutable category, but subject to an evolutionary process. The three aspects of human nature, rationality, morality and freedom, arise materially. Man's capacity for reason and moral judgement, conscience, instinct, and intuition, are all the result of a law-governed system, all arising materially. Morality, therefore, is grounded in the material universe. Seeing natural law categories as vacuous, Roy held that values arise either "sui generes or empirically."

The rationality in the material universe is a basis for human rationality. Human consciousness and conscience arise out of the material universe which is law-governed. History is a determined process, but the individual has free will, Roy contended. It is human reason which "harmonises" the play of human will with the law-governedness of the physical universe. Further, Roy saw a correpondence between the level of human evolution and the level of consciousness. There was an evolution from Hobbesian egotist to Radical Humanist and ultimately to a harmonious and humanist society of free individuals. This reductionist scheme introduced serious problems into Roy's thinking, as will be discussed below.

Roy's "scientific" view of politics included the ideas that the evolution of society is both a determined process and that man is free to remake the world through the application of scientific knowledge. Roy thought that the lack of scientific knowledge about human nature and he world had, numerous times in the past, resulted in the rebirth of religious mysticism and man's continued enslavement. But knowledge acquired through science was the key to human emancipation, Science, for him, was the source of knowledge and the basis for all human progress. Through science, Roy was convinced that it could finally be proven that life, human consciousness and volition arose from dead matter.

Roy persisted in his faith in the inevitability of progress and the belief that the pursuit of Truth would promote freedom and morality. He continued to see religion as enslaving and observed that Liberalism, Socialism and Communism often functioned as secular religions. For human liberation, it was essential for man to regain faith in himself. He must become aware of his rational essence. New Humanism, he hoped, would restore this image of man to himself and release the human initiative and creativity to remake the world rationally. Therefore he rejected the Marxist vision of social transformation, i.e. as the violent organisational transformation of institutions, instead stressing more heavily individual moral transformation as the root of the humanist revolution.

Roy reformulated the concept of democracy to conform with the principles of New Humanism. He insisted that power must be decentralized, that party dominance of society must end, that the State, rather than withering away, must become "coterminous with society," that the Party must be abolished so that power will be dispersed among the people and that people's committees of village *panchayats* must be established. He adopted a Weberian view of the State as a coordinator of autonomous social institutions. It would not constitute itself as a power over and above the people. He said that humanist politics would be the art of public administration. The instutional structure must safeguard the individual moral and intellectual integrity of each citizen. This aspect of Roy's conception of Radical Humanist democracy will be reviewed more fully below.

Roy's view of Radical self-transformation and social change sought to avoid the mystifications of the modern State, rejected the Hegelian conception of freedom and necessity, held that collective freedom cannot be moral, rejected a morality based on a utilitarian standard of ethics and placed the hope for mankind on the individual. Roy concluded that society must be transformed by individual human will and action, and that emphasis must be placed upon both inner moral transformation and external institutional change.

Several criticisms have been leveled at Roy's political thinking. Firstly, it can be argued that Roy's determinist historicism, based on his cosmological presuppositions, limits free will. For Roy, free will arises through natural evolution and its emergence as a mechanical, material and a determined process. Roy argued that his thinking was not teleological, as was Marxism. But this assertion was dubious. Roy did see human potentiality and rationality as unfolding in a teleological way. He believed that man's struggle for freedom, as an element of his essential human nature, must result in greater knowledge, truth, rationality and humanism. Consequently, Roy was faced with the same difficulty which he saw in Marx. He could not have both a determinist historicism and human free will in his system. Human choice and free will were largely reduced to biological functions. It must be concluded that Roy's Radical Humanism, grounded in materialist determinism limited man's free will in the same way as did Marxism.

Further, Roy's concept of human nature could not adequately account for emotion and irrationality. It is difficult for one to understand how the individual can choose to be irrational in Roy's scheme, once scientific knowledge is available and enables the individual to make rational decisions. Roy said that reason harmonizes the play of human will with the law- governedness of the physical universe. But if reason involves conforming the will to physical laws, it is difficult to see how this is different from succumbing to historical necessity in Hegel, and calling this freedom. Since for Roy reason and will as well as values arose mechanically from the material world, they must also be socially determined and it is difficult to understand how the individual can indeed have free will in such a cosmological scheme.

Another problem is that Roy confused fact and value because reason is both a faculty of the individual's personality and the law of the universe. For Roy, values arose "either *sui generis* or empirically." For him, natural law categories were vacuous. He believed that man's values correspond to the level of evolution of human consciousness throughout history.

Roy came to understand and conceptualize freedom as *Moksha*, like others in the Indian tradition. But he differed from Aurobindo, Vivekananda and Gandhi as his conception of spiritual freedom was not based on the teachings of Vedanta but upon materialism. Though it has been pointed out that there is no logical relation between Roy's materialism and his ethical and political ideas. There is no integrated philosophical system.

Jayaprakash Narayan developed a conception of partyless democracy similiar in many respects to that of M.N. Roy. As has been noted, J.P. was influenced by Roy's writings and gained key insights from him. J.P.'s political thought was shaped by three main currents of thought: Marxism, Gandhism and liberal democracy. His ideals concerning equality and brotherhood originally came from Marx, although he found sanction for them in the Indian tradition.

Similiar to Roy, J.P. became a Marxist and a socialist in his youth, looking to the Soviet Union as a model of society, and for a scientific approach to social transformation. He fully accepted the Marxist analysis of society, applying it to Indian society in the 1930s. He saw the solution to India's social and political problems as the orthodox Marxist one, which included political and economic centralization. In 1936 he believed that nationalization of the means of production would effectively transfer power to the masses. He also believed that capitalism in India was based upon imperialism and would vanish when the British departed. The agrarian problem, he thought, could easily be resolved by persuading the peasants to cooperate with collectivization. Even at this point in the evolution of his thinking he found sanction for his socialist ideas in the social organization of ancient India.

As an orthodox Socialist, J.P. bitterly criticized Gandhi's theory of trusteeship. He pointed out that as long as the economic structure of society remained unchanged, the hearts of the landlords and capitalists could not be changed. The mode of production must change before human nature could change, he thought. Human behavior would be reformed through relying upon structural barriers to immorality rather than through Gandhian radical self-transformation. The State would be the mechanism for the moral transformation of society after the Socialists had seized power. So there was a contradiction in J.P.'s thought, seen also in other utopian thinkers, between a faith in the potential of human nature and a reliance upon external organization and formal regulation.

During the 1940s, J.P.'s ideas began to change. By 1942, during the "Quit India" Movement, he was beginning to consider a more indigenous pattern of social change and his thinking moved closer to the Gandhian ideal of *swaraj*, with its reliance upon a greater degree of decentralization. By 1944, J.P. had become disillusioned about the quality of life in the Soviet Union. He began to question Marxist assumptions concerning the economic basis of human behavior. Instead, he became more concerned with moral values. He also began to doubt that desirable values would arise automatically after the structural transformation of society. J.P. increasingly looked to the Indian tradition as a source of societal values, partly accepted the Gandhian path of humanist reformation of society, agreed that non-violence is the most just path, and began to see elements of cultural heritage which all Indians shared as a cohesiver force in society and which transcended class, caste, tribe, religion, community and political persuasion.

J.P.'s thought at this point was in a state of transition. He wanted a non-relativistic code of morality, but still clung to the idea that it might be necessary to violate it to bring about the good society. He argued for a socialist morality which would not serve to preserve the rights and privileges of dominant classes in society. In 1944 he was also not prepared to accept Gandhi's principle that the ends can never justify the means. He stated that he was not prepared to reject immoral means for moral ends.

But by 1946, J.P. had largely accepted Gandhi's constructive programme and he called for the political decentralization of society. J.P.'s Congress Socialist Party launched constructive programmes in the villages at this time, attempting to establish self-governing villages, or a system of *gram raj*. His theoretical perspective was similar to that of M. N. Roy. Firstly, he saw Marxism as a science of society and as such not dogmatic, claiming to be final truth. Secondly, he believed that with greater knowledge, through science, man could more nearly approximate the truth. Thirdly, Marxism was essentially a method to understand and change history.

J.P. believed that the establishment of socialism in India would involve two stages : the transition stage and socialism itself. He envisioned firstly the establishment of parliamentary democracy and after that the transition from parliamentary democracy to socialism. The Congress Socialist Party could, he believed, establish socialism through the ballot box. But he also feared that the Congress might become a "bourgeios party" and fail to bring about the necessary social transformation. In this case a class conflict might result in a violent revolution.

During the 1940s, J.P.'s view of social transformation included other elements. Agricultural organization would proceed through a cooperative and then a collective stage. Legal ownership of land would rest with the village, peasants having proprietary rights. The overall productive operation would be cooperative. Peasants would be allowed to sell land to the *gram panchayat* only, with wages being paid in kind. Economic production would be decentralized as far a is possible to limit the power of the State. J.P. decided that the dictatorship of the proletariat must be rejected as it was a bureaucratic oligarchy in reality.

In 1947, after the Indian National Congress was transformed into the Congress Party, the Congress Socialist Party became the Socialist Party. J.P. hoped it would serve as a party of the peasants and workers. After the death of Mahatma Gandhi in 1948, J.P. became more critical of both, Liberal democracy and Marxism. He accepted Gandhi's position on means and ends and he began to question the utility of power politics, because it led to the idea that the end can justify the means. Valuing the society over the State, he wanted the State to be subsidiary to society. He wanted the State to wither away by strengthening society in relation to the State.

During this democratic socialist phase of his thinking, J.P. questioned the theory of violence in Marxism. He valued democratic change over violent change and wanted socialism to include democratic freedoms. But he continued to believe that the capture of political power was necessary to establish democratic socialism.

After undergoing a fast at Poona in 1952, J.P. made his final break with Marxism. In 1954, he withdrew from the Party and denounced power politics. He took a vow of *Jeevandan*, pledging to dedicate his life to the *Sarvodaya* Movement. Seeing Socialism as *Sarvodaya*, he finally rejected the Marxist tenet that changes in social structure could result in socialism and argued that the means of production does not determine the relations of production. He also addressed the problem of the gap between theory and practice in socialist society, in which an oligarchic power structure and viscious power struggle continues to exist. He charged that Marxism was based on amoralism and the doctrine that the end justifies the means. Good and evil were seen as relative and a one-sided approach taken, which aimed at reconstructing the institutional structure while neglecting the individual.

J.P. saw the moral individual as the true basis for socialist society. One must be sure that what one does is consistent with the ultimate goal, he said.

J.P. argued that materialism can never be a basis for morality. If a philosophical materialist struggled for noble causes, then his action would not be consistent with his philosophy. Consequently, Marxism was internally inconsistent in its theory of action. He also believed that the Marxist assumption of free will was inconsistent with philosophical materialism and he doubted that consciousness could arise out of matter. Consciousness, he thought, could not be understood scientifically and objectively, but only subjectively, because consciousness arises from the spiritual aspect of the individual. The root of morality is in the ultimate spiritual experience of self-realization and this is a source of moral values for the good society.

Concluding that socialist experimentation had failed to discover a viable organisational structure for socialism, he turned to Gandhi's conception of a decentralized socialism or *Sarvodaya*. The State could not bring about such real social change, he concluded. It would have to come about non-violently, through individual initiative. He arrived at Gandhi's belief that the best way to distribute wealth was voluntarily and decided that this could be achieved through *bhoodan, gramdan* and *gram raj* movements.

Sarvodaya was conceived as a democratic, partyless, decentralized and non-violent socialist pattern of society concerned with universal human welfare and the realization of human potential. The *Sarvodaya* image of society is in the modern tradition of anarchism in which economics was to be people-centered, decentralized and subject to a non-relativistic standard of ethics. J.P. was concerned with the struggle for a humanist pattern of society which would restore the individual to the place of primary importance in society, embrace rationality, cooperation, harmony, science and, intellectual and spiritual freedom. He also wished to avoid the atomization, large-scale industrialization and urbanization of Western society and the politics of class interests.

During his work in the *Sarvodaya* movement, J.P. tended to idealize village life and he urged the restoration of the self-governing village as the fundamental unit of social organisation. He became increasingly disillusioned with the Congress Party and Congress rule during the 1950s. Stressing Vinoba Bhave's distinction between *rajniti* (party and power politics) and *lokniti* (non-party and non-power politics) he sharply criticized parliamentary democracy.

J.P. objected to the existing system of parliamentary democracy for several reasons. It was said to be contrary to the nature of human society and the social nature of man, that its basic principles are unsound and that it is a foreign transplant not rooted in Indian soil. He said that the people of India did not understand it, and that it did not contribute to a true community as it emphasized party rather than community. Moreover, it was built upon an improper economic foundation, emphasized rights rather than responsibilities, looked to elitist party rule and did not produce real individuals but rather alienated individuals from themselves. It led to the creation of a mass society, large scale exploitative industrialization, urbanization, uncurbed materialistic desires and the atomization of society, he charged.

J.P. considered parliamentary democracy contrary to the nature of human society and the social nature of man because it saw society as inorganic and man as a grain of sand rather than as an integral part of the organic whole. This criticism was inspired by the Spanish political philosopher, Salvador de Madariaga. He preferred the organic or communitarian view of society wherein man is seen as a living cell in a larger organic unity. He said that the parliamentary system resulted in a fictitious democracy. The ballot box and the party system could not bring democracy because the economic system favoured the propertied interests. J.P. also questioned the rationale of one- man one-vote because of the lack of preparation of the Indian population for voting. Under the party system, it was said, a true community could not be established because such a community must emphasize adjustment, conciliation, harmony and cooperation. The party system, on the other hand, involved a corrupting power struggle. Based on Western society, with its spirit of economism whereby human values became subordinated to "economic progress," it was unsuitable for Indian society. In the parliamentary system was an inherent tendency toward centralization, bureaucratization and a mass society which precluded the development of the personality. The economy could not be balanced with Nature because capitalism encouraged ever greater levels of consumption and perpetuated social and economic injustice.

The essence of democracy for J.P. was self-government of the people and the ideal system to ensure participation was the *Sarvodaya* model of socialism. "Democracy..., is a value: and it is the essence of all democratic institutions and practical processes involved to preserve the value of democracy and to make it possible for it to grow."[6] Representative government was seen as inadequate owing to the lack of popular participation.

Democratic decentralization could provide for the basic needs of the individual and the community. A "human life" can be attained, he said, only in the small primary community, and the essence of human life is in living together. There must be "bonds" between individuals.[7] Not only would decentralization provide for greater participation but it would satisfy a number of other needs. Firstly, the individual wants to be free from coercion, but at the same time, there must be some social restraints. The small community would use persuasion rather than force to discipline its members. Social and economic change would proceed through moral growth. Government would be reduced to a minimum, making for more self-government. The government would be close to the people and this would encourage the self-discipline which a democracy requires.[8] These aspects of decentralization will be delineated more fully in the next section.

J.B. Kripalani was another giant among twentieth century Indian political thinkers. Advocating a ruthless decentralization, he was sceptical of totalistic and apocalyptic solutions, favoring instead a more progressive approach. He recognized the potential for humanity for both great good and great evil. Mistrusting foreign models as a basis for Indian society, he developed a critique of the centralized pattern of society in Parliamentary Democracy, Socialism and Communism.

Kripalani rejected the fundamental tenets of Marxism, seeing genuine revolution as evolutionary. Although violent revolution might remove some of the hindrances to the evolutionary process of history, he believed that it could do no more. He argued that the most radical and effective change was pragmatic and reformist. He saw revolution as a process whereby moral principles were rediscovered and restored as the basis of polity. As a general principle, the least violence brought about the greatest change in the shortest time. In reality he realized that some violence arising from human action in history was unavoidable as there were degrees of truth. But violence to any degree would result in a proportional accumulation of the *karma* of violence.

On the whole, Kripalani was less critical of the Party and the State than M.N. Roy and J.P., although he viewed them as imperfect institutions. The fundamental ethical principle for a moral society, he believed, was that of non-violence. In addition there must be established a decentralized pattern of political institutions and economic production. Kripalani rejected historical materialism, unlike M.N. Roy, arguing that history could not be described by such laws. For Kripalani, the driving force of history was not class struggle but rather psychological and ideological factors. He considered particular individuals and minorities extremely important in history as the masses often resist progress. He firmly believed that class struggle had never existed, but if it had, the result would have been reression rather than progress for mankind as Marx believed. He described the historical movement of society as a "zig-zag" or "ascending spiral" rather than linear progress. Somewhat like M.N. Roy and J.P., true human freedom or liberation was seen in spiritual terms.

Kripalani believed that the fundamental dilemma facing modern society was the concentration of power in the State apparatus. This collectivization of power is necessarily bound up with the centralized economic structure of modern society and affects the cultural and moral values of society. If democracy is to function and moral values are to remain strong, there must be a devolution of political power, Kripalani advocated a balance between local and central units of government so that the strength of the center would depend upon the strength of the local units. Industry must be dispersed and under the control of local authorities.

Kripalani's critique of presently existing politicoeconomic systems charged that each of these displayed over-centralization, both politically and economically. This made machines the masters of men and could not solve unemployment and distribution problems. Each system appeared as an institutional device for achieving economic equality, but undermined moral and spiritual freedom. Finally, each system gave rise to the theory of justification by success. While the logical end of Western liberal democracy was a superior form of democratic socialism, historically, the evolutionary process was derailed by capitalism and imperialism. This destroyed political equality by creating great economic inequality.

"Democratic Centralism" was a myth, according to Kripalani, as "centralism and democracy are really contradictions in terms." He said that the State could not wither away under Communism because it does not preserve the moral integrity of the individual. Instead, the State becomes increasingly powerful. So Communism, it was argued, is regressive in terms of historical progress. The State assumed the duties formerly usurped by the joint family, the caste and the guild. In a bureaucratically complex society, most things must be left to the experts. Communism struck at the root of democracy, i.e. at the principle of the moral autonomy of the individual. The individual is seen as only an "ensemble of social relations."

Kripalani theorized that there existed a historical *karma* and that, in fact, Communist society resulted from the historical *karma* of violence. Under Communism, the leaders are under a "psychology of fear." This is because they came to power by terror and they fear their own overthrow by terror. This begins a chain reaction as leaders rush to build up their power, but in so doing strengthen political and economic centralization. The required rapid capitalization requires a political dictatorship, and the principles of the revolution are soon perverted.

It is clear, Kripalani believed, that both private capitalism and state capitalism result in exploitation, poverty, misery, and ultimately in imperialism and war. Capitalism requires enormous sacrifices under both economic systems. The important principle which Kripalani wished to emphasize was that "economic equality must not be purchased at the price of political and spiritual slavery." There is a need for decentralized industry to help preserve free choice and initiative.

Another objection Kripalani had to socialism was that there was a metamorphosis of moral and spiritual principles into institutional devices to achieve economic equality. Kripalani traced this development to the theory of dialectical materialism, whereby history is treated as scientific and morality is seen in historical terms as an ever changing device for achieving success. He rejected justification by success, arguing instead that human action in history must be based on moral principles.

Kripalani criticized the "scientific socialists" for attacking political democracy, which they confused with the individualism of the capitalist order. Democracy came to be perceived as an "external and organisational device," while the fundamental values of oneness, tolerance and love were obscured. He pointed out that only a few have realized that the moral principle of democracy is inconsistent with economic capitalism.

Kripalani believed that cottage industry could preserve political and individual liberty whilst avoiding the ills of capitalism. It could establish "economic socialism" and avoid imperialism. And in eliminating the factory boss, cottage industry would go far toward eliminating political dictatorships. Further, it could also largely eliminate the arms industry. In terms of the whole system, non-violent methods would be more economical and would provide the soundest basis for democratic socialism. There were nine reasons for this: the principles of cooperation and non-violence would extend democracy to the economic realm, cottage industry would embody spiritual and cultural values, it would eliminate extraction of surplus value from workers, it would eliminate the accumulation of capital either by private industry or the State, science and technology could be brought into harmony with moral and spiritual values, it could eliminate the ills associated with the tedious division of labour and improve the quality of work, it would inculcate independence and self-reliance, the voluntary limitation of wants would encourage self-discipline and mastery of the self, and finally, it would diminish unemployment while boosting collective national wealth.

With cottage industry, mechanization would be acceptable, and even encouraged, but most industry would remain small-scaled. For Kripalani, the cottage pattern of industry was "revolutionary." Another virtue was that it placed moral restraints upon science and technology. Kripalani said that science was basically a search for Truth. To preserve certain higher moral values, he believed, some "practical" results of science might have to remain unexploited.

During the 1930s Kripalani defended the *Sarvodaya* concept of socialism against the criticism of M.N. Roy and J.P. Kripalani believed that Gandhi's constructive program would begin the transition to socialism and prepare the people for political independence. He did not believe that both freedom and socialism could come about simultaneously. At this time he believed that the socialists' programme was, in several ways counterproductive both in terms of reaching political independence from Britain and the broader goal of *swaraj*. He criticized philosophical materialism, viewing the idea as a hypothesis, previously useful to physical scientists and which Marxists had accepted as unquestionable truth and made a pillar of their teaching. With regard to industrialization, he said that the real choice was between development through *swadeshi* or decentralization and centralization, rather than between capitalism and Communism.

Kripalani also developed a philosophy of history which criticized the Marxist view. Violence in history was viewed as regressive. Kripalani argued further that in the social sciences there can be no fixed and inexorable laws. This is because social science deals with dynamic and self-regulative beings and human conduct is influenced by values. Further, social phenomena are in a flux and there are a host of confounding variables often not quantifiable. It would be "material mysticism" to reduce the various aspects of human life to a unitary cause. Consequently, social science can only establish certain tendencies but even these may be altered by human ingenuity, wisdom and will.

Kripalani criticized the concept of class struggle in Marxism. It was based on nine assumptions, he said: that sociology and history are exact sciences with inexorable laws, that the primary moving force in history is economic, that human history has been largely the conflict between two classes—masters and slaves, that the polarization of these two classes had occurred in the industrial West, that polarization means deteriorating conditions for the masses and ultimately class war, that the proletariat will triumph in the struggle, that the dictatorship of the proletariat is necessary for the new society, that in the new society, class and State will fade away and that the interests of the world proletariat are identical, the class struggle being international in scope.

Kripalani argued that history did not support these assumptions. Firstly, social change is not governed by class struggle but by "custom, convention, fixed belief and superstition," as can be seen from a study of ancient Greece and Rome and medieval Europe. He said that Marx over-generalized from one phase of European history when the economic power of industrial and economic classes was dominant. Consequently, he "rationalised a preconceived theory." Secondly, he argued that past revolutions were often the result of conscious tyranny, perceived injustice and departure from convention and tradition rather than class struggle. Generally the wealth of classes, he said, did not cause revolts. Rather, injustice and tyranny caused revolts. The poor generally blamed "fate" for their poverty.

Looking at particular events in history, he said that in Rome the plebians revolted against the patricians for citizenship rights and political power. In seventeenth century England, the struggle was to assert the authority of parliament over the King. The Levellers drew their inspiration from the teachings of Christ. In the French Revolution, the idea of equality was derived from reason, with economic considerations subordinate. The American Revolution was based on "liberty, equality and fraternity" and the Russian Revolution was directed against the Czar and the war rather than against the capitalist class. The Revolution threw up a liberal government under Kerensky, which was overthrown by Lenin's military coup. In the Russian Revolution, society was polarized between the landlords and the tenants and in France, the rebellion was against the aristocracy. So history, he concluded, is not governed by class struggle as Marx had supposed.

Kripalani's own view of history was that social change is evolutionary and revolution is only the last step in a long process. He said that revolutions in all stages of life, geological, biological and socio-political, are evolutionary. Historical evolution, he thought, was generally progressive, moving toward democratic socialism and toward greater honesty, fairness, cooperation and non-violence. Non-violence is the highest stage of social evolution and violence can produce retrogression. Human progress involves both internal and institutional reform and for true reform both must be in balance. The organisation of external social relations must be guided by moral principles.

Kripalani believed that social institutions, although imperfect, could serve the purpose of Truth. But since Truth keeps changing its facets in history, institutions must remain flexible. Kripalani accepted the Platonic Idea of Truth as eternal and absolute, but, like Gandhi, believed that Truth took different forms. Progressive change must involve reverting back to the "fountainhead" of Truth and devising new institutions. But the modern tendency, he contended, had been to abolish moral values rather than the institutions which prevented their application. Individuals, because of this, remained enslaved by class, caste, race and nation.

Kripalani argued that the driving forces in history are psychological rather than material. The essence of revolution is the idea behind it. An array of forces contribute to revolution and human progress, including human ingenuity, will, personality, charisma, spiritual fervor, moral values, ideas, slogans and the irrational element in individuals. Often "the new hope and the new gospel are incarnated in a personality." Individual effort was seen as the major driving force for historical reform, although at a particular time, the reformer may appear to be traditionalist, revivalist or reactionary. Leaders in history need a "clear vision" and an "iron will" and must succeed in institutionalizing ideas. The element of chance in history was important. The physical and economic fields were only the "necessary background" to the psychological and ideological fields. He argued that revolution could never result from poverty alone and, in fact, poverty often rendered the people lifeless.

Kripalani saw as the greatest danger for the revolutionary the doctrine that the end justifies the means. In politics, as in religion, brutality could be employed for the sake of orthodoxy and dogma. Revolutions could destroy their children. In history, the results of human action could never be completely known, and therefore the need for moral values.

Progress in history, for Kripalani, was linked to the trend toward non-violence. This was the fundamental revolution and he believed that Mahatma Gandhi had a historic mission to change both the individual and society. Non-violent action would create a stock of *karma* for peace and good will. So a powerful force could be created for disarmament, international cooperation and a world peace. To the extent that human institutions such as the family, religion, commerce, industry, politics, government and law had embodied the law of non-violence, they had marked progress for humankind.

Kripalani further criticized the concept of class struggle in regard to conditions in India. He pointed out that in all societies cooperation is more important than class antagonisms. In India itself, the concept of class struggle lacked explanatory power as caste was more divisive and pervasive. Further, the major division in Indian society, he believed, was between the urban and rural interests, rather than between the capitalists and the proletariat. Kripalani believed that the decentralization of industry would make the concept of class struggle obsolete in India. He thought that many conflicts in Indian society could best be solved through mutual cooperation and that it was unrealistic to look to the small number of industrial workers for a revolutionary upsurge. Rather, the masses in the villages must be organized for non-violent struggle. Capitalism could be modified through cooperation, democracy, *Satyagraha* and trade unionism. Unity rather than divisiveness was the "way of wisdom." Recently Marxist scholars have re-examined the concept of class struggle and arrived at some of the same objections which Kripalani raised in his writings.

Kripalani was one of the first thinkers to attempt to interpret systematically the ideas of Mahatma Gandhi. He argued that Gandhi's ideas constituted an organic or integral philosophy which could serve as the basis for a fundamental revolution. He said that the period since the French Revolution had produced only two great revolutionaries, Gandhi and Marx. But whereas the ends for the two thinkers were similiar, in some respects, the means to the ends were in dialectical opposition. Gandhi's approach to means was, in itself revolutionary, he said. For Gandhi, the means must not deviate from the principles of Truth and non-violence.

Kripalani saw parliamentary democracy as partially embodying Gandhian principles. There was a movement toward greater individual moral autonomy before retrogressive and exploitative capitalism was introduced through the back door. But he said that the progress in group and inter-group morality had not kept pace with improvements in inter-personal relations. Inter-group and inter-state violence remained due to the acceptance of the principle of moral man and immoral society. Kripalani thought that through *Satyagraha* and decentralization, reform of the group, even on the level of the State, could be carried out. But the Gandhian principles that the end can never justify the means and that there can be no dual morality for the public and private spheres must be accepted. In general, he argued, the "group mind" is morally less advanced and more mechanical than the individual mind and also less amenable to reason and moral influence. But he was convinced that the use of *Satyagraha* would lead to less inter-group violence. Kripalani wrote an interpretation of Gandhi's concept of *Satyagraha* based upon the dilemma of Socrates in *Crito*. He explained the attitude of the *Satyagrahi* to the laws of the State. It is the purpose of the *Satyagrahi* to improve the laws rather than to destroy them. Possible individual choices could be seen in terms of a hierarchy of ethical positions. On the lowest level would be the person who would try to escape from the jurisdiction of the laws and thus tend to harm or destroy the law. On the second higher level would be those who abide by the law but do nothing to improve it. On the highest level would be those who as *Satyagrahis* try to improve the law. Their allegiance is to a higher law and they want the laws of the State to conform with this law, as nearly as possible.

For Kripalani, the laws which provide for the functioning of individual free will, must not oblige the free individual to do that which is against his will. He said, "Only in freedom can there be responsibility." Kripalani's argument hinged upon the contention that the State, realizing the limits of its power, "gives the citizens the choice of either not to break the law or to undergo the punishment for disobedience of the laws."[9] When a person accepts either of the two alternatives provided by the law, according to Kripalani, he has fulfilled the requirements of the law. His "disobedience is only semantical. One who tried to escape the law, on the other hand, would be refusing to accept any of the alternatives provided by the law.

Kripalani argued that the *Satyagrahi* resolved the contradiction between the individual citizen and the State by willingly undergoing the punishment awarded by the state authorities. By doing this, he does no harm to the laws, remains a free and ethical person, and puts pressure on the society to reform and improve the laws, more nearly in accord with a higher ethical standard. Kripalani suggested that most human progress in history had proceeded through this mechanism. This was compared to Gandhi's stand when he was arrested for assisting the peasants at Champaran. According to Gandhi, when one obeys a higher law, he fulfils the requirements of the lower law and helps reform it. Therefore *Satyagraha* was not an "anti-social" activity.

Kripalani saw Gandhi's concept of *Satyagraha* as based upon his Indian background. He pointed out that for the Jains and the Hindus, *ahimsa* was the highest virtue. It was not correct that *Satyagraha* was based on the *New Testament*, he said. The *New Testament's* mission was spiritual but Gandhi did not separate the material and spiritual realms in regard to reform. He said that where Christ was concerned with changing the individual, Gandhi wanted to change both the individual and society.

In Kripalani's interpretation one could see at least four levels of morality in possible human choices. On the lowest level was the cowardly, who did not resist tyranny and evil. Next came the violent resister, who was better that the coward. On the third level was the physically non-violent resister who out of necessity or weakness was non-violent. On the highest level was the non-violence of the strong. This was the action of those, who, following the law of life, were non-violent in thought, word and deed.

A significant distinction was made between Western Pacifism and *Satyagraha*. It could be argued that *Satyagraha* was closer to the Buddhist concept of morality in all spheres of activity. Kripalani believed that non-violent non-cooperation was more effective today than the older doctrines of Buddha, Christ and Mahavira, because their resistance was psychological and not external or organizational. Gandhi also demanded political reform. So *Satyagraha* involved individual, social and political duty.

The idea that the *Satyagraha* method of reform raised conflict to a higher moral level resulting in less conflict was also expressed. Kripalani believed that a degree of organization or institutionalization is necessary although some degree of purity is lost. Overall, in *Satyagraha,* he said, "The gulf between theory and practice is narrowest."

Kripalani suggested that the complex nature of modern society actually allowed *Satyagraha* to work better. Since large-scale cooperation was required for the functioning of modern society, non-cooperation could be very effective, and it became transparently clear that the oppressed forge their own chains by their active cooperation with evil. An industrial strike was viewed as the non-violence of the weak, based upon class antagonism. *Satyagraha*, on the other hand, involved no anger or ill will. The philosophy of non-violence, it was believed, had radical implications for disarmament in the field of international relations, but it was stressed that external organisation was insufficient. Internal will was also required to achieve world peace. *Satyagraha* was seen as a "moral substitute for war," but it was also pointed out that it was better to resist violently than to submit passively to evil.

The first systematic explanation of Mahatma Gandhi's conception of basic education was provided by Kripalani in which he delineated the philosophical basis for craft education. He stressed that the purpose was to prepare the individual to live according to the principles of Truth and non-violence. Another aim was to end the artificial division between the concept of the individual and society. Because the human individual attains his individuality only in a group or in society, Kripalani pointed out that there must be a proper balance, that is, a synthesis between the individual and society.

According to Kripalani, there were three models of education that had aimed at this synthesis. Firstly, John Dewey said education was "the process of remaking experience, giving it a more socialist value through increased individual experience by giving the individual better control of his powers."[10] The second model came from Confucius who said that education promoted duty which has both an individual and a social content. Finally, in the Hindu system, the four duties of *artha, Kama, dharma* and *moksha* were to be performed through the four *varnas* and *ashrams*. The fulfillment of these had reference to both the individual and society.

For Gandhi, the individual was spiritual and so he believed that society must be spiritual. The individual was seen to have a divine destiny which must be worked out in society. This meant that to attain self-realization, the individual must be placed at the center. For the materialist, on the other hand, the individual was seen only as a means for the perfection of society. For Gandhi, it was pointed out, the goal of society must be spiritual rather than material.

Kripalani felt that in the 1930s education in India was too abstract. Cut off from all life and reality, it could not promote practical knowledge. Gandhi called for a system of "Basic Education" which would be centered around a craft. This healthy activity would help develop the will and the personality. It was pointed out that Gandhi's methodology would help combine the intellectual, artistic, scientific and physical development of the pupil: He also argued that Gandhi's Basic Education "follows the natural evolution of the individual and the race, the evolution of all knowledge, art, science, philosophy and religion."[11] Kripalani believed that there was a natural process of education throughout history whereby the human individual came to dominate the forces of nature and know the world and the self. General laws were discovered which were further generalized to create philosophy. Looking inward, the individual created psychology. In society, he said, groups arose through the need for cooperation, and this same process must be emulated in education.

Encouraging self-discovery by the pupils would automatically lead to the habit of scientific thinking. Pointing out that craft education was not new, Kripalani believed that abstract education arose because the priestly class took over education in medieval times. But with the Renaissance, craft education was revived. Rousseau's *Emile* stressed discovery through activity. Others mentioned by Kripalani, whose ideas conformed with this line of thought, were Johann Pestalazzi, Johann Herbert, Friedrich Froebel, John Dewey the Bolsheviks and Peter Kropotkin. Both Lenin and Kropotkin, it was said, opposed the division of society into mental and manual labourers.

Kripalani believed that even though past experiments in craft education had failed, Gandhi's programme was ideally suited to Indian conditions and needs. Past experiments failed, he said, because the industrial revolution wiped out craft industries and the new labourers could afford little education. Secondly, the industrial revolution increased the gap between the urban middle class and the workers, producing an urban and rural proletariat. Education became tailored to the needs of the urban middle class. Thirdly, preparation for war took so much of the national wealth that craft education was not introduced into the schools.

Gandhi's system of Basic Education was intended to provide a basis for a modern scientific education and the means to earn a living for all. Kripalani stated his belief that craft education could avoid what he called "the tyranny of words," that is, the confusion and discord caused by the use of such abstract terms as "materialism." Less disputation over abstract concepts would go far to promote human solidarity, he thought. Most importantly, the principles of cooperative labour would promote Truth, love, justice, peace and discipline.

This section has summarized the approach to democracy of M.N. Roy, Jayaprakash Narayan and J.B. Kripalani. For Roy, a democratic society must ensure freedom, which is defined as "the progressive elimination of all factors, physical, social and psychological which obstruct the unfolding of man's rational, moral and creative potentialities."[12] In such a society, power must be decentralized, party dominance must end and the State must become "coterminous with society." The individual moral and the intellectual integrity of each citizen must be preserved. For J.P., democracy was "a value" and its essence was self- government. This could best be achieved, he thought, through decentralization. For Kripalani, a democratic society must be founded upon the fundamental principles of non-violence and preserve the dignity of the individual. A prerequisite must be political and economic decentralization which gives maximum freedom for the emergence of human creativity and the exercise of the will. A society of autonomous moral individuals adopting the principles of non-violence as the law of life could establish communal harmony and true democracy.

Decentralization

In this section, the vision of future Indian society, which each of the three thinkers discussed in this work set out, will be reviewed. Raghavan Iyer has stated that "Power must be diffused as widely as possible and not concentrated in a few centers if democracy is to secure unity without loss of freedom, equality without mediocrity, variety without sacrificing unity, progress without endangering either unity or liberty."[13] A major tenet of Indian Socialism is that democracy requires decentralization, or the greatest possible diffusion of power. Each of the thinkers discussed in this work contributed to the emerging perspective of decentralized socialism or *Sarvodaya.*

Decentralization was integral to Roy's Radical Humanism, as has been noted previously. In his ideal society the State would function only to "coordinate" autonomous social institutions, party politics would be abolished, society would rely upon local initiative and cooperation and small scaled technology would provide for material requirements. Production would be through decentralized and cooperatively owned units with overall planning of production and distribution. Roy assumed that the Indian peasants, being rational, could be persuaded to cooperate with the establishment of cooperative village based agricultural production. Beyond the village, regional cooperative societies would be established to oversee allied industries. There would be a need for some large-scale industries which would be owned cooperatively. With cooperative industries interlinked into a rationalized economy, Roy argued taht the overall efficiency could be raised to such a level that less efficient private industries would vanish. In this system, political democracy would become a reality and the government would be limited to the administration of the State, the political organisation of society. Sovereign local people's committees would be established to serve as local governments.

M.N. Roy's writings and model for decentralization influenced Jayaprakash Narayan and he further developed the model, which later played a crucial role in the establishment of the *Panchayati Raj* system by the Indian Government. The fundamental principle of decentralization, he pointed out, was that the basic unit must have freedom to do all that is in its competency.[14] As a general rule, J.P. said, "The system that rests on individual votes has invariably a tendency towards concentration of power at the top." The *panchayat* system, on the other hand, tends toward dispersal of power.[15] There were other important contrasts. In the parliamentary system organized parties are run by a small elite, but in the *panchayat* system, communal bodies working from below have a decisive influence. He noted that representatives elected by unorganized voters cannot be under their control in the parliamentary system. But in the *panchayat* system, voting would be structured so that electing bodies could exert a continuing influence over their representatives to the higher circles of organization. Further, in the parliamentary system participation is largely limited to casting votes, but in the *panchayat* system, local participation is encouraged through the *gram sabha.* Another advantage of the *panchayat*, according to J.P., was that both the enormous expense and the propaganda and emotional excitement of elections would be kept to a minimum. He also believed that in the *panchayat* system, the voters were more likely to understand the issues than in the parliamentary system.[16]

It has been noted that J.P.'s vision of Indian Socialism or *Sarvodaya* was grounded in the Indian tradition. *Sarvodaya* (the social good, public interest or universal welfare) involved three facets: *Gramdan, Gram Swavalamban* and *Gram Swaraj. Gramdan* involved the pooling of resources in the community. It would be "a revolution of mind, in values and in attitudes toward property." Gram *Swavalamban* signified the concept of village self-sufficiency. It was felt that the quality of life would be far superior in small communities. Gram *Swaraj* was the concept of village self-government. In the absence of political parties, the community would be homogeneous and human. Differences of opinion could be settled locally using a non-violent approach. With "moral" individuals, there would no longer be a basis for a state.

In the local community, J.P. said, the individual *dharma* of duty would translate into *Gram dharma*. The contradiction between liberty and freedom could only be solved through communitarianism and trusteeship, he concluded. *Dharma* was seen to include duty, moral law, social and personal morality, natural law and natural obligation. In Indian thought, *dharma* helped to knit the political into an organic whole. For Gandhi, *dharma* was similar to the Kantian concept of a universal categorical imperative of duty. For J.P., *dharma* was the moral basis for *Sarvodaya*, It signified identification between human beings and the entire human community, and held moral and spiritual values to be more fundamental than material values .. Spiritualism implied a concern for universal human welfare.

J.P. worked to establish *Sarvodaya* through Vinoba Bhave's *bhoodan* movement launched in 1951. He saw the movement as a process whereby inward human change could result from outward social change. This non-violent revolution, it was said, was more likely to put power in the hands of the people and establish a consensus in the community than a violent revolution. *Sarvodaya* would satisfy the three basic psychological needs of the citizen. Fristly, the individual must have personal independence and responsibility within and toward a self-governing group. Secondly, work must possess a certain aesthetic value and human significance. Finally, the individual should be related to his natural environment in some organic, rooted and symbiotic way. In Gandhi's "grand conception" of society, individuals would stand at the center of ever-widening oceanic circles. Primary communities would form regional communities and these would, in turn, form district communities. District communities would form provincial communities, and these, national communities. In this way, a world community might come into being.

J.P. and others set up experimental *Gramdan* villages during the 1950s. The moral qualities and mental attitudes for communitarian society were: a concern for Truth, aversion to violence, love of liberty and courage to resist oppression and tyranny, a spirit of cooperation, concern with community interest, tolerance and respect for others' opinions, willingness to take responsibility and a faith in human nature.

But J.P. believed that the resulting system of *Panchayati Raj* in India grafted onto the parliamentary system was a failure because, he said, like oil and water, the two systems would not mix. The center was certain to establish its authority over the weaker local units of government under such an arrangement.

J.B. *Kripalani's* perspective on decentralization was expressed through an evaluation of Gandhian economics. Kripalani viewed Gandhian economics as an alternative conceptual framework to Western economics. Firstly, it held that economic systems must not be built upon abstract economic formulations or laws as it deals with living human beings and life does not move in consonance with the rules of formal logic. Instead, it is dynamic and always transcending these rules. Secondly, he said, Gandhian economic thought placed people and their material, moral and spiritual needs at the center. It embodied human values in accord with an open view of human nature. Kripalani agreed with Gandhi that in India, the welfare of the individual should be the highest concern and the village should be the basic unit of organisation.

For Kripalani, capitalism, Socialism and Communism were all within the same economic conceptual framework. They each accepted the principle of accumulation. Further, the concept of the economic man was seen in both systems. In the West, the individual was seen as seeking to maximize economic interest and Marxists saw the basic conflict between economic classes, ideology and culture as having an economic basis. For Gandhi, however, economic activity was only a part of social activity.

Total Revolution

The movements launched by the thinkers in this study, taken collectively, may be seen as part of the continuing revolution or "Total Revolution." The concept of a total revolution is based upon the Renaissance ideals of M.N. Roy's Radical Humanism and Gandhi's philosophy of non-violence. It is grounded in an open view of human nature which sees the individual as perfectable and institutions, as imperfect, malleable or capable of improvement. It places the human individual at the center of the cosmos and seeks to create a moral society which will encourage the release of free creative initiative. It is basically non-materialist in philosophy, emphasizing psychological and spiritual factors over the material. J.P. described the movement as follows:

> I visualize this movement as a total revolution that will bring about fundamental changes in the social, economic, political, cultural, educational and moral spheres ...Exploitation will disappear.
>
> ... [W]e will have to free our minds from the straitjacket of the Western concept of democracy and break new ground.[17]

The transformation of society through total revolution is based upon Gandhi's conception of social change, or what J.B. Kripalani called his "organic philosophy." The principles and programmes, he said, together form an organic whole. The unity running through them made it a complete system of philosophy. Kripalani pointed out that Gandhi believed that all aspects of human life should form a harmonious whole. The religious, moral, political, economic, social, individual and collective cannot be divided into separate compartments. This "synthetic" approach was seen as consistent with the Indian tendency to assimilate the new. It was a dialectical progression, but without the negative or destructive, it was said.

Gandhi's programme was seen by Kripalani as the foundation of the ethical reconstruction of society. A dynamic revolutionary such as Gandhi demonstrated four characteristics. Firstly, he had the ability to recognize a revolutionary situation and take appropriate action. He recognized the existence of material and historical forces but thought that these could, to a large extent, be overcome by human will. Secondly, he recognized that genuine revolutions are movements of the masses. The people lend their will and collective spiritual force to the struggle. He compared revolution to the spiritual rebirth of a people. But even though revolutions are mass movements, they may be initiated by an individual, group or class. Thirdly, the revolutionary leads under a compelling sense of urgency. Finally, he sees every action in terms of the revolution. Within the concept of total revolution, freedom is seen in terms of moral and spiritual freedom and as the goal of the individual in history and society. In the words of Kripalani:

> ....Gandhi sought to coordinate and synthesise social, political and economic life, establish effective democracy and lay the foundation of a new social order based on justice and equality and prove the way for peace.[18]

Jayaprakash Narayan's call for total revolution in the Gujarat and Bihar student movements of 1974-75 represented a shift in his conception of the most effective methodology of social change at the time, rather than a change in the overall objectives of the movement. J.P., who had spent more than a decade working in the *bhoodan* movement in the villages decided that a mass *Satyagraha* must be launched and that the students and urban intelligentsia must be given the central role of leadership. He came to believe that for real social change, these segments of the people must be in a state of frustration and alienated from authority.

The goals of J.P.'s total revolution included the Gandhian concept of inner moral change. It was to be a social, economic, political, moral and cultural revolution. It would deal with the fundamental ills of Indian society, including poverty, lack of opportunity, inequality, the dowry system, caste distinction, untouchability, communalism and lack of social and cultural integration. It demanded morality in the public sphere. The general *Satyagraha* would be a "permanent revolution."

Under J.P.'s total revolution, committees for people's struggle would be set up and later become people's governments. Urban intellectuals would serve in the campaign by explaining the principles of Gandhian socialism to the people. In J.P.s words:

> I came to the conclusion that the people would have to fight their own battle ...Let there be a people's struggle ... I concluded that the movement would have to be peaceful and of a non-party character and the students and youths would have to be its vanguard. [The] aim is to change the whole system.This is the call for a total revolution.[19]

> ... [T]he foundation of a new type of politics will be laid on its [the present system] ruins and the new politics will be completely different from the old. It will be *lokniti* or the people's politics, not *Rajaniti*, or the elitist politics. The seed of that new politics is slumbering in the soil of India ...This new politics will be born from the womb of the people's power.[20]

This chapter has summarized the political thinking of M.N. Roy, Jayaprakash Narayan and J.B. Kripalani on democracy, decentralization and total revolution. Although diverse ideological strands were woven into their thought, taken as a whole, there is a unitary theme concerning the ideal nature of society and a common approach to human liberation. Their thinking contributed enormously to the synthesis between the East and West which comprises the emerging conception of Indian Socialism or *Sarvodaya*.

References

1. D.G. Dalton, "M.N. Roy and Radical Humanism: The Ideology of an Indian Intellectual Elite," in *Elites in South Asia*, eds. Edmund Leach and S.N. Mukherjee T Cambridge: Cambridge Univ. Press, 1970), pp. 169-170.
2. Robert C. North, *The World That Could Be* (Stanford, California: Stanford Alumni Association, 1967), p. 31.
3. M.N. Roy, *Beyond Communism* (Calcutta: Renaissance Publishers, 1960), p. 64.
4. M.N. Roy, *Materialism* (Calcutta: Renaissance Publishers, 1940), p. 233.
5. M.N. Roy, *New Humanism* (Calcutta: Renaissance Publishers, 1947), pp. 52-53.
6. Jayaprakash Narayan, "Decentralised Democracy: Theory and Practice," *The Indian Journal of Public Administration* 7 (July-Sept. 1961): 271.
7. *Ibid.*, p. 274.
8. *Ibid.*, pp. 272-273.
9. J.B. Kripalani, *Freedom In Peril* (Madras: Gandhi Samaj, 1977), pp. 44-47.
10. J.B. Kripalani, *Latest Fad* (Allahabad: The Hindustan Talimi Sangh, 1939), p. 73.
11. *Ibid.*, p. 14.
12. Roy, *New Humanism*, pp. 52-53.
13. Raghavan Iyer, *Parapolitics* (New York : Oxford Univ. Press, 1979), p. 177.
14. Jayaprakash Narayan, "Decentralized Democracy," p. 276.
15. *Ibid.*, p. 284.

16. *Ibid.*, pp. 284-285.
17. Jayaprakash Narayan, *Total Revolution*, trans. Monmohan Chaudhury (Rajghat, Varanasi: Sarva Seva Sangh Prakashan, 1975), pp. 68-74.
18. J.B. Kripalani, *Gandhi: His Life and Thought* (New Delhi: Publications Division, Minister of Information and Broadcasting, Government of India, 1970), p. 356.
19. Jayaprakash Narayan, *Total Revolution*, pp. 19-21.
20. *Ibid.*, p. 67.

9

Conclusion: Socialism and Sarvodaya

Indian socialism or *Sarvodaya* is firmly grounded in the Gandhian concepts of Truth (*Sat*), non-violence (*ahimsa*) and the principle of trusteeship. While drawing inspiration from the classical Indian tradition, it also integrates themes from the Western classical tradition, Renaissance Humanism, Utopian Socialism and Liberalism. Offering a viable alternative to the demonstrably deficient contemporary ideologies, it encourages perceptive individuals to see beyond enervating conceptual blinders.

Sarvodaya emerges from a radical break with the political thought which laid the ideological foundations for today's mass societies. The political thought which forms the basis of *Sarvodaya* rejects the central assumptions concerning power and social action, which have come to be taken for granted. First, with respect to power, *Sarvodaya* rejects the traditional bases of power which were seen to lie in the power of force or law. Instead, *Sarvodaya* bases power on love of humanity thereby establishing people's power.

Accordingly, *Sarvodaya* rejects the use of violence as a method of social change. A fundamental objective is to establish institutions through which the principles of 'non-violent social action can function to create harmony between all groups in society'. It should also be stressed that non-violence in *Sarvodaya* is not passive resistance, but rather active resistance to all forms of evil. *Sarvodaya* deems inaction where evil exists as cowardice. It is not a pacifist doctrine, as violent action in the defence of a good cause is held to be superior to inaction. The ideal form of social action in *Sarvodaya* is *Satyagraha*, whereby the perpetrators of violence and exploitation in society are converted into adherents of a harmonious and non-violent society. *Satyagraha* or insistence upon truth seeks to change the human psychology. This is deemed necessary for permanent and meaningful social change. It is believed that this development of "soul force" or leavening of society may swell into a mass movement whereby people's power may be established and, resting on a firm moral foundation, be maintained. The power struggle will end and for the first time in modern history, there will be a genuine possibility of the "withering away of the State."

It is recognized that this method of social change involves self-suffering for the purpose of the moral, spiritual and material uplift of every member of society. *Sarvodaya* goes beyond utilitarianism, as it insists upon the greatest all round good of all, physical and spiritual, rather than the greatest good for the greatest number. Through trusteeship the strong help the weak and promote the welfare of all.

Sarvodaya emphasizes education and the rationality of the individual. It recognizes the self-perfectibility of every member of society. As such, it takes an open view of human nature, recognizing that while human nature is shaped by material factors, it is more than a historical product arising from social and economic factors. The role of the will as a force in human action is stressed, as well as the individual potential for good and evil, rationality and irrationality.

Sarvodaya insists upon the dignity of all and the opportunity for individual development. It insists upon the preservation of individual moral autonomy in a truly democratic social order. Finding negative freedom insufficient, it seeks the guarantee of positive social welfare to eliminate poverty and unemployment and successively narrow inequality.

Sarvodaya insists upon the radical decentralization of political and economic power and the establishment of democratic local people's government with universal participation. The State and the Party, as we know them today, are absent, the State becoming, an instrument for the administration and regulation of society.

The decentralized *Sarvodaya* institutions are conceptualized as the nucleus of the emerging global community. The power configuration is radically altered with power being vested in the sovereignty of the autonomous moral individual. In Gandhi's conception, the individual stands at the center of ever widening concentric circles. Power then radiates outward and when the citizen is a moral individual, it will be a moral force which will radically transform society and promote a truly global community, where harmony and peace is assured.

A crucial concern of *Sarvodaya* is the individual. As opposed to Liberalism, where the individual will is resolved into the general will or the will of the majority, and Western Socialism, where the individual will is merged into an alternative conception of the collective, *Sarvodaya* preserves individual moral autonomy, basing political sovereignty in the individual. Consequently, it achieves a fundamental objective of liberal democracy which, historically, could not be realized due to the contradictions of *laissez faire* economics and the reliance upon a centralized power structure. In practice, Liberalism and Socialism became secular elitism, where underlying the illusions of freedom, existed an entrenched power structure.

It is also significant that in *Sarvodaya*, political obligation is not to the State or to abstract law, but rather to the community first, and, in turn, this obligation extends outward to the edges of the concentric circles. Therefore one cannot fulfil his or her political obligation in *Sarvodaya* while engaging in actions which exploit and promote violence. Fulfilling political obligation must also serve to reduce poverty, exploitation and degradation in the community. It must reduce violence, change hearts and promote world peace.

Sarvodaya can also be distinguished from other political ideologies in its approach to the problem of human history. In the West the goal of human history is seen, largely, as the perfection of society. The individual is transient and subservient to the final goal of history. In *Sarvodaya*, on the other hand, the moral individual is placed at the center. Perfection of the individual is the fundamental project of history, the institutional structure of society remaining imperfect. Self-perfection is seen in spiritual terms as *Moksha*.

Sarvodaya differs from Western political thought again in its approach to science and technology. Asserting that the individual in society is the measure of all things, it insists that science and technology serve the needs of humanity and that a non-relativistic ethics guide the development and use of technology. Science and technology must serve to promote the goal of *Sarvodaya* which is the uplift of all. The Calvinistic imperitive to conquer nature and exploit natural resources is absent. *Sarvodaya* insists upon an ecological balance between human society and nature, as the individual is seen as an integral part of nature. Finally, it is recognized that most problems do not have technological solutions but involve human relations.

Sarvodaya also presupposes deep spiritual foundations. An underlying theme is the essential unity or "oneness" underlying all of humanity, all of nature, and ultimately all of existence. From this is derived the concept of interdependent humanity which provides a basis for human solidarity.

In the twentiety century, M.N. Roy, J.P. Narayan and J.B. Kripalani contributed enormously to the development of the philosophy of *Sarvodaya* and the revival of traditional thinking upon which it is based. They demonstrated remarkable conceptual flexibility and willingness to transcend a narrow faith in ideologies. This is seen in the great lattitude of their thought.

Moreover, their critique of liberal and Marxist thought is vitally important and provides crucial insights into modern political society. The works of these thinkers deserve to be studied widely.

Further, these thinkers greatly contributed to the revival of classical political thought, both Western and Eastern, and demonstrated its continued relevance to contemporary society. The concept of positive freedom embodied in *Sarvodaya* is extremely relevant to global social and economic conditions. The philosophy of non-violence embodied in *Sarvodaya* has important implications for international relations and disarmament.

The three thinkers considered in this work greatly enriched contemporary political philosophy. Because they insisted upon the crucial need for individual moral change as well as upon radical structural change in society, their thought goes to the root of the contemporary social dilemma. By insisting upon the establishment of non-violent relations not only between individuals but also between groups, and by the insistence of morality in public life, they helped to lay the basis for a non-violent society and the emerging global community.

Appendix

PRINCIPLES OF RADICAL DEMOCRACY

Thesis 1

Man is the archetype of society. Co-operative social relationships contribute to develop individual potentialities. But the development of the individual is the measure of social progress. Collectivity presupposes the existence of individuals. Except as the sum total of freedom and well-being, actually enjoyed by individuals, social liberation and progress are imaginary ideals which are never attained. Well-being, if it is actual, is enjoyed by individuals. It is wrong to ascribe a collective ego to any form of human community (viz., nation, class, etc.), as that practice means sacrifice of the individual: Collective well-being is a function of the well-being of individuals.

Thesis 2

Quest for freedom and search for truth constitute the basic urge of human progress. The quest for freedom is the continuation, on a higher level—of intelligence and emotion—of the biological struggle for existence. The search for truth is a corollary thereof. Increasing knowledge of nature enables man to be progressively free from the tyranny of natural phenomena, and physical and social environments. Truth is the content of knowledge.

Thesis 3

The purpose of all rational human endeavour, individual as well as collective, is attainment of freedom, in ever increasing measure. Freedom is the progressive disappearance of all restrictions on the unfolding of the potentialities of individuals, as human beings, not as cogs in the wheels of a mechanized social organism. The position of the individual, therefore, is the measure of the progressive and liberating significance of any collective effort or social organisation. The success of any collective endeavour is to be measured by the actual benefit for its constituent units.

Thesis 4

Rising out of the background of the law-governed physical nature, the human being is essentially rational. Reason, being a biological property, it is not the anti-thesis of will. Intelligence and emotion can be reduced to a common biological denominator. Historical determinism, therefore, does not exclude freedom of the will. As a matter of fact, human will is the most powerful determining factor. Otherwise, there would be no room for revolutions in a rationally determined process of history. The rational and scientific concept of determinism is not to be confused with the teleological or religious doctrine of predestination.

Thesis 5

The economic interpretation of history is deduced from a wrong interpretation of Materialism. It implies dualism, whereas Materialism is a monistic philosophy. History is a determined process: but there are more than one causative factors. Human will is one of them, and it cannot always be referred directly to any economic incentive.

Thesis 6

Ideation is a physiological process resulting from the awareness of environments. But once they are formed, ideas exist by themselves, governed by their own laws. The dynamics of ideas runs parallel to the process of social evolution, the two influencing each other mutually. But in no particular point of the process of the integral human evolution, can a direct causal relationship be established between historical events and the movement of ideas. ('Idea' is here used in the common philosophical sense of ideology or system of ideas.) Cultural patterns and ethical values are not mere ideological superstructures of established economic relations. They are also historically determined—by the logic of the history of ideas.

Thesis 7

For creating a new world of Freedom, revolution must go beyond an economic reorganisation of society. Freedom does not necessarily follow the capture of political power in the name of the oppressed and exploited classes and abolition of private property in the name of production.

Thesis 8

Communism or Socialism may conceivably be the means for the attainment of the goal of freedom. How far it can serve that purpose, must be judged by experience. A political system and an economic system which subordinates the man of flesh and blood to an imaginary collective ego, be it the nation or the class, cannot possibly be the suitable means for the attainment of the goal of freedom. On the one hand, it is absurd to argue that negation of freedom will lead to freedom: and, on the other hand, it is not freedom to sacrifice the individual at the alter of the imaginary collective ego. Any social philosophy, or scheme of social reconstruction which does not recognise the sovereignty of the individual, and dismisses the ideal of freedom as an empty abstraction, can have no more than a very limited progressive and revolutionary significance.

Thesis 9

The State being the political organisation of society, its withering away under communism is a utopia which has been exploded by experience. Planned economy on the basis of socialised industries presupposes a powerful political machinery. Democratic control of that machinery alone can guarantee freedom under the new order. Planning of production for use is possible on the basis of political democracy and individual freedom.

Thesis 10

State ownership and planned economy do not themselves end exploitation of labour: or do they necessarily lead to an equal distribution of wealth. Economic democracy is no more possible in the absence of political democracy than the latter is in the absence of the former.

Thesis 11

Dictatorship tends to perpetuate itself. Planned economy under political dictatorship disregards individual freedom on the pleas of efficiency, collective effort and social progress. Consequently, a higher form of democracy in the socialist society, as it is conceived at present, becomes an impossibility. Dictatorship defeats its professed end.

Thesis 12

The defects of formal parliamentary democracy have also been exposed in experience. They result from the delegation of power. To make democracy effective, power must always remain vested in the people, and there must be ways and means for the people to wield sovereign power effectively, not periodically, but from day to day. Atomised individual citizens are powerless for all practical purposes, and most of the time. They have no means to exercise their sovereignty and to wield a standing control of the State machinery.

Thesis 13

Liberalism is falsified or parodied under formal parliamentary democracy. The doctrine of ·*laissez-faire* only provides the legal sanction to the exploitation of man by man. The concept of economic man negativates the liberating doctrine of individualism. The economic man is bound to be a slave or slave-holder. This vulgar concept must be replaced by the reality of an instinctively rational being who is moral because he is rational. Morality is an appeal to conscience, and conscience is the instinctive awareness of, and reaction to environments. It is a mechanistic biological function on the level of consciousness. Therefore, it is rational.

Thesis 14

The alternative to parliamentary democracy is not dictatorship; it is organised democracy in the place of the formal democracy of powerless atomised individual citizens. The parliament should be the apex of a pyramidal structure of the State reared on the base of organised democracy composed of a country-wide network of People's Committees. The political organisation of society (the State) will be coincident with the entire society, and consequenty the State will be under a standing democratic control.

Thesis 15

The function of a revolutionary and liberating social philosophy is to lay emphasis on the basic fact of history that man is the maker of his world—man as a thinking being, and he can be so only as an individual. The brain is a means of production, and produces the most revolutionary commodity. Revolutions presuppose iconoclastic ideas. An increasingly large number of men conscious of their creative power, motivated by the indomitable will to remake the world, moved by the adventure of ideas, and fired with the ideal of a free society of free men, can create the conditions under which democracy will be possible.

Thesis 16

The method and programme of social revolution must be based on a reassertion of the basic principle of social progress. A social renaissance can come only through determined and widespread endeavour to educate the people as regards the principles of freedom and rational co-operative living. The people will be organised into effective democratic bodies to build up the socio-political foundation of the post-revolutionary order. Social revolution is required in rapidly increasing the number of men of the new renaissance, for a rapidly expanding system of People's Committees, or an organic coordination of both. The programme of revolution will similiarly be based on the principles of freedom, reason and social harmony. It will mean the elimination of every form of monopoly and vested interest in the regulation of social life.

Thesis 17

Radical Democracy presupposes economic reorganisation of society so as to eliminate the possibility of exploitation of man by man. Progressive satisfaction of material necessities is the precondition for the individual members of society unfolding their intellectual and other finer human potentialities. An economic reorganisation, such as will guarantee a progressively rising standard of living, is the foundation of the Radical Democratic State. Economic liberation of the masses is an essential condition for their advancing toward the goal of freedom.

Thesis 18

The economy of the new social order will be based on production for use and distribution with reference to human needs. Its political organisation excludes delegation of power which in practice, deprives the people of effective power; it will be based on the direct participation of the entire adult population through People's Committees. Its culture will be based on universal dissemination of knowledge and on minimum control and maximum scope for, and incentive to, scientific and creative activities. The new society, being founded on reason and science, will necessarily be planned. But it will be planning with the freedom of the individual as its main purpose. The new society will be democratic, politically, economically as well as culturally. Consequently, it will be a democracy which can defend itself.

Thesis 19

The ideal of Radical Democracy will be attained through the collective efforts of spiritually free men united in a political party with the determination of creating a world of freedom. The members of the party will function as the guides, friends, and philosophers of the people rather than their would be rulers. Consistently with the goal of freedom the political practice of the party will be rational and therefore ethical. The party will grow with the growth of the people's will to freedom, and come to power with the support of enlightened public opinion, as well as intelligent action of the people. Realising that freedom is inconsistent with concentration of power, its aim will be the widest diffusion of power. Its success in attaining political power will only be a stage in that process, and by the logic of its own existence, the party will utilise political power for its further diffusion until the State becomes coterminous with the entire society.

Thesis 20

In the last analysis, education of the citizen is the condition for such a reorganisation of society as will be conducive to common progress and prosperity without encroaching upon the freedom of the individual. The Radical Democratic State will be the school for the political and civic education of the citizen. Its structure and function will enable detached individuals to come to the forefront of public affairs. Manned with such individuals the State machinery will cease to be the instrument in the hands of any particular class to coerce others. Only spiritually free individuals in power can smash all chains of slavery and usher in freedom for all.

Thesis 21

Radicalism integrates science into social organisation and reconciles individuality with collective life; it gives to freedom a moral-intellectual as well as a social content; it offers a comprehensive theory of social progress in which both the dialectics of economic determinism and dynamics of ideas find their due recognition; and it deduces from the same a method and programme of social revolution in our time.

Thesis 22

Radicalism starts from the dictum that "man is the measure of everything" (Protagoras) or "man is the root of mankind" (Marx), and advocates reconstruction of the world as a commonwealth and fraternity of free men, by the collective endeavour of spiritually emancipated moral men.

Bibliography

Books:

Agarwal, Shriman, *Gandhian Constitution for Free India*. Allahabad: Kitistan, 1945.

Ahuja, B.N., *"J.P.", India's Revolutionar Number One*. Lahore: Varma Publishing Company, 19 47.

Aristotle, *The Politics of Aristotle*. Translated and edited by Ernest Barker. London: Oxford University Press, 1979.

Basham, A.L., *The Wonder that was India*. New York: Grove Press, 1954.

Bhargava, G.S., Acharya Kripalani. New Delhi: Popular Book Service, 1967.

Bhattacharjea, Ajit, *Jayaprakash Narayan*. Delhi: Vikas Publishing House, 1975.

Bhattacharjee, G.P., *Evolution of Political Philosophy of M.N. Roy*. Calcutta: Minerva, 1971.

Bhave, Vinoba, *Bhoodan Yagna. Ahmedabad:* Navajivan Publishing House, 1953.

Third Power, Rajghat, Varanasi: Sarva Seva Sangh Prakashan, 1972.

Bondurant, Joan V., *Conquest of Violence*. Berkeley: University of California Press, 1971.

Brecher, Michael, *Nehru, A Political Biography*. Bombay: Jaico, 1969.

Brown, D. Mackenzie, *The White Umbrella*. Berkeley: University of California Press, 1958.

Deva, Acharya Narendra, *Socialism and the National Revolution*. Bombay: Padma Publications, 1946.

Fischer, Louis, *Gandhi, His Life and Message for the World*. New York: Signet 1954.

Gandhi, M.K., *Basic Education*. Edited by Bharatan Kumarappa. Ahmedabad: Navajivan Publishing House, 1951.

Gandhi, M.K., *My Socialism*, Edited by R.K. Prabhu. Ahmedabad: Navajivan Publishing House, 1959.

Gandhi, M.K., *Sarvodaya*. Edited by Bharatan Kumarappa. Ahmedabad: Navajivan Publishing House, 1954.

Gandhi, M.K., *Towards New Education*. Edited by Bharatan Kumarappa. Ahmedabad: Navajivan Publishing House, 1953.

Gandhi, M.K., Godwin, William, *Enquiry Concerning Political Justice*. Edited by Isaac Kramnick. Baltimore: Penguin, 1976.

Haithcox, John Patrick, *Communism and Nationalism in India.* Princeton, N.J., Princeton University Press, 1971.

Hoffman, Daniel P., *India's Social Miracle*. Healdsburg, California: Naturegraph Co., 1961.

Iyer, Raghavan, *The Moral and Political Thought of Mahatma Gandhi*. New York: Oxford University Press, 1973.

Iyer, Raghavan, *Parapolitics*. New York: Oxford University Press, 1979.

Iyer, Raghavan, *Utilitarianism and All That, The Political Theory of British Imperialim*. Santa Barbara, Calif.: Concord-Grove Press, 1983.

Kripalani, J.B., *Class Struggle*. Rajghat, Kashi: Akhil Bharat Sarva Seva Sang Prakashan, 1958.

Kripalani, J.B., *Fateful Year*. Bombay: Vora and Co., 1948.

Kripalani, J.B., Freedom in Peril. Madras: Gandhi Samaj, 1977.

Kripalani, J.B., *Gandhi: His Life and Thought*. New Delhi: Publications Division-Ministry of Information and Broadcasting, Government of India, 1970.

Kripalani, J.B., *Gandhi The Statesman*. Delhi: Ranjit Printers and Publishers, 1951.

Kripalani, J.B., *Gandhian Thought*. New Delhi: Gandhi Smarak Nidhi, 1961.

Kripalani, J.B., *The Indian National Congress*. Bombay: Vora & Co., 1946.

Kripalani, J.B., *The Latest Fad*. Allahabad: The Hindustani Talimi Sangh, 939.

Kripalani, J.B., *Minorities In India*. Calcutta: Manoranjan Guha, N.D.

Kripalani, J.B., *The Nightmare and After*. Bombay: Popular Prakashan, 1980.

Kripalani, J.B., *Planning*. New Delhi: Praja Socialist Party, 1957.

Kripalani, J.B., *Politics of Charkha*. Bombay: Vora & Co., 1946.

Kripalani, J.B., *Some Stray Thoughts*. Ahmedabad: Navajivan Publishing House, 1979.

Kripalani, J.B., Where Are We Going. Calcutta: Vigil Publishers, 1958.

Kumarappa, Bharatan, *Capitalism, Socialism or Villagisrn*. Rajghat, Varanasi, Sarva Seva Sangh Prakashan, 1965.

Lal, Lakshmi Narain, *Jayakrakash, Rebel Extraordinary*. New Delhi: Indian Book Company, 1975.

Lanza Del Vasto, Joseph Jean, *Gandhi to Vinoba*. New York: Schocken Books, 1974.

Laslett, Peter and W.G. Runciman, eds., *Philosophy, Politics and Society*. Oxford: Basil Blackwell, 1964.

Leach, Edmund and S.N. Mukherjee, eds., *Elites in South Asia*. Cambridge: Cambridge University Press, 1970.

Linton, Erica, *Fragments of a Vision*. Varanasi: Sarva Seva Sangh Prakashan, 1971.

Mahadevan, T.K., ed., *Jayaprakash Narayan and the future of Indian democracy*. New Delhi: Afiliate East-West Press, 1975.

Marx, Karl and Friedrich Engels, *The Communist Manifesto*. New York: Appleton-Century-Crofts, Inc., 1955.

Marx, Karl, *Early Writings*. Translated and Edited by T.B. Bottomore. New York: McGraw-Hill, 1964.

Masani, Minoo. *J.P. Mission Partly Accomplished*. Delhi: Macmillan, 1977.

Mehta, Vadilal Lallubhai, *Equality Through Trusteeship*. New Delhi: Tata McGraw-Hill Pub. Co., 1977.

Misra, B.R., V. *For Vinoba, The Economics of The Bhoodan Movement*. Bombay: Orient Longman, 1956.

Morris-Jones, W.H., *Politics Mainly Indian*. Bombay: Orient Longman, 1978.

Myrdal, Gunnar, *Asian Drama*. 3 Vols. New York: Pantheon, 1968. Vol. 2.

Naravane, V.S., *Modern Indian Thought*. Columbia, Mo.: South Asia Books, 1978.

Narayan, Jayaprakash, *Communitarian Society and Panchayati Raj*. Varanasi: Navachetna Prakashan, 1970.

Narayan, Jayaprakash, *Jayaprakash Narayan on Some Impressions of My European Tour*. New Delhi: Office for Asian Affairs, Congress for Cultural Freedon, 1958.

Narayan, Jayaprakash, *Nation Building in India*. Edited by Brahmanand. Varanasi: Navachetna Prakashan, N.D.

Narayan, Jayaprakash, *Socialism, Sarvodaya and Democracy*. New York: Asia Publishing House, 1964.

Narayan, Jayaprakash, *Three Basic Problems of Free India*. New York: Asia Publishing House, 1964.

Narayan, Jayaprakash, *Total Revolution*. Translated by Manmohan Chaudhury. Rajghat, Varanasi: Sarva Seva Sangh Prakashan, 1975.

Narayan, Jayaprakash, *Towards A New Society*. New Delhi: Congress for Cultural Freedom, 1958.

Narayan, Jayaprakash, *Towards Total Revolution*. Bombay: Popular Prakashan, 1978.

Narayan, Jayaprakash, *Towards Struggle*. Edited by Yusuf Meherally. Bombay: Padma Publications, 1946.

Narayan, Jayaprakash, *The Tragedy of Tibet*. New Delhi: Afro-Asian Committee on Tibet, 1959.

Narayan, Shriman, *Vinoba, His Life and Work*. Bombay: Popular Prakashan, 1970.

Nargolkar, Vasant, *J.P.'s Crusade For Revolution*. New Delhi: S. Chand & Co., 1975.

Nehru, Jawaharlal, *An Autobiography*. New Delhi: Allied Publishers, 1962.

Nehru, Jawaharlal, *Toward Freedom*. Boston: Beacon Press, 1967.

North, Robert C, *The World That Could Be*. Stanford, California: Stanford Alumni Assoc.,1976.

Oommen, T.K., *Charisma, Stability and Change*. New Delhi: Thomson Press Ltd., 1972.

Ostergaard, Geoffrey and Melville Currell, *The Gentle Anarchists*. London: Clarendon Press Oxford, 1971.

Overstreet, Gene D. and Marshall Windmiller, *Communism in India*. Berkeley: University of California Press, 1959.

Prasad, Bimal, ed. *A Revolutionary's Quest*. Delhi: Oxford University Press, 1980.

Radhakrishnan, Sarvepalli and Charles A. Moore, eds., *Indian Philosophy*. Princeton, N.J.: Princeton University Press, 1957.

Rao, V.K.R.V., *The Gandhian Alternative To Western Socialism Bombay*: Bharatiya Vidya Bhavan, 1970.

Rao, V.K.R.V., *Indian Socialism; Retrospect and Prospect*. New Delhi: Concept Publishing Co., 1982.

Roy, Ellen and Sibnarayan Ray, *In Mants Own Image*. Calcutta: Renaissance Publishers, 1948.

Roy, M.N., *Beyond Communism*. Calcutta: Renaissance Publishers, 1947.

Roy, M.N., *The Communist International*. Bombay: Radical Democratic Party, 1943.

Roy, M.N., *Constitution of Free India*. Delhi: The Radical Democratic Party, 1944.

Roy, M.N., *Fragments of a Prisoner's Diary*. 3 Vols. Calcutta: Renaissance Publishers, 1943-1952. Vol. 1: *Crime And Karma, Cats And Women*.

Roy, M.N., Fragments of a Prisoner's Diary. 3 Vols. Calcutta: Renaissance Publishers, 1943-1952. Vol. 3: *Letters from Jail.*

Roy, M.N., *The Future of Indian Politics*. Calcutta: Calcutta: Minerva Associates, 1971.

Roy, M.N., *The Historical Role of Islam*. Calcutta: Renaissance Publishers, 1939.

Roy, M.N., *India and War*. Lucknow: Radical Democratic Party, 1942.

Roy, M.N., *India In Transition*. Geneve: Edition de la Librairie J. Target, 1922 reprint ed., Bombay: Nachiketa Publications Ltd., 1971.

Roy, M.N., *Materialism*. Calcutta: Renaissance Publications, 1940.

Roy, M.N., *M.N. Roy's Memoirs*. New Delhi: Allied Publishers, 1964.

Roy, M.N., *M.N. Roy on Communist China*. Calcutta : Renaissance Publishers, 1963. My Experience in China. Calcutta: Renaissance Publishers, 1938.

Roy, M.N., *National Government or People's Government*? Calcutta: Renaissance Publishers, 1944.

Roy, M.N., *New Humanism*. Calcutta: Renaissance Publishers, 1947.

Roy, M.N., *New Orientation*. Calcutta: Renaissance Publishers, 1946.

Roy, M.N., *Our Differences*. Calcutta: Saraswaty Library, 1938.

Roy, M.N., *Our Problems*. Calcutta: Barendra Library, 1938.

Roy, M.N., *Politics Power and Parties*. Calcutta: Renaissance Publishers, 1960.

Roy, M.N., *Poverty or Plenty*. Calcutta: Renaissance Publishers, 1943.

Roy, M.N., *The Problem of Freedom*. Calcutta: Renaissance Publishers, 1945.

Roy, M.N., *Radical Humanism*. New Delhi: Eastern Economist Pamphlets, 1952.

Roy, M.N., *Reason, Romanticism and Revolution*. 2 Vols. Calcutta: Renaissance Publishers, 1952-1955.

Roy, M.N., *Scientific Politics*. Calcutta: Renaissance Publishers, 1942.

Scarfe, Allan and Wendy Scarfe, *J.P. His Biography*. New Delhi: Orient Longman, 1975.

Schilpp, Paul Arthur, ed., *The Philosophy of Sarvepalli Radhakrishnan*. New York : Tudor Publishing Co., 1952.

Schumacher, E.F., *Small is Beautiful*. New York: Harper & Row, 1973.

Seetaramayya, B. Pattabhi, *Socialism and Gandhism. Rajahmundry*, Andhra Pradesh: Hindustan Pub. Co., 1938.

Seth, H.L., *The Red Fugitive, Jai Prakash Narayan*. Lahore: Indian Printing Works, 1944.

Sharma, B.S., *The Political Philosophy of M.N. Roy*. Delhi: National Publishing House, 1965

Spratt, Philip, *Communism and India*. New Delhi: Eastern Economist Pamphlets, 1952.

Talwar, Sada Nand, *Political Ideas of M.N. Roy*. Delhi: Khosla Publishing House, 1978.

Tandon, P.D., ed., *Acharya J.B. Kripalani*. Bombay: Hind Kitabs Ltd., 1948.

Tandon, P.D., ed., *Vinoba Bhave*. Bombay: Vora & Co.

Tandon, Vishwanath, *The Social and Political Philosophy of Sarvodaya After Gandhi*. Rajghat, Varanasi: Sarva Seva Sandh Prakashan, 1965.

Tennyson, Hallam. *India's Talking Saint*. New York: Doubleday, 1955.

Wofford, Harris, Jr., Lohia and America Meet. Madras: Shehalata Rama Reddy, ND.

Dictionaries and Encyclopedias:

A Dictionary of Marxist Thought, 1983 ed., S.V. "Class Conflict," by Tom Bottomore.

A Dictionary of Marxist Thought, 1983 ed., S.V. "Human nature," by Mihailo Markovic.

The Encyclopedia of Philosophy, Reprint ed. (1972), S.V. "Materialism," by Kieth Campbell.

Journals:

Aveneri, Shlomo. "Marx's Vision of Future Society." *Dissent* 20 (Summer 1973): 323-31.

Barua, B.P. "The Political Philosophy of Jayaprakash Narayan." *The Indian Political Science Review* 15 (January-1981): 67-77.

Haithcox, John Patrick. "Left Wing Unity and the Indian Nationalist Movement: M.N. Roy and the Congress Socialist Party" *Modern Asian Studies* 3, No. 1 (1969): 17-56.

Hettne, Bjorn. "The Vitality of Gandhian Tradition." *Journal of Peace Research* 13, No. 3 (1976): 227-45.

Naik, J.P. "Development and Gandhian Tradition in India." *The Review of Politics*, 45 (July 1983): 345-65.

Narayan, Jayaprakash. "Decentralized Democracy: Theory and Practice." *The Indian Journal of Public Administration* 7 (July-Sept. 1961): 271-86.

Palmer, Norman D. "Experiments in Democratic Decentralization in South Asia." *The Indian Political Science Review* 1 (Oct.1966-Sept.1967): 49-68.

Pantham, Thomas. "Thinking With Mahatma Gandhi." *Political Theory* 2 (May 1983): 165-188.

Prasad, Ganesh. "Democratic Decentralization, A Lay-man's Approach." *Indian Journal of Political Science* 25 (Jan.-March 1964): 5-15.

Sankhdher, M.N. "Political Theory and Spirituality: Search For A Multi-Disciplinary Paradigm." *The Indian Political Science Review* 13 (July 1979) : 197-204.

Magazines and Newspapers:

Ashtavakra. "He Was A Satyagrahi All His Life." *Illustrated Weekly of India*, March 28-April 3, 1982, p. 19.

Krishnan, V.R. "Sevagram going to Seed." *Overseas Hindustan Times*, October 14, 1982, pp. 8-9.

M.V.K., "A Latter Day Rama." *Illustrated Weekly of India*, October 21-27, 1979, p. 27.

Masani. Minoo, "Homage To J.P." *Illustrated Weekly of India*, October 14-20, 1979, pp. 6-7.

Radhakrishnan, J. "For the Union of Hearts." *Overseas Hindustan Times*, Sept. 23, 1982, p. 9.

Ramabhai, "Bhave—The Man and His Message." *Overseas Hindustan Times*, Dec. 23, 1982, pp. 8-9.

"A Stalwart goes." *Overseas Hindustan Times*, 1 April 1982, p. 116.

Index

K

L

M

N

O

P